CREATIVE FIDELITY

GABRIEL MARCEL

Creative
Fidelity

Translated and introduced
by Robert Rosthal

CROSSROAD · NEW YORK

LIBRARY
ATLANTIC CHRISTIAN COLLEGE
WILSON, N. C.

To Jeanne Delhomme, Maxime Chastaing,
Charles Lapicque

THEIR FRIEND G. M.

1982
The Crossroad Publishing Company
575 Lexington Avenue, New York, N.Y. 10022

Copyright © 1964 by Farrar, Straus and Giroux, Inc.
Originally published in French as
Du Refus à L'Invocation by Editions Gallimard.

Printed in the United States of America

Library of Congress Catalog Card Number: 81-70385

ISBN: 0-8245-0446-1

TRANSLATOR'S ACKNOWLEDGMENTS

I wish to thank the following publishers for permission to quote the original English version of passages for which Marcel has provided a French translation: Edward Arnold Co. for a passage from E. M. Forster's *Howard's End,* Bodley Head for a passage from G. K. Chesterton's *Orthodoxy,* and Dodd, Mead for a passage from the same author's *Heretics.* Wherever possible I have used the authorized English translations of the French works to which Marcel has referred. Elsewhere I am responsible for the English translation either in whole or in part. Grateful acknowledgment is therefore due to Random House for a passage in Marcel Proust's *The Captive,* to Beacon Press for permission to quote from Katherine Farrer's admirable translation of Marcel's *Être et Avoir (Being and Having);* despite certain minor changes I have made, Miss Farrer's translation has been preserved essentially intact. Also to Henry Holt & Co. for a passage from Bergson's *The Two Sources of Morality and Religion.* The following French publishers have kindly given their consent to my translation of passages quoted by Marcel: Aubier for passages from Louis Lavelle's *De l'Acte* and Eugene Minkowski's *Vers une cosmologie* and *Le Temps vécu;* Editions du Cerf for passages from Father Conger's *Chrétiens Désunis-Principes d'un oecuménisme catholique;* Desclée de Brouwer for passages from *La soif* and *Le Monde cassé;* Gallimard for passages from Marcel's *Journal Métaphysique;* Plon for a dialogue from Marcel's play, *Quatuor en fa dièse,* and Presses Universitaires for a quote from Léon Brunschvicg's *Le Progrès de la conscience dans la philosophie occidentale.* Material from Jacques Maritain's "Le Sens de l'Athëisme Marxiste" in *Esprit* (October, 1935), and from a critical article by Marcel in *Revue Hebdomadaire* (January 27, 1923), has also been translated. In order to clarify textual references I have found it convenient to quote from the English translation of Paul Hazard's *The European Mind,* published by Yale University Press, and from The Tudor Press edition of *The Philosophy of Karl Jaspers,* edited by Paul Schillp. Finally, I am indebted to those persons who have helped in various ways with my translation of *Du Refus à l'invocation:* to Wallace Fowlie for his help in the translation of a passage from Paul Claudel's play *La Ville,* to Dr. Seymour Cain of the Philosophical Institute in San Francisco without whose encouragement the present translation would not have been begun, and to Mrs. Marjory Memory of the Library staff of the University of North Carolina, Greensboro.

Contents

Translators introduction

The present translation of *Du Refus à l'Invocation* fills a significant lacuna for readers of Marcel who have patiently awaited an English translation of this important collection of lectures and essays first published in France in 1940. The only major work of Marcel which has unaccountably remained untranslated, it has continued to offer in its author's own estimation the best introduction to his philosophical thought. *Creative Fidelity* is noteworthy for the richness of its descriptive analyses, for its systematic application of Marcel's "concrete approaches" to philosophical questions, and for its diversity of themes. In addition to Marcel's more characteristic themes, *Creative Fidelity* includes chapters on religious tolerance and orthodoxy together with a critical chapter on Jasper's ultimate situations which serves to exhibit the crucial points of *rapport* and of difference between the two philosophers. In general, *Creative Fidelity* offers us a more sustained and less fragmentary analysis of the typically Marcellian themes of fidelity and faith, incarnate being and participation, the metaproblematic, than has appeared in earlier published works.

Marcel is best known in this country as a leading "Christian existentialist." But he prefers to be called a "Neo-Socratic," both to avoid the doctrinaire implications of the above title, and more positively, to suggest the essentially dialogical, unfinished nature of his thought. Perhaps he may be best described in Hocking's phrase as a "reflective empiricist," the originator of a widened empiricism which encompasses in the subtlety and sensitivity of its analyses those inner, decisive experiences of our existence such as love, faith, hope, and despair. Distinguished in France not only as a philosopher, but also as a music and literary critic as well as dramatist who has written over a score of plays, Marcel is largely known in this country as the author of philosophical works such as *Being and Having* (1935) and *The Mystery of Being* (1951). More recently, the publication of books such as *Man Against Mass Society* (1952) and *The Decline of Wisdom* (1954), which are concerned with the techniques of personal degradation in modern society, reveal Marcel's growing awareness of the social import of his philosophical doctrines.

Born in Paris in 1889, the son of the French ambassador to Stockholm, Marcel was the beneficiary of a rich cultural upbringing involving extensive travel, a constant frequenting of literary and political milieux, and a wide reading, particularly in German and Anglo-American philosophy. At the age of 18 he took his *Diplôme* with a thesis on *The Metaphysical Ideas of Coleridge and their Relation to the Philosophy of Schelling.* Two years later he passed his *agrégation* at the Sorbonne. His reading was early concentrated on the Anglo-American idealists, Bradley, Royce and Hocking. His work on *The Metaphysics of Royce* still remains one of the best critical works on that philosopher; his own conception of creative fidelity owes much to Royce's philosophy of loyalty, as his analysis of sensation and its continuity with the higher forms of spiritual life owes much to Hocking. Already reacting against Bradley's monism in his *Metaphysical Journal* of 1914, and attempting to replace it with a philosophy of personal participation and freedom, Marcel's thought nevertheless echoes the idealist dialectic of immediacy, thought, and their fusion in the Absolute, in its own themes of existence, objectivity, and being or the Ontological Mystery. It is in his elucidation of mystery and the metaproblematic that Marcel has exerted a substantial influence on the current, analytically oriented movement in philosophical theology in England.

Marcel has taught only intermittently, earning his living primarily as an editor, publisher's reader, and as a literary, drama, and music critic.

II

Certain themes of Bradley may be clearly discerned in Marcel's analysis of conceptual thought and in his views on the relation of existence to being. First, for Marcel as for Bradley, philosophical thought is at once too abstract and too systematic for a reality which does not possess the unity of a system but rather that of immediate experience. Secondly, for both we find in immediate experience, although in a more rudimentary form, what re-emerges in its perfection in being; being is, in Marcel's terms, the "recuperation" of immediate experience on a higher level. Hence immediate experience provides the model for a supra-relational experience of the Absolute. Finally, if thought is inadequate to its object and can never do justice to existence,—an inadequacy whose symptoms are self-contradiction,—this is because thought separates itself from a reality of which it is essentially a part and of which we are only dimly aware in our unreflective experience. It is from here, however, that Marcel first takes his *point de départ*. For if thought is somehow "within experience," and if to know experience thought must somehow *be* immediate experience, then a fully concrete thought must follow the contours of that experience with all its singularities and deficiencies on pain of losing what is essential in it. Philosophy, Marcel declares, is experience *transmuted* into thought. Hence the attempt to construe experience as an objectively analyzable datum, or to construe the whole of reality in terms of a system of logically related propositions, is a betrayal of experience.

We shall see more fully what is implied in this withdrawal of thought from experience when we examine Marcel's concept of objectivity. But it is clear that it is this disability which inspires Marcel's "concrete approaches" and which gives substance to his translation of the familiar categories of philosophical thought into experiential terms: space and time become "paired modes of absence," the object, "what does not take us into account," solipsism and the viewpoint of the cogito, "egotism" and "autolatry," and conceptualization an "exorcism."

Despite the above similarities, it would be a mistake to identify Marcel's views with the idealist dialectic between thought and experience and the inclusion of both in a higher reality, whether this reality is an impersonal reason as for Hegel, or more congenially, an Absolute that has the quality of immediate experience as for Bradley. For Marcel's being is an "Absolute Thou," not the whole of reality, a particular being, not being in general. Moreover, that being is an exigence to which we are somehow bound, a reality immanent in yet transcending our experience, to which we have access by an act we are at liberty to realize or not; if being is capable of being felt as an aspiration of our nature or as a need, we are nevertheless free to accept or reject the "appeal" addressed to us. Thus in the inefficacy of thought to achieve by dialectical means a reconciliation with being; in the primacy of the act with which we respond to the appeal of being, whether that response be one of acceptance with its consequent feeling of plenitude, or rejection with its attendant despair; and in his theistic rather than monistic conception of being as an Absolute Thou, Marcel differs from the idealism he had earlier espoused.

While Marcel's philosophical or expository writing appears to emphasize the discontinuities in our experience, his drama, on the contrary, seems to stress a certain continuity. Here the related themes of existence, objectivity and being may be construed as three stages in a "dialectic" embodying three stages of increasing self-awareness. Here being is illuminated from "below," the meaning of being is approached by way of an analysis of human being, as it is for Heidegger, and the response to the question, "What am

I?" has a methodological priority to that of "What is being?" The first stage, existence, is a state of being characterized by aspirations which are vague and indeterminate because they exist on a purely sensuous or prereflective level; the protagonist of the drama is usually aware of his anxiety or self-alienation, but is unaware of its origin. Frequently, as in Marcel's play, *Le monde cassé* (A Broken World), there is an obscure presentiment that "something is wrong;" this awareness is usually followed by a frenetic activity in which the individual blindly engages himself in various projects to restore his sense of participation in the world. The second stage, objectivity, is characterized by an attempt to discover a rational solution to one's situation. In a sense, it represents an attempt to recreate the affective unity I had with the world by thought alone. Finally, being, involves the sought-for-restoration or "recuperation" of existence on a higher level, since it implies a degree of self-awareness or reflection which did not exist on the lower level of intelligibility. If we stress this aspect of Marcel's thought as it is revealed in his drama, we may envisage being or "ontological participation" as a "clarification" of existence or of what is indeterminately implied in existence. In his drama Marcel discloses the effects of this itinerary on the three principal relationships: to oneself, to other persons, and to the Absolute Thou.

It may be supposed that the exigencies of dramatic development here impose an artificial constraint on Marcel's dialectic. To this Marcel has responded that his goal was to restore to existence its *dignité tragique,* for life itself trembles with tragedy. It is not his purpose to present us with a *pièce à thèse* or to provide us with a purely rhetorical exposition of spiritual conflict, but rather to show how tragic conflict is rooted in the *ambiguité foncière* of our situation as existing beings. And here reflection, the search for rational solutions or justifications, has a fundamental role. Hence while in his philosophical writing Marcel stresses rational thought as a bar to communion, and in his plays views it as a necessary stage through which we must pass on the road to communion, this must not be regarded as a contradiction, for it is both. We must now turn to the different stages in this ascent, bearing in mind that these are not logical categories of thought and that a relapse is always possible. For if existence offers the possibility of a consummation which transcends my life, it also presents us with the permanent possibility of despair.

III

A. EXISTENCE. The central datum of existence is *incarnate being,* i.e., the affective unity I have with my body. The elucidation of this unity requires an analysis of sensation or feeling. Marcel's approach to the nature of incarnate being and sensation has both a negative and a positive aspect. First, he attempts to exhibit the inadequacies of the traditional solutions to what is familiarly known as the "mind-body problem," together with an allied conception of the nature of sensation. And secondly, he attempts more positively to elucidate the nature of both by means of his "concrete approaches," i.e., the presentation of exemplary experiences which suggest the direction in which his meaning is to be sought. The indispensability of the latter method is seen to rest on the incapacity of conceptual thought to express without distortion the experience of a feeling unity which eludes the distinction between subject and object. Hence incarnate being precludes the possibility of either identifying the person with a certain body (materialism), construing the person as a mind, distinct from the body, (idealism), or as related as a distinct entity to the body (dualism). Briefly, his argument against the materialist view which identifies the self with an ostensively defined body or ensemble of sense-organs, relies on the fact that I can adopt certain attitudes toward my body, evaluate it, alter my relations to it, hence cannot be identified *with* this body. Frequently, he appeals to a "principle of intimacy," i.e. an *experience* of my body which is not one of detachment and which therefore does not allow us to construe the body I call mine as an *object*. His argument against the dualist view exploits the meaning of the instrumental relation. On the dualist view that he considers, the body is construed as the instrument of the mind, i.e. something *used* by the mind to extend its powers. An instrument requires an instrumentalist or agent, however, and this agent in turn must be the instrument of a still further instrumentalist. The instrumental view therefore leads to an infinite regress. Marcel also invokes the related view that dualism can only lead to a hypostatization of the mind, i.e., the mind is simply endowed with those potentialities which are realized by the body; the mind itself is necessarily construed as something on the model of the body or as possessing the attributes of body. Finally, there is the idealist view which Marcel associates with the cogito, and to which he accords most of his attention. Briefly, the view in question involves the effort to identify the self or "I" with a mind, i.e. something existing by itself in a disembodied or disincarnate state and at no particular place or time. The "I," Marcel affirms, cannot be identified with "thought in general" or with "whatever thinks," as in the case of the Cogito; the "I" is not an abstract "epistemological subject." Marcel buttresses his argument against the Cogito by pointing to the self-contradiction in attempting to say something about the world from a point of view outside the world in which the self finds itself. But generally he relies on his concrete approaches to point up the *practical* impossibility of disincarnation.

A corollary to all of the above views is the "message-view" of sensation. This asserts that sense-data are transmitted by external objects and are picked up by a body which, as an ensemble of sense-organs, may be construed as a "receiving-set"; the data are then "translated" by the mind. The view is a familiar one, and has been dubbed by Ryle the "para-mechanical hypothesis of sensation"; sensation occurs "only if the object causes something to go on in my body which in turn causes something else to go on in my mind." Marcel's objections to this theory are similar to those of Ryle, and he rejects the term "impression" for the same reason, viz., that it presupposes a special causal theory which conflicts with our ordinary use of the term. Similarly, his argument that the "translation" of events into sense-data or sensations *presupposes* the existence of the latter, hence that sensation cannot itself be construed as a "message," is parallel to Ryle's argument that since the perception of objects implies the having of at least one sensation, sensation itself cannot be a perception.

The more positive aspect of Marcel's approach with respect to these two themes consists (a) in the distinction between *a* body or a body-object, and *my* body, or the body-subject, and (b) the view that sensation is an action, not an affection or an "impression," and that it implies a "centrifugal tendency" towards the external world. Both of these views converge on Marcel's notion of *existence*.

(a) *My* body, Marcel affirms, is not to be confused with *a* body, i.e. this particular body which is ostensively definable. In his *Journal Metaphysique* he notes that I have an inner awareness of my body which is not based on observation, although my body is something, one and the same thing, which can also be perceived by myself or another on that basis. The person or "I" then, is at once a body-subject and a body-object, something which is at once the content of an inner awareness and an object of public knowledge. An analysis of sensation, moreover, discloses that the inner experience or awareness I have of my body, my sense of embodiment or existence, so to speak, is fused with an awareness of myself as in the world, as being there for others; my existence, Marcel affirms, is "manifestory." Now it is clear that the results of such a phenomenological analysis are not conclusive with respect to the *"objective"* existence of the self. For we cannot infer *objective* existence from a *sense* or *feeling* of embodiment. It would seem, however, that Marcel's Sensualist metaphysics which is based on such an analysis, would require an identification of "existence" with the "sense of existence" while "objective existence" becomes what he terms "objectivity." This however, entails a subjectivism which Marcel seeks to avoid, and moreover ignores the dual nature of incarnate being. Hence while he often stresses the *antithesis* between existence and objectivity (the object is *by definition* what has being independently of my awareness of it); although he habitually focusses his attention on the various modalities of our *inner* experience of our body, stressing the affective unity I have with my body and contrasting "being" thus understood with an objective "hav-

ing," his more technical "definition" of existence takes account of
the two inseparable aspects of incarnate being. Thus the function
"X exists" is equivalent to "X is related to me as I am related to my
body." That is, incarnate being is the paradigm case of existence;
so that (formally) when suitable values other than "I" are substituted for X the above function expresses a proposition; "I exist" is
itself tautologous. ("X exists" is not equivalent to "X is related to
his body as I am related to mine," for then the existent is converted
into an object and the existence of other selves becomes problematic). It is clear that existence is not a general property or concept since it has a unique reference whenever the "existential orbit,"
as Marcel terms it, differs. If however, incarnate being implies a
center or an orbit, hence *a body,* it is less clear how other selves can
be as intimately related to me as I am to *my body,* how existential
participation can be extended to interpersonal communion. At one
time, Marcel conceived of this relationship in metapsychical terms,
where the presence of the other person was not mediated by an
alien body. Generally however, Marcel regards the affective unity I
have with *other* selves in terms of what he calls "disponibilité"
or disposability, i.e., openness, permeability to the other, spiritual
availability, which are best illustrated in connection with the relations of love and fidelity. It would seem, then, that we must construe interpersonal communion as an *analogue* of the affective
unity characteristic of incarnate being or existential participation.
Sympathy, feeling *with* the other person, or putting oneself in his
shoes, are phenomena which would adequately illustrate Marcel's
formula: *Esse is Co-esse.* Marcel, however, is also intent on showing
how the relationship I bear to myself is a *function* of the relationship I bear to others, how these relationships vary directly with one
another. Hence there is not merely an *analogy* between the two, but
also, we are tempted to say, a *causal* or *psychological* relation.
Marcel's remarks concerning the nature of sensation and affectivity,
however, point to his conviction in a still closer relation which can
only be called "mysterious."

(b) Sensation, Marcel maintains, is not an affection or an impression, but an action. Marcel is concerned mainly with two fea-

tures of sensation: (1) a primordial relation of ourselves to the world in sensation, the full significance of which is best brought out in connection with the phenomenon of alienation or "désorbitation." And (2) the continuity of sensation with the "higher affectivities" or higher forms of spiritual life, i.e., inter-subjective relations. The analysis of the first is based on the phenomenon of "feeling at home," exhibited for example, in the sailor's attachment to the sea or the farmers attachment to his land, and offers no special difficulty: we readily recognize these features of the primitive affective unity we have with a circumambient world. The second aspect, however, presents a greater challenge to our comprehension and is one of the more intriguing as it is one of the more puzzling aspects of Marcel's doctrine. For sensation is seen to possess a complexity, a resonance, we had not anticipated. Thus Marcel develops his analysis of the centrifugal tendencies of sensation in terms of "receptivity," "extending hospitality," etc. which imply an active initiative of the agent and a differentiation of the world not to be discovered in immediate experience. These in turn lead to the fuller forms of communion such as charity and love, and ultimately to fidelity and faith. Nevertheless, I think it would be a mistake to overstress this continuity. For if we consider Marcel's analysis of fidelity, it is clear that the spiritual relations to which Marcel refers are ultimately contingent on an act or decision of the agent which is superimposed on feeling, and which implies a radical *discontinuity* with feeling.

B. OBJECTIVITY. The terms "object," "objectivity," and their cognates are persistently used by Marcel in a pejorative context, and possess such latitude of meaning, that the reader begins to suspect that Marcel uses it as his most general term of opprobrium, and that it has emotive but no descriptive meaning. We can, however, discriminate three related contexts of meaning. (1) Objectivity refers to any exercise of *conceptual thought* which is, as for Bradley and Bergson, inadequate to a reality incapable of being grasped by concepts or by a language which is both general and artificial. As we have noted in connection with Marcel's analysis of incarnate being, thought is relational and abstracts from a reality which is essentially non-relational. The evidence of this inadequacy is moreover exhibited in the contradictions which ensue when we attempt to think reality. (2) The term is also employed to refer to *scientific methods and procedures:* to scientific generalization where the particular case has significance only as an instance of a universal law; to the method of successive approximations to a truth which is therefore construed as eternally elusive: empirical truth in this sense possesses degrees of probability and never certainty; (the existence of the "object" of religious faith cannot, on the other hand, be expressed in terms of postulates or hypotheses); alternatively, the term may imply the concept of the standard observer or the intersubstitutability of observers, the postulation of normal conditions of observation, the establishment of criteria of evidence which are wholly public and therefore "impersonal." Or it may refer to whatever is verifiable in experience as distinct from events or states of affairs for which "objective" evidence is irrelevant or impossible in principle to obtain. Finally, (3) the term may refer to an *attitude* one can adopt towards oneself or others which Marcel, however, clearly regards as either motivated by or as inspiring the above exercises of thought. Usually the attitude in question implies a posture of detachment towards others and towards the world, a spectator-view of reality, a fear of involvement, egocentrism, impermeability to others, impersonality, etc. Marcel's drama is particularly rich in personages who answer this description, and who are dominated by the spirit of abstraction: the pedant, the ideologist, the religious man whose acts are motivated by a false professional charity, the dramatist whose family life has significance only as a source of dramatic material. The objective attitude is ordinarily accompanied by the emotions of fear, distrust, self-alienation, anxiety and despair, the renunciation of this attitude by a sense of unity, harmony and peace.

In his more recent works Marcel has been concerned with the consequences of the extension of the scientific method and mentality on the individual and society, as he was interested in the motives underlying these in his drama. His animus is directed against the substitution of an abstract thinking subject for the concrete existing individual whose destiny must emerge from a particular situation that is his own and no other's; against the *homo spectans* as opposed to the *homo participans,* against the individual who construes existence as an abstract category and who thinks the world rather than lives in it. Hence he inveighs against the *fachmensch* of a technological society made possible by the growth of science, the application of science to society with the consequent rationalization of every phase of existence; the growth of bureaucracy in which man becomes an enumerable list or inventory of objective properties, and the general impersonality of human relations. Ideology and mass fanaticism, the use of ideas as weapons for ulterior purposes, the "democratization" of thought, the *nivellement* of individuals and the elimination of standards of excellence with a disregard for what is rare and distinctive, all seem to be associated with the objective habit of mind. It is clear, however, that Marcel refers here to the pernicious consequences of this attitude on the individual and society and does not intend to impugn the actual criteria of scientific investigation themselves; what Marcel condemns is not so much science in itself, as the inappropriate extension of its techniques and procedures to interpersonal *rapports* where it is not only inapplicable but also destructive of human relations. It is the abuse not the use of these methods which leads to dehumanization. The scientific habit of mind *can* lead to a detachment from the lives of others, an *insouciance* with respect to the needs of other persons, a pragmatic outlook with respect to both oneself and others where the same motives of scientific control and mastery operate. And yet it is plain that Marcel's critique is sometimes directed against the scientific enterprise itself and not merely against its more undesirable consequences. For Marcel also suggests that scientific inquiry is based on the fear of error and that this fear is the very antithesis of faith and confidence, of a creative fidelity which restores us to being.

It should be noted that Marcel's description of objectivity, apart from its independent value as a critique of science and society, is an integral part of Marcel's concrete approaches to being. For it implies the adoption of a *via negationis* in which the metaproblematic nature of ontological participation may be suggested by a method of exclusion, i.e., by revealing to us its antithesis, what it is not, and thereby conveying to us by indirection the nature of this reality. Furthermore, it must not be assumed that *all* thought is inadequate to the particular reality Marcel wishes to convey. For there is a "Secondary reflection" which is synonymous with an authentic philosophical inquiry, and whose role it is to "join what objective thought has disjoined." The nature of this philosophical reflection is ambiguous, although it too may be described negatively as a meditation on one's personal experience which rejects any concession to the requirements of abstract thought for systematization, generalization, unity. Sometimes Marcel associates it with a Bergsonian act of recollection which restores unity and continuity to experience, sometimes with an obedience to the injunction *Il faut pas juger*. But it is clear that these are rather preliminary to the kind of reflection which is best exemplified in Marcel's own philosophical thought.

C. BEING. Marcel asserts that he came to the question of being in terms of particular beings and their relations. There is no Being in general, no being "emptied of individual characteristics." Indeed our understanding of being is restricted to our understanding of interpersonal relations with particular beings in the relationships of love and fidelity, etc., Being itself is indefinable, and the Absolute Thou, God, whom Marcel identifies with being, is not the object of a rational theology: any attempt to prove his existence or define his nature is futile. It is in the mutuality or reciprocity of personal relationships, of which fidelity is the supreme example, that we gain access to being, that we can have some intimation of the Absolute Thou. "The more we are able to understand the individual being," Marcel affirms, "the more we shall be oriented, and as it were directed towards, a grasp of being itself."

Fidelity towards a thou provides us with an insight into faith in the Absolute Thou. Marcel plainly intends that the term "fidelity," as it is used in ordinary contexts of discourse retain this sense in its religious employment, even though it must be "semantically stretched" to accommodate the religious use of "faith." As a recent writer, R. Hepburn, has pointed out, "religious language emeshes a new expression in a nest of accepted expressions," with words sometimes being "wrested" from their normal use to convey what ordinary language cannot completely convey. The same author, however, suggests that "an appearance of meaning can be given by showing the direction in which we are to look for the meaning which will finally elude us; "an expression can be "cashable in part," and in connection with certain religious concepts such as the dependency of the world on God, it is possible "to recount the dependence relations that we can describe, annul them all, and hope that they will have made possible the non-linguistic or "prelinguistic" movement of thought that can alone begin to grasp what language cannot state." This is, I believe, an accurate description of Marcel's own practice.

Marcel characteristically approaches the question of fidelity to another person in terms of sincerity; in his earlier plays such as *Le Chemin de Crete* (Ariadne), he questions the metaphysical possibility of sincerity. Sincerity to oneself, as fidelity to another, implies an element of spontaneity, of genuine feeling or love, and must therefore be distinguished from "constancy" or from obligation, which are coercive. Marcel rejects the ethical rigorism of a Kant for whom the rightness of an act is based on duty or obedience to an imperative, and which implies an inner conflict between one's inclinations and one's obligations. The fulfillment of an obligation *à contre-coeur* is devoid of love and cannot be identified with fidelity. Indeed Marcel questions whether I do in fact have the *right* to fulfill an obligation under these conditions, and not merely whether I *can* in fact do so. Marcel's concrete critique of the ethics of obligation emerges clearly from his drama. In one play, Marcel attempts to show that an ethic of obligation can be based on egoism, on an image of oneself as "coming up to one's own standards," and that it can, as in the case of a pastor who forgives his wife's infidelity, be based on a "professional charity." The ethics of obligation, then, may be construed as one symptom of that "fanaticism of the ideal" which Marcel persistently combats. Thus the problem for Marcel is how to define a commitment which avoids both the Kantian solution on the one hand, because willed out of a positive feeling or desire, and a valetudinarianism which destroys the possibility of any commitment by making every decision contingent on one's state of feeling in the future. A creative fidelity is neither coercive nor contingent.

The possibility of an absolute fidelity or of a commitment satisfying the above conditions, lies in the collaboration of two acts, one of which depends on our own initiative, the other of which does not. In the first place, commitment implies a *refusal* to put a future state of mind or attitude in question. And this in turn is based on an *interpretation* of any future conflict between how I feel and what I ought to do, as a temptation or *épreuve* (trial). Hence conflict becomes something which I can actively resist, although the apprehension of the possibility of conflict is what makes commitment a risk. This, however, is clearly not sufficient to defeat the doubt that my resolution could have been mistaken (the object has become unworthy, conditions have altered, I was deceived, etc.). For the relation I have entered into to become unshakable and for the above reflections to be construed as a betrayal or a temptation, my commitment must become infused with *hope*. Hope, however, is ultimately an invocation or appeal to what lies *outside* our unaided efforts; fidelity, in short, is only possible in faith, i.e. when fidelity to the other is seen to be "the shadow of a more absolute fidelity to the Thou." Fidelity, then, is metaproblematic, for it is dependent on a "response" to my appeal, a transcendent revelation. The supreme examples of fidelity for Marcel are those which do not merely imply the abrupt termination by the agent of a series of reflections seeking to justify a changed attitude toward the other. For in *le mort de l'être aimé,* the death of the beloved, the "object" of fidelity is not *in principle* an object of empirical investigation or rational inquiry. The analysis of fidelity does not of course preclude any approach which would help to elucidate its nature, and Marcel also attempts to offer logical distinctions which would clarify the nature of faith. Thus he distinguishes between *belief that* such-and-such is the case, and *belief in* something or someone. And his analysis of what we might call *attestatory judgments,* which "witness" one's faith, and do not communicate any factual information either about the content of one's belief or one's subjective state, offer fruitful suggestions for a further analysis of this class of religious statements. Marcel regards any skeptical attempt to separate a "subjective" state from its intended object a misconstrual of the meaning of such judgments.

The metaproblematic or the ontological mystery is the central notion in Marcel's philosophy, and has led critics like Gilson to see in Marcel's thought an attempt to establish the philosophical foundations of mysticism. The metaproblematic is not a definable concept, and Marcel habitually refers to it in negative terms, i.e. as what is not-problematic. Indeed, he asks how something not reducible to a problem can be thought at all. It is nevertheless used by Marcel in a technical sense and its meaning is circumscribed both by Marcel's concrete approaches, and in opposition to the problematic.

The metaproblematic, Marcel affirms in his few positive utterances on this subject, is something which encroaches on its own data, upon the intrinsic conditions of its own possibility. What is meant by these cryptic utterances? Marcel here is referring to the contradictory consequences of attempting to "problematize" the metaproblematic, to pose it in the form of a problem. However, if we restrict ourselves to this characteristic of the metaproblematic, we are likely to confuse it with what we may term the *pseudoproblematic.* This is illustrated by our earlier discussion of incarnate being: the attempt to conceptualize a non-relational unity alters the nature of the object of our analysis. (This is also true of the "problems" of evil, personal encounter, love, etc.) In general, the pseudoproblematic refers to the attempt to state something that cannot be thought; but this difficulty can be ascribed to the *inherent inexpressibility* of its object, or to a *logical* difficulty which can be clarified. We can make this distinction clearer if we consider the conception of the pseudoproblematic held by a contemporary linguistic philosopher, Strawson. Here the statement of the problem, Strawson affirms, "involves the acceptance of a conceptual scheme and at the same time the silent repudiation of one of the conditions of its existence. . . . Such problems are in the terms in which they are stated, insoluble." Hence the "solution" would seem to lie in the clarification of the logical difficulty which would show the senselessness of the "problem." It is clear that what we are confronted with is not a mystery but an apparent mystery that can be dispelled. But Marcel does not mean by the metaproblematic something which is due to "a misunderstanding of our language" and which can be remedied by linguistic analysis.

The metaproblematic can best be illuminated in opposition to the problematic. A problem is something that can be solved in accordance with some technical procedure. Thus the propositions of empirical science which fall within the province of the natural world, are all problematic. This, of course, refers equally to statements about natural phenomena which are still unexplained. Such propositions can be formulated so as to make sense even if we cannot now decide on their truth values. But a mystery, Marcel affirms, is not a lucuna in our knowledge or a void to be filled, since this is only a limiting case of the *problematic*. Hence the metaproblematic is neither a pseudoproblem which can be "remedied" by linguistic analysis, nor an as yet unsolved problem due to a lack of knowledge resolvable in principle by further scientific inquiry. *A mystery is something which while insoluble in principle, is yet not senseless.* It is an aspect of our experience which is inexpressible, hence inaccessible to communicable knowledge. But it can still be spoken of in a *suggestive* if not in an informative way. The view that "all and every experience is expressible and communicable," is as Maslow points out in his study of Wittgenstein's *Tractatus,* "a case of a presumptuous and dogmatic rationalism," one which Wittgenstein himself presumably avoided. Cognitive knowledge does not exhaust the whole of reality, and "what cannot be said need not be nonsense; it can also be mysterious." We cannot of course speak of it in any cognitive way: "Whereof one cannot speak, thereof one must be silent."

In conclusion, we must, as M. B. Foster points out in his *Mystery and Philosophy,* distinguish elimination of mystery from revelation of mystery. The latter is not something to be acquired from God by any technique; it is not the object of a knowledge "obtainable by the application of a technique which man can control," nor is there any public scientific evidence for it. "Since it is an accommodation of God's revelation to our creaturely capacities, it is hidden so that some will see it, others not." The problematic approach, on the other hand, excludes revelation as a source of truth, and it is ultimately on this ground that we must understand Marcel's denigration of the "objective" approach. "Belief in Divine Revelation," as Foster affirms, "seems to involve something like a repentance in the sphere of the intellect." Thus the "peace, unity, reconciliation, harmony, and community" of which Marcel finds an intimation in our spiritual relations with others, is a goal not finally achievable by scientific techniques but by the response to an appeal transcending the self.

Robert Rosthal

CREATIVE FIDELITY

Introduction

The reader will find nothing in the present volume remotely resembling a system of metaphysics in which the mind suddenly descends to some vantage point from which it can, by a rational sequence of steps, get back to the data of ordinary experience; such a procedure gives us the false impression that experience has been reconstructed by the creative movement of a dialectical process. I do not deny that I have a nostalgia for system-building, and I admire the rigor with which Louis Lavelle, for example, ties up the loose ends of his doctrine. But I cannot hide the fact that my admiration is mingled with a certain distrust; that the persistent feeling of nostalgia that I sometimes catch in myself, is not entirely justified in the light of a reflection which is soon able to uncover its unsuspected source. Indeed, how could I ignore the fact that the need for systematization embodies, on the one hand, a desire to perfect the network of communications which links our ideas together, transforming them into a unified domain over which we can exercise increasing control; on the other hand, the desire to make our thought more communicable, to embody it in a system which can be called our own the way in which an object or a piece of property is our own. Moreover, it is clear that a system based on definitions and theorems decidedly diminishes the inferiority complex philosophers have had for the past fifty years with the development of the empirical sciences; philosophers have often been accused of responding to this development with the same time-worn truisms, with their equally sterile paradoxes, or with fruitless excursions into the nebulous realms of the unverifiable.

In succumbing to the temptation of system-building, however, isn't there a tendency to forget that any philosophy worthy of its name is impossible without an investigation of our condition as existing and thinking beings; that we must first ask whether that condition warrants the act whereby the metaphysician "claims to install himself at the center of being or to rediscover the primitive act on which both his being and that of the world depends?" [1] For my part, I am convinced that the transcendent cannot be identified with any conceptual point of view. Yet the expressions "install" and "rediscover" are meaningless unless they imply such an operation however clearly it is realized. From a metaphysical point of view the most significant step that can be taken is one which enables me to see that I cannot without self-contradiction conceive the absolute as a central observatory from which the universe may be contemplated in its totality, instead of being apprehended in the partial and oblique way it indeed is by all of us. For I cannot conceive of the existence of such an observatory unless I somehow place myself in it mentally; and it is this very notion which must be declared self-contradictory. It would seem however, that we here encounter a paradox: how indeed can I even refer to "my point of view" without presupposing that "absolute point of view" I have declared inconceivable? Perhaps the only reply that can be given to this question is that the notion of a true order of the world as it would be discovered to an observer who occupied a privileged position or who observed it under optimal conditions of perception, is implied in the awareness of this world as it is originally given to me according to a perspective which is mine and no other's; this, however, does not entail that such a notion expresses or embodies the advance to a higher level of being urged by all the great philosophical rationalisms. It may very well be—and this will be one of the recurrent themes of the following meditations—that depersonalized thought cannot admit us to a realm worthy of being called metaphysical, or even help us to formulate the idea of such a world. In my opinion, it is Karl Jaspers, following in the steps of Kierkegaard and in all likelihood Heidegger too, who merits the important distinction of having shown that existence (and *a fortiori* transcendence) can only be apprehended or evoked in a realm beyond that of thought in general which must operate by means of signs on the contents of the objective world.

It will be convenient at this point to repeat, or rather paraphrase, the unpublished text of a talk I gave to the *Union pour la Vérité* shortly after the publication of my *Journal Métaphysique,* when I was still unaware of the philosophy of existence. I addressed an audience which was for the most part rationalist in its convictions, hence I thought it necessary to clarify my position with respect to that of Léon Brunschvicg who had earlier published his huge work on the *Progrès de la Conscience.* "Believe *or* verify, the alternative is exhaustive. To construe disbelief as a negative state is to play on words. Disbelief for the philosopher is a positive quality just as courage is for the soldier." [2] The formulation has the merit of being unequivocal. Believe *or* verify. In other words, adopting an attitude which is profoundly, yet consciously intolerant, the advocates of the *monad* construed as infinite subjectivity of thought dismiss all non-empirical or non-social interpretations of the claim expressed by *I believe.*

"I believe it would be accurate to say that the kind of vital reaction such a claim formerly evoked in me has been one of the sources of all my subsequent thought. Global response—refusal, rejection, the exact nature of which is not easy to describe. It could perhaps be compared to what occurs when we try to recall a name we have forgotten, and when someone suggests a name which we know with certainty 'is not that one.'

"Beginning with this initial refusal, Idealism gradually seemed to me to be a doctrine which did not 'work,' which indeed did not claim to 'work,' and even claimed not to 'work'; on the contrary, it tried to transcend vital questions, i.e. evade them, as far as I was concerned, free to varnish over a number of simple negations: denial of God, of Providence, or immortality, camouflaging these denials with solemn utterances such as the moral order, spirituality, eternity.

"My uncompromising opposition was due to a massive belief, so to speak, that some of the supreme human experiences implied the apprehension or state of something transcending any possible verification: to illustrate this point I have only to evoke love or adoration the objects of which are impossible in principle to exhaust, and which cannot be specified by the successive approximations typical of the procedures of empirical verification.

"Furthermore, when I affirm that a certain proposition is verifiable, I imply that there is a set of conditions which are general in principle, i.e. are understood as normal or as applicable to any agent capable of uttering valid judgments. This view eventuates in the notion of a depersonalized subject, which means that A can be substituted for B if B possesses the necessary equipment for a veridical experience. Hence, we are now in an area where vulgarization is in principle possible. It is important to note by the way the relation between the intrinsically vulgarizable nature of objective thought and the idea of democracy; democracy has consolidated itself in everyone's mind in the measure that positive science has succeeded in subjugating the mind.

"However, if we fix our attention on the idea of normal conditions of experience, the latter will seem to crystallize into a postulate. While the propriety of postulating certain normal conditions of apprehension in the case of an objective experience is obvious, there is no ground for denying infra- or supra-objective experiences, or levels of existence where the postulate is no longer applicable. For instance, on the level of appreciation or of esthetic creation, the idea of a postulate is devoid of meaning. A particular musical composition, for example, seems a pure chaos of sound to my neighbor while I discern an order which completely escapes him: shall we say that one of us is experiencing it under normal conditions while the other is not? This is plainly an improper way of speaking. It would be more appropriate to say that I am somehow in harmony with the work while my neighbor is not. The example is sufficient to indicate that there are realms of experience which possess a particular order or intelligibility subject to conditions which cannot be properly specified; if they are unspecifiable, it is because they inhere in the subject himself insofar as he is identified with a living experience which cannot by its nature mirror itself.

"There are several reasons for assuming that the question of miracles can be illuminated on the basis of the above considerations. It is not inconceivable that there are beings who satisfy a set of spiritual conditions capable of modifying their apprehension of reality; indeed this claim is too restrictive since there is the closest relation between the mode of apprehension and the thing apprehended. We can also concede that there are events which occur to such beings which have a maximum improbability from the point of view of our ordinary experience. It is unnecessary to add that from the religious point of view, the events in question cannot be separated from the meanings they possess for those who experience them; nothing would be further from the truth than to construe the meaning as arbitrarily associated *a posteriori* by the mind with an historical occurrence which is in itself indifferent.

"On the above view, we can no longer agree with traditional empiricism that the deliverances of experience are decisive, for what is in question is knowing *what* experience is decisive and how that experience should be internally qualified, so to speak. The dangers in this view, of course, should not be concealed. We require in this case too, a frame of reference, but it will not be that of thought in general or of a reason immanent in ordinary experience; one must be within the privileged world where these events take place in order to discern, appreciate or sanctify them. For this reason miracles can only be acknowledged and authenticated by the Church, and only insofar as they are related to the Incarnation. For the miracle is both the present and remote witness to it, a radiation, so to say, of it.

"In evoking in this context the role of the Church, I am referring to a real community, to an existent universal, as it were, which obviously cannot be identified with the monad referred to above. Mr. Brunschvicg assumes that because I can reach an understanding with my neighbor on computations or business affairs, I have a foundation for and even a guarantee of, an authentic spiritual communion. It is to be feared however, that reflection confirms our experience in revealing the illusory nature of this expectation. Indeed there is no real community in this case because there is no real plurality, no distinctions acknowledged as such. Instead, we are dealing with an external mode of correspondence which thought has with itself, such as what I observe when I check the validity of an arithmetical proof. A community is only possible when beings acknowledge that they are mutually different while existing together in their differences.

"It would be relevant at this point to refer to a few simple, immediate experiences which philosophers have either wrongly ignored because they seemed trivial, or unduly intellectualized by applying to them the traditional normative criteria. If we adopt the religious point of view, it can be said that the universal is the awareness of participating together in a unique adventure, in a fundamental and indivisible mystery of human destiny. What brings me closer to another being and really binds me to him is not the knowledge that he can check and confirm an addition or subtraction I had to do for my business account; it is rather the thought that he has passed through the same difficulties as I have, that he has undergone the same dangers, that he has had a childhood, been loved, that others have been attracted to him and have had hope in him; and it also means that he is called upon to suffer, to decline and to die. It seems clear that it is only in these terms that a meaningful content can be ascribed to the term *fraternity* whose use has been abused by rationalism. Rationalism has introduced an abstract element into human relations which depersonalizes beings; and the democratic, secular philosophy which is a degraded aspect of rationalism, is also a distortion and complete perversion of that evangelical thought to which the temper of abstraction is wholly alien. In this connection it may be observed that the idea of the fatherhood of God which Mr. Brunschvicg interprets as the relic of an infantile anthropomorphism, actually assumes preeminent value. For it is only in terms of this idea that an effective, authentically existing human community is even conceivable, whereas for philosophic rationalism it is an idea which is so impoverished that it is no more than a mere logical skeleton, a line of logical possibilities."

In my talk to the *Union pour la Vérité* I doubtless failed to emphasize sharply enough that this community or living universal does not transcend the natural order of things. It must be clearly shown how it creates a region in human nature itself in which an authentic religious life, a life of grace can be led, although to be sure, this is accomplished by movements, the origin of which lies outside of our own possibilities and volitions. If, however, we try to abstract from these concrete grounds as every philosophy does which bases itself on thought in general, i.e. on a depersonalized mind, then the religious reality becomes unintelligible; the only remaining alternative is to make it the object of a systematically depreciatory analysis, involving psycho-pathological interpretations, Freudian or otherwise; or of a sociological analysis which inevitably seems to confuse the infra- and the supra-individual, and whose results are least subject to challenge precisely in those areas where religious consciousness has been silenced and methodically choked off.

The objection will be raised, however, that after all it has been in the name of religion that the "religious consciousness" has been betrayed; isn't it an evasion to construe one as authentic and the other as a crude alloy? To answer the objection we do not have to appeal to Bergson's distinction between the open and the closed, although the distinction is still fully meaningful today, for we cannot deny the existence of the above contraries, and even more, we must concede that they are grounded in being itself; unless, that is, we want to convert human existence into an intermittent dream or a delirious stream of images, justifying thereby every abandonment and every disavowal. The only positive counter-weight to the nameless horror of our age perhaps, has been the simple fact that the martyr has recovered for men of good will and faith his traditional value as witness, or better, as *creative testimonial*.

In the final analysis, the paradox expressed in these two last words is the main theme of the present book. Roughly, it is that it would be a complete mistake to construe the essence of creation as a *making* or as a productive activity whose source is in the agent itself. The same presence and the same appeal to the soul by the Being within it can be found in any creative act whether visible or not; the act, the same with itself despite the inexhausti- bility of its manifestations, testifies to this same presence, and the soul can challenge or annul it insofar as it is a soul endowed with freedom. On the threshold of the catacombs which may soon swallow us up, it should be remembered that it is basically the same power of creative fidelity concentrated in more favorable times in architecture, music and poetry, which tomorrow will strengthen the fierce resolution of those who reject the consum- mation by themselves or others of man's denial of man, or to formulate this in a more profound way, the denial of the more than human by the less than human.

G. M.

NOTES

1 Louis Lavelle *De l'acte* (Paris: Aubier, 1937), Ch. I, Art. 1, p. 9.
2 *Le Progrès de la Conscience dans la philosophie occidentale* (Paris: Presses Universitaires, 1953.) Vol. II, p. 744.

I

Incarnate being as the central datum of metaphysical reflection

A few weeks ago I was walking in the Luxembourg Gardens thinking over certain familiar themes, when I apparently strayed into one of those badly kept gardens where everything had been trampled on and crushed and where no surprise nook remained to spur the imagination. A shocking impression but one with which I am admittedly familiar. The English term *stale*—a word which is practically untranslatable and which refers particularly to bread that is no longer fresh but also to anything that is repetitious or worn by the passage of time—occurred to me. Immediately, the experience I had just been exposed to took on substance through the efficacy of the word itself, became an object of reflection, then just as swiftly and as if by magic, I was free of it. I had revived a theme which has often caught my attention but which I have never been able to exploit fully, which for that very reason preserves a certain freshness. . . . The feeling of staleness only occurs in the stagnant regions of the mind. The stagnant coincides with the repetitious; and here, as in the sensible world, stagnation seems to be the beginning of putrescence. From a cognitive point of view, there is no experience which has less significance and which is less capable of being understood; for the rationalist the only toxic principle is error—and he finds it difficult to understand it or to conceive it as a possibility. In the present case, however, we are dealing with something revealed to us by experience which must be elucidated. I think I may say without exaggeration, that my whole philosophical career has been devoted to the production—I dislike using this physical term—of currents whereby life can be reborn in regions of the mind which have yielded to apathy and are exposed to decomposition. The inner event has an unusual significance for this reason, even though we find it impossible to relate it to any specific, objective situation. In the past I have frequently had the occasion to stress the metaphysical significance of the encounter, never having seen eye to eye with the rationalist who prefers to construe it as a simple, accidental meeting; but I had not noticed until now that encounters can also occur on the level of thought. To encounter someone is not merely to cross his path but to be, for the moment at least, near to or with him. To use a term I have often used before, it means being a *co-presence*. We have a number of thoughts with which we get by without really encountering them; they are not revealed or present to us, and it might be added, we do not expose ourselves to them. A real encounter with one of these thoughts, if we consider the matter carefully, is something which does not happen accidentally, and one can ready oneself for it—as for a visible encounter—but it still involves one of those shocks which punctuates the career of the soul.

These reflections require further elaboration; their full meaning will not be obvious until I have finished; nevertheless they may help orient your thoughts towards a concrete philosophy which views what is cut and dry and what is depersonalized with distrust. It is a philosophy whose aim it is to restore those links which a certain type of idealogy has conceived it as its task to break. I acknowledge the slightly bergsonian overtones of these words, but certain nuances of meaning should be pointed out. Bergsonism as a system must be distinguished from bergsonism as a mode of thinking, and I would not be so ready to invoke Bergson in this context unless I could construe him in the latter sense. He offers us something which, while it does not fully account for, yet enables us to come nearer to, the concrete life of the mind as investigation and creative inquiry—provided we disregard the theory of intellect that bergsonism as a system presents. The defect in that system, it may be noted, is the failure to sympathetically apprehend and, as it were, commune with the intellect, to provide instead an already intellectualized schema of intelligence to which intelligence is reducible only if we confuse it with its products. In short, the primary distinction we must make in this context is not between intellect on the one hand, and instinct or even intuition, on the other, but between *pensée pensante* and *pensée pensée*.

A concrete philosophy is a philosophy of the pensée pensante; it can be developed only by acrobatic feats which place one in continuous jeopardy. I know beforehand that the reader will find the terminology and the expression of what follows, inadequate, and I can only do my best to help him adjust his inner vision in a way which will let him see behind the words I am forced to use.

In order to eliminate any serious misunderstandings, however, it should be understood that this philosophy of the *pensée pensante* has nothing in common with subjective idealism; in a way, it is the inverse of such a doctrine; for myself, as for Mr. Maurice Blondel, the *pensée pensante* can be developed only if it is constantly replenished in such a way that its uninterrupted communication with Being is guaranteed; it cannot really break off that communication but it can abolish it in thought; however, insofar as it nurses such an illusion, it is in danger not only of devitalizing itself in fact, but of tending towards the worst of autolatries.

The first step in any philosophical inquiry would seem to be finding a point of departure. However, we must be forcibly reminded that there is an absolute polarity between a point of departure and the type of finality according to which the thought of a philosopher is defined. Hence before finding a point of departure, I have to determine as clearly as possible how and towards what goal I am oriented.

It is clear, for example, that if my aim is to construct a conceptual system whose propositions are rigorously connected by dialectical relations, then I should have grounds for finding some principle which is *logically* certain—i.e., a principle which cannot be denied without self-contradiction.

However, as my philosophical efforts became more fully self-conscious, it was evident that they did not tend towards this kind of systematization—even though the systems of the postkantian philosophy at the beginning had a great influence on me. At the same time, however, a problem continued to obsess me: how could I succeed in integrating into a rational system my own experience, with the qualities it has *hic et nunc,* with its singularities and even its deficiencies which in part make it what it is. As I reflected on this question, it became clear that such integration could not be accomplished nor even seriously attempted; as a result, I was led to arraign before an inner court not the ideal, but the real, metaphysical value of the idea of a rational system; at the same time, I began to examine with growing uneasiness the inner structure of experience, of my own experience, viewing it not merely in terms of its subject matter, but in terms of its quality, its being as experience. From that moment on, my philosophical orientation was radically altered. My work which before seemed to be a scaffolding enabling me to construct a building, assumed a value, an intrinsic significance. The problem now was not so much one of building as of digging; philosophical activity was now definable as a drilling rather than a construction. The further I went in the examination of *my experience,* and into the hidden meaning of these two words, the more unacceptable became the idea of a particular body of thoughts which was my system, one I could call my own; the presumption that the universe could be encapsuled in a more or less rigorously related set of formulas, seemed absurd. I should stress that my own critical reflection was concentrated on the alleged relation between the system and the individual who considered himself its inventor and patent-holder. The truth is that there is nothing which is less patentable than philosophy, nothing more difficult to appropriate. In this connection it should be noted that the teaching of philosophy, especially in Germany after Schopenhauer and Nietzsche, has had a pernicious influence; the philosopher who teaches his philosophy invariably seems to be selling his own product, a particular brand over which he has indefeasible rights. We may also note by the way that there is no area where it is less possible to establish with any degree of certainty what is borrowed, what the outside influences are, or, conversely, the agreements or spontaneous convergencies of thought. This is not merely a factual difficulty but a quasi-logical impossibility. The more authentic the thought, the less its historical filiations or the outside contributions to its development can be traced. A simple phrase accidentally hit upon can be for the fertile mind the incentive or point of crystallization for a whole series of complicated reflections. This simple fact is sufficient to show why the expression *my philosophy* is practically meaningless.

The kind of inquiry I have in mind will be governed by an obligation which is not easy to formulate; it is not sufficient to say that it is an avowal of fidelity to experience; an examination of philosophical empiricism shows the extent to which the term "experience" is vague and ambiguous. Philosophy provides the means for experience to become aware of itself, to apprehend itself—but at what level of experience? and how can such a hierarchy be established or defined? My only comment here is that we must distinguish not only degrees of clarification but degrees of intimacy with oneself and with one's surroundings—with the universe itself.

This inquiry must be based on a certitude which is not rational or logical but existential; if existence is not at the beginning it is nowhere, for I do not believe that any transition can be made to existence which is not cheating or deception.

A final preliminary remark of a general nature should be made which should preface every existential philosophy: Propositions of the type "Nothing exists," "It is possible that nothing exists," need not be construed as internally self-contradictory but rather as empty and meaningless. Indeed, I cannot deny the property of existence to "all things" (I deliberately use an expression which is as vague as possible), without presupposing a certain idea of existence and such an idea is here by definition without content or application. The above propositions possess the semblance of a meaning only because I am careful not to explain the nature of this indeterminate idea of existence which I have refused to ascribe to this, that, and the other particular. Thus to assert "something exists" is to maintain that it is meaningless in principle to deny existence, that such a denial is wholly verbal, and an unwarranted extrapolation of meaningful particular propositions such as "A does not exist," or "It is possible that A does not exist."

We must now determine whether there is some privileged existent to which this quality cannot be denied if not without self-contradiction, at least without absurdity, absurdity and nonsense here being identified.

I am strongly tempted to say that this existent-type is myself, but this cannot be maintained without further qualification. If the self that I am is construed as a subject, a subjective reality, if the "I" in "I exist" is identified with this subjective reality, then the assertion cannot stand up under scrutiny. What justifies the assertion, the criteria of validity, cannot be determined. The assertion "I exist" is valid only if it signifies, in an admittedly loose and inadequate way, an original datum which is not "I think" nor even "I am alive," but rather "I experience," and this expression must be accepted in its maximal range of indefiniteness. Here the German is much more adequate than our own language: *ich erlebe*, again to be understood in connection with the infra-discursive unity of its terms, hence on the hither side of the question, "wer erlebt?" and of its appropriate response, *"Ich* erlebe (nicht Du or nicht Er—*Ich* erlebe, is understood here). In this context *Ich erlebe* cannot be distinguished from *Es erlebt in mir,* another translation which is probably not any better, and which by definition substitutes for an immediate unity a plurality of further determinations which such a unity does not imply.

Clearly, this qualified formulation is not satisfactory, and besides it is based on meditation. It is difficult to clarify the meaning in question since we have to dig under experience, so to speak, without losing contact with it.

Of course, by a conscious act of abstraction I can apprehend myself as a being of pure feeling. On this basis I can, in the cartesian mode, infer that I am. But when I assert: I exist, I certainly mean something more than this; I vaguely imply that I am not only for myself but that I manifest myself, or rather am manifested; the prefix *ex* in exist, has primary significance because it conveys the meaning of a movement towards the external world, a centrifugal tendency. I exist: that means I have something by which I can be known or identified, either by another person or by myself insofar as I assume for myself a borrowed otherness; none of these characteristics are separable from the fact that "there is my body." For the time being I want to preserve a certain looseness of meaning as I do in connection with the expression "there is my body." And I want to refer to a presence of my body to me without which the fact of existing would not have the density it has for me. Presence of my body to me: concentrating on these words, I immediately run into difficulty: Do not these words imply a duality between myself and my body, an externality of one with respect to the other? However, have we even any justification for affirming this externality? does our affirmation have any clear, determinate meaning? The same question constantly arises: wouldn't it be more appropriate to assert the presence of a body to *itself?* This possibility, however, is immediately nullified: does my body construed as a physical object imply a self? This is clearly not the case.

It is evident that we have been forced to present a rigorous analysis of what I have called my body. Before beginning this inquiry however, it must be pointed out in connection with what is to follow, that my body is the datum relative to which there are other existents, and, it may be added, the basis of the division between existence and non-existence. I want to cite with a few changes and without any alteration of meaning, a passage from the first part of my *Journal Métaphysique:* "When I affirm Caesar has existed,—I am borrowing an example which refers to the past since it is here that my thesis can best be challenged—I do not mean merely that Caesar would have been perceived by me; I mean that there is between the existence of Caesar and my existence, i.e. my psycho-physical presence to myself, an objectively determinable temporal continuity; this presence is the datum to which I relate the infinite variety of anything I can think of as existing; any existent can be related to this datum and cannot be thought of apart from this relation except by abstraction." [1] Furthermore, the chain of spatial, temporal, and spatio-temporal relations can be compressed by the imagination to the point where the existent that is thought becomes co-present with me. The magnetic field in which these various chains are distributed with respect to my present existence, is what I shall call the existential orbit.

Thus however odd or contradictory the characteristics of this privileged existent turn out to be, they will necessarily be found in any other existence we can conceive of. It must be observed, however, —and this will become clearer in what follows—that existence, strictly speaking, is not conceivable; what is incorrectly called conception in this context is really an imaginative and sympathetic extension of a datum, partly opaque to itself, which is the basis of all experience.

My body. What exactly is the meaning and value of the possessive index? We will find insoluble difficulties no matter what way we try to explain it. Should I maintain, for example, as I have been tempted to do many times before, that my body is my instrument? If so, we must start by examining the instrumental relation. It seems plain that any instrument is a means of extending, developing, or strengthening an original power possessed by the person who uses it; this holds for a knife as much as for a lens. These powers or aptitudes are active properties of an organic body. If I consider my body from the outside, I can evidently think of it as a mechanism or as an instrument. But we are now examining the nature of *my body* insofar as it is mine. *This* body (*Hoc corpus* not *illud*), this instrumentalist, can I construe it as itself an instrument —and if so, of what? It is clear that there is the danger of an infinite regress; if the instrumentalist is itself an instrument, of what is it the instrument, etc.? If I think of my body as an instrument, I thereby ascribe to the soul of which it is the instrument, as it were, those potentialities which the body ordinarily realizes; thus the soul is converted into a body and the same regress will now occur in connection with the soul.

It should be possible to show that this conclusion is valid for any objective relation which is alleged to hold between myself and my body, what I call *myself* being construed in this context as the *ignotum quid* to which my body as mine, is purportedly bound. Reflection discloses that any kind of communication between myself and my body is inconceivable.

To silence or eliminate questions such as these, which are inherently insoluble, couldn't one execute a logical *coup de force* by asserting that the alleged dualism between myself and my body does not exist and that I really am my body?

Here, however, we must exercise caution. Does I and my body mean: I am identical with my body? Can this identity be maintained in the light of reflection? Clearly not. The alleged identity is absurd; it is possible to affirm it only if the I is first implicitly denied, thereby becoming the materialist assertion: my body is myself, only my body exists. But this assertion is absurd. For it is a property of my body that it does not and cannot exist alone. Can we, then, find haven in the concept of a world of bodies? What, however, confers unity on such a world? Furthermore, in a purely objective world, what becomes of the principle of intimacy (*my body*) around which the existential orbit is created?

In asserting "I am my body" one is actually making a negative judgment: "It is neither true nor meaningful to assert that I am other than my body"; more precisely, "It is meaningless to assert that I am a certain thing bound in some manner to a certain other thing which is or would be my body." We cannot assert any truths about the relation R between an unknown X and my body, which means that the relation cannot be thought.

We should understand clearly what these remarks entail. They do not imply agnosticism; we cannot find refuge in the convenient idea that the relation is not knowable for me but that it would be for a mind more richly endowed than mine; for it is the very idea of such a relation that is incapable of formulation. Hence we are led to a definition of incarnate being, interpreting the word "being," here, in its verb rather than substantive form.

To be incarnated is to appear to oneself as body, as this particular body, without being identified with it nor distinguished from it—identification and distinction being correlative operations which are significant only in the realm of objects.

What clearly emerges from the foregoing reflections is the fact that there is no distinct haven to which I can repair either outside of or within my body. Disincarnation is not practically possible and is precluded by my very structure.

However, there is a counterpart to the above which should be emphasized.

If I abstract from the index characterizing *my* body—insofar as it is mine—if I construe it as one body among an unlimited number of other such bodies, I will be forced to treat it as an object, as exhibiting the fundamental properties of objectivity. It then becomes an object of scientific knowledge; it becomes problematic, so to speak, but only on condition that I consider it as not—mine; and this detachment which is essentially illusory, is the very basis of all cognition. As knowing subject, I re-establish or claim to re-establish that dualism between my body and me, that interval which, we have learned, is inconceivable from an existential point of view. A subject of this kind can be established only if existence is first renounced; it is, it can be said, only on condition that it considers itself not to be. This paradox is fundamental for the object, for I can really think about the object only if I acknowledge that I do not count for it, that it does not take me into account. This is the only valid response—and it is decisive—that can be made to the annoying question asked by empirical idealism; can objects continue to exist when I no longer perceive them? the truth is that they are objects only on that condition.

However, by an anomaly which disappears when it is reflected on, the more I emphasize the objectivity of things, thus cutting the umbilical cord which binds them to existence and to what has been termed my psycho-organic presence to myself, the more I affirm the independence of the world from me, its radical indifference to my destiny, to my goals; the more, too, this world, proclaimed as the only real one, is converted into an illusory spectacle, a great documentary film presented for my curiosity, but ultimately abolished simply because it disregards me. I mean that the universe tends to be annihilated in the measure that it overwhelms me—a fact forgotten whenever the attempt is made to crush man under the weight of any data of astronomical proportions.

What this amounts to is that the act of trying to break the nexus uniting me to the universe, because of a fear of anthropocentrism, nexus of my presence to the world, my body being this nexus manifested, is a purely abstract act. I grant that this remark will cause some serious misunderstanding. I am not postulating any kind of dependence of the universe on me; this would be a relapse to an extreme subjectivism. What I am asserting, first of all, is the primacy of the existential over the ideal, with the added proviso that the existential must inevitably be related to incarnate being, i.e. to the fact of *being in the world*. This expression which was not part of the philosophical vocabulary, at least not before Heidegger, adequately renders something which, it is now understood, must be construed as a participation not as a relation or communication. The term "participation", which I constantly used between the years 1910-1914 with a meaning altogether different from the meaning conferred on it by Plato, reappears in the philosophy of Mr. Lavelle, and in some respects is similar to my own use of the term. The difficult task I gave myself then, was to determine the possibility of thinking that participation without denaturing it, i.e. without converting it into an objective relation. Doubtless there is little worth saving in these exploratory writings which have never been published and probably never will. But it should be said that my main views have not changed even if the terminology has.

If the foregoing comments are consolidated and an attempt made to clarify what may be called with Jaspers, my fundamental situation, the results are the following:

First, it must be observed that this situation, because it is fundamental, cannot in any way be construed as contingent, relative to some independent entity which would "occupy" that situation but which could as easily occupy some other. In my earlier writings just mentioned, I called this somewhat crudely "the non-contingency of the empirical datum." If we explained this as carefully as possible, we would find that in this region metaphysics joins not so much the ethical but the spiritual life, strictly speaking.

On the one hand, the capacity I have to perceive my body to a certain extent from the outside (for example, figuratively, as when I see myself in a mirror), invariably tempts me to divorce myself from it ideally and to disavow it—just as one might disavow a friend or a relative; the crucial significance I give to the theme of possible disavowal will be patent in what follows.

On the other hand, reflection detects the fallacious nature of such a divorce; as we have noted, reflection compels me to acknowledge that this separate entity, this self relative to which the possession of this particular body is accidental, cannot be thought of either in isolation or in relation, nor yet as identical with that from which I claim to separate it.

I should note in passing that such a reflection of the second degree or power whose object is another original reflection, is to my mind synonymous with philosophy itself viewed as an effort to restore the concrete beyond the disconnected and discontinuous determinations of abstract thought; despite undeniable differences, I am aware how closely this corresponds not so much with Hegelianism as such, but with certain doctrines which have extended it and made it more supple, particularly the doctrine of Bradley.

The participation which involves my presence to the world, however, cannot be affirmed, cannot be found again nor restored, unless I resist the temptation to deny it, i.e. to assume that I am a separate entity.

An objection may be raised: There is no reason to use the term "temptation" here. If your argument is valid we have no choice. Can there be a choice between what is reasonable and meaningful and what is absurd: There can be, for the essence of the absurd for a being like myself is just its capacity to be preferred, usually on the condition that it is not identified as such. This reflection of the second degree or philosopical reflection exists only for and by means of freedom; nothing external to me can force me to exercise it in this respect; the very notion of constraint in this context is devoid of content. Thus I can choose the absurd either because it is easy for me to convince myself that it is not the absurd, or because I prefer it inasmuch as it is the absurd; to this end I need only interrupt arbitrarily a certain chain of reflections. My undeniable ability to pursue or not a sequence of thoughts, is, in the final analysis, only a mode of attention, and can be immediately exercised; hence we can confirm the fact that our freedom is implied in the awareness of our participation in the universe.

The premises of what I venture to call concrete or existential philosophy have thus been established in a somewhat indirect and unexpected way.

This philosophy is based on a datum which is not transparent to reflection, and which, when reflected, implies an awareness not of contradiction but of a fundamental mystery, becoming an antimony as soon as discursive thought tries to reduce or problematize it.

I have indicated above the impossibility of construing my body as an instrument or appendage, as belonging in any way whatever to a distinct entity which could be identified with myself. It has also been noted that it would be arbitrary and even absurd to interpret this impossibility materialistically. There are two inversely related positions which the mind is in danger of oscillating between like a pendulum, as long as it is not aware of the disconcerting fact that there is nothing in this context which can be construed as a relation—given that relations can only exist between terms, I mean symbols of objects or ideal objects. Existence, or better, existentiality, if I may be allowed to used this barbarism, is participation insofar as participation cannot be objectified. However, we must not be misled by words. It is only too clear that we irresistibly tend to objectify this participation and to construe it as a relation; it is only our free act which intervenes to prevent us. Our essential immediacy is disclosed in this act alone, and our discovery of it may occur in rather different areas which nevertheless communicate with one another—the areas of metaphysics, poetry, and art.

We can make this somewhat clearer by focussing our attention on what is usually called the problem of sensation but what is in reality the mystery of feeling.

When I observe any organism including my own from the outside, I cannot refrain from describing and equipping it—and am even forced to do so—with the properties of an emitting, transmitting and receiving set all at once. It is then impossible for me not to interpret the sensory faculty with which the organism is endowed, as the capacity to grasp something which comes to it "from the outside;" the form that this organism has for the percipient, moreover, necessarily lends itself to this interpretation.

If, however, attention is focussed on sensing as it really is, i.e. on the *I feel*, it is clear that, to think of sensation in this way is at bottom not to think of it at all, for it is to subsitute something for sensation to which it cannot be reduced. Let me explain. When we use the terms receiver, emitter, etc., we identify the organism with a radio set which picks up a certain message. More accurately, what is grasped by the set is not so much the message as a group of data which can be transcribed by means of a code. Hence the message, strictly speaking, implies a double transmission, the first of which occurs at the start, the second on arrival; there are, of course, an infinite number of material modalities according to which this can take place but this is not important for our present purposes.

Now the problem is that of knowing whether sensation in itself can be identified with a message. Reflection shows that this is impossible and that we are deluded when we obscurely believe that a receptive consciousness succeeds in *translating* into sensation something originally given to it as a physical phenomenon, as a motion, for example. What does the word "translate" mean actually? At the very least it means to subsitute one set of data for another set. But the term "data" must be construed in a strict sense. The contact experienced by the organism or by any of its parts is by no means given; more precisely, it is a datum for the external observer who perceives it in a certain way, but not for the organism which undergoes it. I am only persuaded of the contrary because, as spectator, I put myself mentally in the organism's place and impute to what it undergoes the idea I have formed of it. I have a tendency to give a psychological coloration to a phenomenon which I, moreover, try to define in exclusively physical terms. The vocabulary we use here is of primary importance and I believe that ambiguous words such as "affection" should be systematically rejected. If we carefully consider the implications of any datum—of the fact of being given (of *Gegebensein*), we will note that the externality of this relation, granting that it is a relation, presupposes a fundamental internality, i.e. consciousness itself. The essence of the physical event as such, considered as the basis of sensation, is that it is not and cannot be given to the consciousness which purportedly translates it into sensation. Here we are in danger of falling into the same infinite regress, symptomatic of an insoluble contradiction, as in the case of the description of my body. It is really meaningless to construe sensation as a translation; sensation is immediate, the basis of all interpretation and communication, hence not itself an interpretation or communication. The difficulty is that whenever I claim to relate it to an object, I inevitably interpret it as a kind of emanation of the object that I must grasp; when I do so, however, I am no longer referring to sensation. Action, nevertheless, is impossible, unless I can identify and define objects, unless that is, I can construe sensations as messages without bothering about the absurdity of describing them in this manner. Hence it is inevitable that I envisage sensation from two contradictory or incompatible points of views; for there is a metaphysically ultimate sense in which it is true to say that sensation is immediate, and another sense in which it may be construed as a message which is emitted and transmitted and hence capable of being intercepted.

It is not too difficult to see that this disconcerting dualism corresponds exactly to the dualism indicated previously in connection with my body. From the point of view of what I shall venture to call the body-subject, the body I am without being logically identified with it, sensation is immediate; from the point of view of the body-object, on the other hand, sensation seems to be a communication. This distinction, nowever, which seems so clear, must be held at arms length; as soon as we relax our efforts, the distinction is lost in the inextricable tangle of experience where the immediate and the objective mingle and are constantly lost from view.

The starting point for an authentic philosophy, and by this I mean a philosophy which is experience transmuted into thought, is a clear understanding of that paradoxical situation which is not only mine but which makes me what I am. But it must be remembered that that situation, however fundamental it may be—and I wish to emphasize as forcibly as anyone can the ultimate value of a certain *ecceity*—can only be understood relative to a freedom which is primarily the power of self-affirmation or denial.

Here, in particular, we must be on our guard against the pit-fall of abstractionism. How can a freedom which is as essential as immediacy of feeling, positively affirm itself? It recently occured to me that metaphysics should be defined as the logic of freedom; the formulation is not impeccable but is has the merit of clarifying an essential truth: progress in philosophy consists in the sum of successive steps whereby freedom, aware of itself as a simple capacity of affirmation and denial, incarnates itself, or, if one likes, becomes a real power of conferring a content on itself so as to discover and acknowledge itself for what it is. It will be clear from what follows that a philosophy of freedom so conceived cannot be opposed to a philosophy of being; more precisely, such an opposition is justified only if one wrongly identifies being and thing, if, as is the case with a literal bergsonism—I do not refer to an authentic bergsonism which points beyond its own formulations—one believes that being must be given an exclusively static interpretation. I am convinced, however, that being, as it has been conceived by all the great metaphysicians, perhaps without exception, transcends the opposition between static and dynamic; I intend to supply elements of an interpretation oriented in just this direction, although the terminology in which it is expressed may be somewhat unprecedented.

At this point we must analyze the concrete with more care and indicate how a number of assertions which have a deceptive generality and which I have formulated until now in terms which were too abstract, may be made more specific.

I shall continue the present analysis along the same lines as the analysis I attempted to give elsewhere of receptivity. The analysis continues the observations I made in connection with feeling which were elaborated in the first part of the *Journal Métaphysique*.

What does it actually mean to *receive*? In answer to this question, the loose and, as we shall discover, metaphorical use of the term where it is associated with a piece of wax receiving an imprint, must first be set aside; in this context, to receive is to undergo. We should consider instead the specific complex human relationship we want to indicate when we say of someone that he has received another person. To receive in this context is to admit in or welcome an outsider into one's home. One's home, it must be repeated. I suggest, first of all, that the intimate and mysterious relation expressed by the phrase "feeling at home" has scarcely caught the attention of philosophers up to now. There is only a "feeling at home" with respect to a self (*soi*), and that self can be the self of another person, i.e. a being capable of asserting *I*. There is a mystery here, and to be convinced of it we need only mention certain specific experiences such as the following: I have just moved into an apartment; the furniture is mine but it may happen that I don't feel at home. One has such experiences in mind when one affirms that the American has far less feeling of being at home than the Frenchman or Englishman, the proof of this lying, for example, in the fact that it is easier for him to live at a hotel, that it is natural for him to eat out, etc. . . . I cannot refer to *my feeling at home* unless I grant or imply that the self does or can seem to itself to impregnate its environment with its own quality, thereby recognizing itself in its surroundings and entering into an intimate relationship with it.

If this is the case, it must be maintained that to receive is to introduce the other person, the stranger, into a region which has these qualities, and to admit him in to participate in it. I would assert *a priori* that an historical-sociological inquiry into hospitality could only have significance if it began with such data, difficult to describe in abstract terms, but which a careful analysis of experience could disclose without difficulty. It is very probable that the social protocol we observe, only the tattered remains of which still survive among us, is the relic of something involved in our very condition. We should observe in passing the primitive significance of this word, "condition." I believe that a contemporary philosopher who wanted to rewrite Humes *Treatise* would have to entitle it *A Treatise of Man's Condition* rather than a *Treatise of Human Nature*.

If we devote our attention to the act of hospitality, we will see at once that to receive is not to fill up a void with an alien presence but to make the other person participate in a certain plenitude. Thus the ambiguous term, "receptivity," has a wide range of meanings extending from suffering or undergoing to the gift of self; for hospitality is a gift of what is one's own, i.e. of oneself.

These simple observations have great importance to my mind, and for the following reasons.

In the first place, they help us to understand, indirectly to be sure, but far more profoundly than we were able to before, that feeling is not and cannot be passivity; this view is opposed to what the philosophical doctrines of the past have generally maintained, at least when they took issue with Aristotle who had, I think, some penetrating views on the subject. The current, almost automatic identification of receiving with undergoing, as it seems to emerge from Kantism, is explicable only because of a faulty first analysis. When we have clearly understood that feeling is not reducible to undergoing although it is still a receiving, we will be able to discover the presence of an active element in feeling, something like the power of taking upon oneself, or better, of opening oneself to . . . I am ending here with an ellipsis; for if I should replace it with the name of an objective or objectifiable datum, I would fall again into the contradictions I indicated earlier.

On the basis of the above, a continuity may be discovered between the fact of feeling and creativity—something which would be inconceivable if we were concerned with simple passivity, on the one hand, and pure activity on the other.

The foregoing account does not exhaust the subject nor is it perhaps the most essential aspect of the subject. In my opinion, the foregoing considerations can be most fruitfully applied to the relationship with other minds.

This raises an extremely difficult problem for any philosophy, and for idealism especially. One is tempted to ask whether the question isn't insoluble strictly speaking, if it is viewed from my perspective. For by emphasizing the irreducibility and metaphysical primacy of feeling, the *I feel*, haven't I locked myself in a prison from which the only escape is an illusory escape by thought? Don't I end up in solipsism? I do not think that this is the case, and the fear that it is, is based on a misunderstanding which should be dispelled.

Even if we concede that solipsism is theoretically tenable—a thesis I strongly deny—it is meaningless unless I take the Schopenhaurian formulation literally: the world is my representation, or in its more restricted interpretation: the world is only my representation. Reflection again bids me ask how I can in fact think of that restriction, and where the idea of something beyond my representation comes from even if my idea of it is only sufficient to permit me to affirm its inconceivability.

For a philosophy of participation, however, Schopenhauer's for-mulation must be completely rejected; in any case, it loses its metaphysical significance. To use a phrase I have used before, I am in the world only insofar as the world is not a representation, but as something shaping me as in a womb. The only condition in which the above view could be meaningful would be where I thought of myself as an entity claiming that *aseity* which in the past was considered the exclusive property of the Absolute. I think it could be argued that there exists a rigid and inconsistent philosophy of the person which indeed implies this degradation and this transference of meaning.

At this point it should be remembered that our freedom has the power to deny itself when it believes it is affirming itself, to become lost in an *impasse* while it claims to be expanding. This is exactly what happens when it deifies itself in fact—without always being fully aware of its act of self-divinization, i.e. when it claims that the world revolves around itself. We cannot stress too strongly that Kant's Copernican revolution could and did degenerate for many into an anthropocentrism of the second degree; an anthropocentrism which does not share the simplicity of the traditional anthropocentrism, and where the pride of reason is not counterbalanced by the theocentric affirmation of divine sovereignty.

I will doubtlessly be blamed for ignoring the fact that a thought which is anchored in experience, is not your property or mine, but fortunately exists apart from all these impoverished descriptions which distort it. It remains to be seen whether such thought which is exercised in the search for truth and which is the source of our universal judgments, does not change into an idol when it is objectified, when it considers itself a reality and confers being on itself—an idol because it represents man dehumanized, man claiming to take the form of the absolute. No progress will be made in our understanding of scientific inquiry if we grant in principle that it is not the personality of the expert with its good and evil capacities that is involved, but an impersonal mind instead, which for some unknown reason is embodied in this contingent individual, this absurd and ephemeral spokesman. As a matter of fact, we are thereby prevented from grasping a feature of that inquiry which is at once personal and dramatic—whereby it belongs not merely to history in general, but is, more importantly, the fulfillment of an individual destiny. We should pause over these last two words which are meaningless in the context of a philosophy of thought in general.

As we have noted, my freedom cannot fully affirm itself unless it embraces my personal destiny and does not claim merely to survey it. However, this destiny is not deepened or enriched unless it is open to others. Scheler has fittingly described sympathy in terms of the irreducible phenomenological datum that it is, and nothing more need be said on this subject. Nevertheless, I would have liked to transcribe here the admirable analysis of Hocking on the awareness of other selves, if only because at a decisive moment in my life, it helped to free me from some residual monadistic views. I shall limit myself, however, to my discovery of the solution to the problem of communication in the transition to the thou. It should be added that the terms of the problem do not altogether correspond with those of the solution, as we shall see.

I had been encouraged to think about the thou as such when I was reflecting on the idea of response and its implications. The empirical, non-abstract and non-speculative channels in which my thought on this theme ran from the start, were however, manifold; and since the reader has been negotiating arid terrain long enough, I shall assume the prerogative of introducing certain biographical aspects of the investigation, including inner experiences, which possess a certain significance for me. I have already indicated that the biographical, on the one hand, and the spiritual and even the intelligible, on the other, cannot be separated.

I was not mobilized during the war because of my health, so I was induced to pursue investigations of a particularly difficult and unfortunate kind, since they were related to the fate of soldiers who had disappeared under extremely obscure circumstances, circumstances which were from a practical point of view, inscrutable. They were such that I found myself compelled to reply to questions frequently addressed to me by persons of flesh and blood whose anguish was immediately conveyed to me by voice and glance . . . This experience of a truly human contact made on the level of a shared emotion with unknown persons who were X's and Y's for me at the start, but whose anxiety I was aware of before long, and which in a way I made my own, has, I am convinced, played a fundamental role in the development of my thought; just how, will be seen shortly. This, however, was not the whole of the story.

During the war I sometimes performed metapsychical experiments with my friends, the results of which were to a certain extent ambiguous; they nevertheless forced me to raise certain fundamental questions which may have seemed unprecedented or unusual when judged in terms of the philosophical proprieties. It would not be feasible to describe these experiments in any detail, experiments which had at that time, and still do, a peculiar significance for me. I can, say, however, that I was the medium and yet possessed of such perfect lucidity that I was a spectator at the same time. The experiments were performed with the help of a ouija board. We began with questions and answers as in the case of the use of a table; but I was aware of being the instrument rather than the source of the frequently unpredictable answers given by the board. In no sense could it be said that I was the one who responded. *Who* then was it? and in a further act of reflection I asked what the meaning of the question itself was, the meaning of the question *who*? The postulation of the unconscious seemed to me then, as it does now, intellectual laziness, an attempt to evade a set of problems which are extremely obscure and among the most difficult to formulate in coherent terms.

I have limited myself to these few remarks which should nevertheless give a glimpse of the concrete sources of my reflections on the relation between I and thou and the metaphysical implications of the thou.

Let us return to our preceding remarks concerning the object; it is what does not take me into account, something for which I do not count. Conversely, I address the second person when what I address can respond to me in some way—and that response cannot be translated into words. The purest form of invocation—prayer—embodied imperfectly in the uttered word, is a certain kind of inner transfiguration, a mysterious influx, an ineffable peace.

When I consider another individual as *him,* I treat him as essentially absent; it is his absence which allows me to objectify him, to reason about him as though he were a nature or given essence. However, there is a presence which is yet a mode of absence. I can act towards somebody as though he were absent. This can be illustrated by examples drawn from our daily lives. In this connection I want to transcribe with certain additions a page from my *Journal Metaphysique:* "I meet someone I don't know on the train; we talk about the weather, the war (the text dates from April, 1918), [2] but even though I am addressing him, he continues to be "someone", "that man there;" he is in the fullest sense a Mr. so-and-so, the particulars of whose biography I get to know bit by bit. It is as though he were filling out a questionnaire, as if he were providing me with fragments of an account with which he identified himself. It can also be imagined that you are confronting some employee who asks you to state your identity. The remarkable fact, however, is that the more my questioner is external to me, the more I am by the same token external to myself; in confronting a Mr. so-and-so I also become another Mr. so-and-so, unless I literally happen not to be a person anymore—a pen which traces words on paper or a simple recording apparatus . . . It can happen, however, that a bond of feeling is created between me and the other person, if, for example, I discover an experience we have both shared (we have both been to a certain place, have run the same risks, have criticized a certain individual, or read and loved the same book); hence a unity is established in which the other person and myself become *we,* and this means that he ceases to be *him* and becomes *thou*; the words "you too" in this context take on primary value. Literally speaking, we communicate; and this means that the other person ceases to be for me someone with whom I converse, he ceases to intervene between me and myself; this self with whom I had coalesced in order to observe and judge him, while yet remaining separate, has fused into the living unity he now forms with me. The path leading from dialectic to love has now been opened.

The being whom I love can hardly be a third person for me at all; yet he allows me to discover myself; my outer defenses fall at the same time as the walls separating me from the other person fall. He moves more and more into the circle with reference to which and outside of which there exist third persons who are the "others."

This can be expressed more clearly in terms of the observation that I communicate effectively with myself only insofar as I communicate with the other person, i.e. when he becomes thou for me. Such a transformation can be accomplished only by an inward relaxation in which I abolish the sort of constriction which makes me shrink into myself and which deforms me. Recently I heard André Gide taken to task in connection with a passage of the *Nouvelles Nourritures*. "Know thyself. A maxim which is as pernicious as it is unbecoming. Whoever observes himself arrests his own development." [3] I believe that the expression of the meaning here sins only in its want of elaboration. The self-knowledge Gide attacks is the kind one finds by retracting into oneself, and this is no more than a diminished and mutilated awareness of a reality attainable only through other persons—and here too only insofar as we maintain with them a living relationship animated by charity.

We must apply these conclusions to the metaphysical realm, strictly speaking, not—or at least not yet—extrapolating them but rather reflecting them. We are able to perceive then that the correlative but rudimentary categories of the same and the other have been transcended. If I had the opportunity I would illustrate what I mean with reference to a play such as the *Quartet in F Sharp*,[4] which is revelatory from this point of view. In the last scene of the play, and one of the most significant in my entire dramatic work, we witness the mystery of a reconciliation between Clair and her second husband, Roger, the brother of Stephane (her first husband whom she had divorced because he was unfaithful). Feeling a wall growing thicker between them, a wall which for one was the memory of a man who represented an enduring fraternal fellowship, for the other, the bitterness of a betrayed love,—through the mediation of music—Stephane is a composer—they reach an understanding of their relationship which is deeper and more intimate than before; Clair is led to ask herself, although she at first did not suspect it, if it was not really her first husband whom she still loved although she thought herself forever free of him, and she is led to do this through his brother who resembles him and who has never wished to judge her. I will only cite a bit of the dialogue from the scene, enough to give a clearer meaning and a more immediate value to this part of my exposition.

CLAIRE If I told you that there were times—yes, I sometimes wonder whether you haven't been mostly a means of avenging my hurt vanity. Something else too. The illusion of a resemblance. . . . But I really thought I was attracted to you only because you were different from him. How I opposed you to one another! How sure I was that I preferred your friendship to his capricious affections!

ROGER All you care for in me is a reflection.

C. An exalted image.

R. But an image just the same.

C. If you could only know how clear everything became for me when I found you.

R. The clarity of a satellite!

C. Roger, we mustn't. . . . I was wrong; what is the use of exploring what is past and gone? It is so distant from us already.

R. No. Ah it's awful to think that I wasn't loved for myself.

C. Yourself, himself. . . . Where does a personality begin? It was really you after all; don't you believe that each one of us is prolonged into whatever he creates?

R. That thought is soothing.

C. Think. It was really you after all.

R. Still it was he. . . .

"Yourself, himself. . . . Where does a personality begin?" What is revealed to the protagonists in a flash and what may never be revealed to them again, is that there is a region of fructifying obscurity transcending the closed systems in which thought imprisons us, where beings may communicate, where they *are* in and by the very act of communication. The theme of freedom clearly emerges again as before. The indistinctness of the I and thou, of the thou and him, does not imply the existence of a neutral environment in which one can lose oneself and abdicate, so to speak; on the contrary, it is a kind of vital milieu for the soul from which the soul draws its strength and where it is renewed by testing itself. Once again a will to participate must operate which alone can rescue us from total confusion.

I believe that this will become clearer as soon as the question of the reality of the thou is posed with any clarity: what does it mean to say that the thou as such, is or is not, real? It is plain that we are not concerned with some further quality which could be rightly or wrongly attributed to a him. What is relevant rather, is the act by which I expose myself to the other person instead of protecting myself from him, which makes him penetrable for me at the same time as I become penetrable for him. Whereas objectification particularly for the him, implies a dialogue between me and myself, hence a triadic relation, in the presence of the thou, I attain an inner unification which makes possible a dyadic relation. The above question only arises if I detach myself from this living relation in order to examine it, hence if I destroy it. To be sure, when the thou can also be given to me as an object, it is impossible for this reflection and distinction not to disappear whenever the concrete relation is re-established; Proust recognized in a similar context that this kind of intermittency was the rule in the natural order of things.

Where the thou is absolute, however, i.e. when it is not subject in principle to objective interpretation, when it is not merely accessible but present only to invocation, i.e., prayer, the problem is different. Of course religious consciousness or mystical experience also have an intermittent character—equally tied to the structure of the creature that I am; nonetheless, the absolute *Thou* is not merely unattainable but can only be thought of apart from all those questions which the creature never ceases to raise: who is he? what does he want? what is he thinking? I have always had the conviction that the attributes of God as defined by rational theology: simplicity, immutability, etc., have value only if we succeed in discovering behind them the qualities of a Thou which cannot be construed as a him without being denatured or reduced to our absurd, human proportions. "When we speak of God it is not of God that we speak," I wrote not so long ago. I cannot overstress the fact that theological affirmations as such are a snare; for the "properties" I have just mentioned, if construed as predicates, seem to be the most impoverished that exist; if they are construed as principles of the understanding it must be conceded that they are in a sense more inadequate than those which are conferred on the humblest and most ephemeral creature in our world. To achieve that conversion of our outlook which is indispensable, and to reveal what seems an infinite deficiency as the infinite plenitude that it really is, consciousness must, by an act of decisive conversion, sacrifice itself to the One whom it must alone invoke as its Principle, End, and only Resort.

NOTES

1 (Paris: Gallimard, 1935), p. 15.
2 [The entry in the *Journal,* pp. 145-146, is dated August 23, 1918. Transl. note]
3 *Les Nourritures terrestres et les Nouvelles Nourritures* (Paris: Gallimard, 1947), p. 266.
4 Paris: Librairie Plon, 1925, p. 190.

II

Belonging and disposability[1]

The task I shall take up in the present chapter may be aptly described as clearing the ground; I apologize to the reader for the circuitous and perhaps *perplexing* nature of my exposition.

Orginally, the theme which I proposed to myself for reflection consisted in extricating the roots of indisposability as I had described it in *Etre et Avoir*. However, I soon realized during the course of my inquiry that it was first necessary to deal with a set of problems the discovery of a definitive solution for which has up to now aroused little concern; these gravitated around what I have to call "belonging"; i.e., the fact or the act of belonging.

I shall follow my usual method of analyzing the content rather than the fact of consciousness, i.e. what consciousness actually discerns in a number of clearly distinct situation-types.

Belonging to. This object belongs to Paul. This means;

(a) this object is Paul's property,

(b) or more accurately, is part of the possessions or holdings of Paul.

In this sense of the term, what belongs to someone is that the possession of which can be contested or disputed. The assertion: this object belongs to Paul is, implicitly at least, a warning addressed to others: make no claims on the object in question, it belongs to Paul. That is why I often have occasion to say: such-and-such a thing, such a painting, belongs to me; however, there is no reason to assert: my nose belongs to me (since it is not assumed that a claim can be made on my nose); the question must be framed somewhat differently for the instrumental parts of my body (i.e. for my arms, hands) which someone else may want to use as tools.

Formulation (b) has the merit of illuminating the existence of a cleavage within belonging; indeed, it shows that on the one hand, there is a relation between the object and the whole of which it is a part, and on the other hand, a relation far more difficult to explain between this same object and a certain *who* who claims it as his own.

It is evident that this latter relation can be idealized, so to speak, as for example when I assert: it is my job to perform such-and-such an act; belonging here means approximately, incumbent on; we are now completely outside the objective realm in which we first seemed to be imprisoned.

We must now inquire whether the relations implied in belonging are completely personalizable, whether they are truly applicable to persons and if so, in what sense.

If I assert of a servant: *he belongs to me,* my audience would obviously be stupefied; assuming that I am not treated with the silent commiseration due an idiot, and am asked what right I have to assert that this servant belongs to me, I will explain that I treat him as a thing I have acquired or something that has been given to me, etc. Whatever the specific nature of the response, however, it is clear that it has every chance of not satisfying my questioner; on the contrary, it will seem to him an extravagant and unacceptable claim. Of course, this would not have been the case when slavery still existed.

It is curious to note that the question is completely transformed if I happen to declare to another person: *I belong to you.* Here we have completely shifted our ground.

First, it must be observed—and this is fundamental—that I am evoking a situation which cannot really be objectified, strictly speaking; one, in any case, which cannot be objectified without its nature being radically changed.

Let us examine closely the original relation: Jack, I belong to you. This means: I am opening an unlimited credit account in your name, you can do what you want with me, I give myself to you. This does not mean, at least not in principle: I am your slave; on the contrary, I freely put myself in your hands; the best use I can make of my freedom is to place it in your hands; it is as though I freely substituted your freedom for my own; or paradoxically, it is by that very substitution that I realize my freedom.

We must determine what the response to this offering will be, however, not necessarily a verbal response, perhaps, but one involving actions. In other words, how is the "you belong to me" which seems the required response to the act whereby "I give myself to you," to be described? Ultimately, it seems to be the expression of a disenfranchisement; *you belong to me* means *you are my thing;* I will dispose of you as I want.

It is conceivable, however, that this response can be inflected in a completely different way and that it means: "I welcome you as a participant in my work, in the undertaking to which I have given myself."

It is also clear that while the two cases can be theoretically distinguished by reflection, they are actually very difficult to distinguish in fact. The distinction, however, should be maintained at all costs, for the fundamental question is still that of knowing whether you are appealing to my freedom as such or whether on the contrary, you want to alienate it.

A related problem arises in connection with the attitude I adopt in my innermost being.

When I declare: I belong to you, do I perform an act of total abdication? Do I resign as a thinking and willing being? And what will be my subsequent reaction to an eventual disenfranchisement? If I have not merely consented to but also desired the latter, I have no reason to rebel against it when it occurs. Everything depends on the attitude with which I have given myself. Unfortunately, there are sufficient grounds for believing that this attitude cannot be clearly identified in any given case, given the impossibility of knowing what such an impulse conceals of the erotic— and there is a collective eroticism.

It should be stressed that insofar as I accept being treated as a thing, I make a thing of myself, and it is then significant to ask if I am not betraying myself.

At this point we are prompted to pose the question on which these reflections are based and which can be formulated as follows: what does it mean to belong? can I indeed dispose of myself if I do not belong to myself?

If we recall the introductory remarks where we asked what it meant for an object to belong to someone, we will at once perceive the difficulties raised by the present question.

(a) Can I somehow treat myself as an object belonging to the subject I at the same time am? what is the relation which connects this I and this me?

(b) If such objectification is impossible in practice, if, that is, it converts me precisely into what *I am not,* can the term *belonging* still express a relation?

(c) In any case, it is essential to elucidate the meaning of what is inadequately expressed by the statement that I belong to myself; it may be convenient in this context to substitute for belonging the expressions *being to oneself* or *not being to oneself.* The main problem consists in determining the nature of the concrete relation joining me to myself—or more accurately, in determining whether the idea of such a relation should be transcended.

(d) If the term "object" is strictly construed, and if we mean by it something which can be possessed or which can be part of a collection, it is clear that the answer to the first question (a) above should be negative with a qualification I shall introduce presently.

Moreover, "I" is the very negation of objectivity, whereas in the present case, the "I" is capable of being treated as a "him," hence is completely meaningless on such an analysis.

However, it is impossible to adhere to the pure and simple goal of not receiving. "I belong to myself" is intelligible only if we carefully personalize the relation in question; if, in short, we interpret it in the following way, for example: I have custody over myself or am trustee of myself; it is interesting to note that "I belong to myself" has a scale of meanings which is symmetrical with the meanings disclosed in the analysis of "you belong to me."

Ultimately, I can dispose of myself as some thing I can get rid of; this is what happens in the case of suicide. But we can scarcely find anything of this sort in life, except in a case where life closely imitates death—in total prostitution, for example.

If the expression "I belong to myself" is to be understood as *I am responsible for myself*—and we cannot identify the expressions without a considerable shift in our thought—I am then led to assume that everything must be interpreted as though I were two persons—as though I were, for example, at once the older and younger brother of myself. (I assume in this context that there are two orphaned brothers one of whom is responsible for the other.)

We should observe the absolute convergence and even identity of

I belong to you
You belong to me
I belong to myself

An equilibrium is attained if:
(1) The distinction of older and younger is actually effective, i.e. the older brother assumes authority; (2) this authority is recognized by the younger brother.

(1) If we assume the existence of some being who is completely dominated by his impulses and caprices, living only for the moment, it seems that this distinction can only be applied nominally or theoretically; it may well be—and this should be investigated

further—that this is only a limiting case, situated on the border of the human: it is the case of a being deprived of conscience. This makes it possible to understand the profound meaning of the word "conscience," the way in which psychological consciousness and moral conscience are united.

(2) On the other hand, we can evoke without difficulty a being for whom the moral conscience is not inexistent, but who nevertheless rejects its claims and denies it the authority to prescribe or prohibit.

It is a curious phenomenon that for the anarchist in the pure state—if such a being can exist—the *I belong to myself* is defiantly hurled at the conscience construed as traitor or as a spokesman of an abhorrent society. It would be interesting to determine the extent to which the conclusions of my previous analysis are valid for this extreme case.

It would seem that in the anarchist's mouth, the formulation has an exclusively negative import; it means, I belong to nobody, no individual or community has the least right over me. To affirm *me* in this context is really to affirm *nobody else;* the content of the me is determined by that exclusion and in no other way.

Now the whole question is one of determining whether such a purely polemical affirmation which merely has the value of an act of defiance, is sufficient to effectively orient one's life and behavior. The evidence points to a negative conclusion. Whether he likes it or not, the anarchist will be forced in his actions to adopt a position with respect to certain values; some values will be accepted, others rejected, and these latter always on behalf of other values which are more or less implied. Whatever these values may be, they cannot be identified with the principle of exclusion or repulsion to which his self seems to be reduced. Hence there is a dualism in his thought which cannot be resolved for the reason that the anarchist is not even aware of it.

Moreover, reflection shows that the reason the anarchist refuses to submit to an individual or to the community, is in order not to fail in his own eyes, a refusal which implies that he considers himself both a man of faith and a divinity. At the bottom of every consistent anarchism there is a deification of self which is usually unavowed.

Doubtless, this formulation is too simple and obvious, and so is still inadequate; there would be greater advantage in breaking into it as one would a shell or outer crust in order to expose what may be termed the pulp of the anarchist's affirmation; basically, this may be formulated as follows: *at present and whatever the circumstances, I intend to do what I please*; the defiance and the attempt to provoke which we have alluded to is also to be found here; this time, however, something additional has been made explicit. We must be careful in determining what this affirmation implies and what it clearly does not imply.

When I assert that I intend to do what I please, or act as I see fit, I completely abstain from making any judgment about the invariance, or conversely, the possible fluctuations of this *as I see fit*. It may be that what pleases me now still pleases me in six months; in that case I will act in six months as I am acting now. But the contrary may also be the case and I may act in an inverse manner.

If an identity is being affirmed, then—and this is clearly the case—it refers neither to me (construed as a set of dispositions), nor to the object of my desire or aversion—but solely to a certain relation between two terms which, moreover, can vary with one another.

It would seem, however, that the above considerations bring us back to the negative formulation given earlier. In asserting the identity of this relation, we are, of course, not making any judgments about the metaphysical relation—or if one prefers, the psycho-physiological relation—which unites the mental and the physical; the point is rather one of simply refusing to allow another individual to place any obstacle on the path leading from one term to the other.

This ultimate-situation which, again, involves a pure exclusion, cannot be evaded without the acceptance of an individual constant, a value to which we are committed; but then the meaning of *I belong to myself* is radically transformed; it comes close to passing into its contrary, into an "I do not belong to myself" but rather to such-and-such an Idea (justice, truth, etc.).

Hence we are forced to draw the apparently paradoxical conclusion that at one end of the scale, *I belong to myself,* is a self-defeating affirmation because the I is the negation of any objectively specifiable content—while at the other end, it is equally self-defeating and changes into its contrary: I belong to such-and-such a value. It would be appropriate to ask whether that value may not be negative, whether a being cannot therefore belong to Evil, Hate or to the Devil. In my opinion this possibility cannot be lightly dismissed; it seems plain that our structure is capable of being totally perverted, for a human being is capable of devotion to what seems to be a positive principle but what is in reality a radical negation of such principle.

If we carefully analyze the moral reality we seek to grasp, in its rhythm and dramatic pulsations, as it were, we generally seem to find again the dyadic relation joining the younger and older brother in the metaphor or parable with which we started; it is possible that this relation can be construed as pluralizable, i.e., that there is no familial or other human relationship which cannot be found in a transposed form inside the society of individuals that I form with myself. The specific relationship described above, however, is sufficient to show what I mean.

The latter has the advantage of correcting the current idea of autonomy which has the serious defect of being too inflexible as well as equivocal. Indeed, the legislative or *nomothetic* principle can be mistaken only verbally for the me or self whose independence, it seems, one wishes to proclaim. It may be possible to show how the historical shifts observable in the meaning of democracy ultimately derive from this basic equivocation. My parable at least has the merit of clearly showing that it is less a question of identity than of kinship, of what may be called a basic *dymorphism* which must not be hypostatized but rather interpreted in terms of its functional value.

A difficult question arises at this point: doesn't this dymorphism necessarily presuppose a unity as the ground of its possibility? It seems plain that we can, or in principle should assert, that this dualism is not and cannot be basic; it does not even exhibit the property of relative irreducibility characterizing the distinction between two different bodies, or more generally, two beings given to one another in corporeal form. However, we may assume that the dual question concerning the type of unity presupposed and the manner in which it is differentiated is of no concern to our present inquiry. My concluding remarks which will be of a metaphysical order, should shed some light on these obscure questions. However, it is important to note that the determinations of which the dyadic relation is capable, are directly related to well-defined species of self-love and self-hate; I omit self-indifference, the existence of which may be argued, although I personally tend to think it possible. In any event, a very large field is opened to phenomenological investigation.

As to self-love, it is easy to discern the complete opposition which exists between an idolatrous love, a heauto-centrism—and a charity towards oneself which, far from treating the self as a plenary reality sufficing to itself, considers it as a seed which must be cultivated, as a ground which must be readied for the spiritual or even for the divine in this world. To love oneself in this second sense is not the same as self-complacency, but is rather an attitude towards the self which permits its maximum development; it is clear that there is an infatuation which is in itself unfavorable to the development of any truly creative activity whatever; I do not limit myself in this context to artistic or scientific creation since I speak also of the radiance shed by any generous soul. On the other hand, it can be assumed that a harshness or an excessive malice towards oneself can also be paralyzing although for inverse reasons; hence there is need for patience towards oneself, a patience that may be reconciled with complete lucidity and which has been recommended by several teachers of the spiritual life, by a St. François de Sales, if I am not mistaken. However, this is possible and meaningful only when the distance from and nearness to the self which define the act of charity, are realized in and relative to, oneself. In practice we usually sin because of our inability to see ourselves, or—less often if we have managed to reach such objectivity—through our failure to maintain that contact with ourselves that we should always have with our fellow-man. This second possibility could be illustrated by a close study of pure rational psychology which so often seems to be alienated from itself.

The foregoing remarks will help us to clear up the unfortunate confusion associated with the relations between egoism and self-love, particularly in connection with the notion of salvation which is inevitably considered from the outside by those who believe it to be some sort of supra-terrestrial accomplishment. This mistake is corrigible if we forcibly recall that for Christian thought, there can be no individual salvation in the privative and atomic sense of this term. We can find a portent of this, moreover, in the realm of artistic creation, for the true artist does not create for himself alone but for everyone; he is satisfied only if that condition is fulfilled and I may add that there is no artistic creation without a permanent dislocation of the agent.

The foregoing reflections have precedence over all those inquiries relating to disposability, properly speaking, insofar as disposability is realized not only in the act of charity but also in hope and, I might add, in admiration, whose enormous spiritual and even metaphysical significance is still not recognized.

The verb *lift* forcefully and accurately denotes the kind of effect admiration evokes in us, or rather realizes in us as a function of the object which evokes it. This is so evident that when, for example, we communicate our enthusiasm to someone who does not share it at a musical performance or poetry reading, it not only seems that the other person is earth-bound while we are soaring, but we also have a painful impression that he is dragging or weighing us down; the violence with which we protest against his attitude is in a sense a measure of the effort with which we resist him.

It is clear that the function of admiration is to tear us away from ourselves and from the thoughts we have of ourselves; doubtless there is no realm with respect to which the reductive analyses of a

La Rochefoucauld seems more inadequate. There is perhaps no example on the psychological plane which better illuminates the ex-
tensions of meaning the Bergsonian distinction of the closed and
open is capable of receiving.

In fact, to affirm that admiration is the active negation of an
inner inertia is inadequate; it is particularly necessary to note that
it can be conceived not only as an *élan* but even more as an
irruption (the verb "innundate" refers here to an unmistakable
reality); that irruption can only occur in a being who is not a
closed or hermetic system into which nothing new can penetrate.

More precisely, but without elaborating the question any further,
I shall say that admiration is related to the fact that something is
revealed to us. Indeed, the ideas of admiration and revelation are
correlative and a subjective psychology is bound to misunderstand
completely the nature of admiration and substitute for it certain
data to which it is entirely incapable of being reduced. This reduction is, in fact, one of the foundations of realism. We should,
together with these simple observations, study first the *refusal*
to admire, then the *inability* to admire, in order to determine how
both imply a basic indisposability.

Not so long ago a dramatist affirmed during an interview that
admiration was for him a humiliating state which he resisted with
all his force. This affirmation may seem grotesque, but I am afraid
that it embodies a state of mind which is becoming more wide-
spread. There is hardly anything which is more characteristic of
our present state of degradation than the tendency to view with
suspicion any acknowledged mark of superiority. An analysis
similar to the one Scheler has given of resentment should disclose
that there is a burning preoccupation with self at the bottom of
this suspicion, a "but what about me, what becomes of me in that
case?" Admiration, insofar as it may be rendered in the form of a
judgment, however, is precisely the affirmation of a superiority
which is not relative but absolute; absolute, I repeat; the word
incomparable has a clearly distinct meaning in this context.

The spirit of comparison doubtless intervenes after the event
(one says: it is as beautiful as . . . it is more beautiful than . . .);

but this is relatively contingent with respect to the original datum which is the awareness of a certain absolute.[2] I come to think of myself relative to that absolute and become uneasy about the position I occupy with respect to it, only by a reflex motion. It is here that a choice is forced on us: depending on whether I act or not—and it is primarily an inner act I envisage in this context—as a system of claims, I will or will not be suspicious of that absolute which has just risen up before me. How rich in meaning the expression *take umbrage* is in this context! It admirably indicates that this new light can make me pale into insignificance in my own eyes or in those of others whose judgment I must consider since that judgment directly influences the judgment I tend to have of myself. There is plenty of scope to continue these reflections on the conditions which either invite or conceal such a revelation.

To affirm: admiration is a humiliating state, is the same as to treat the subject as a power existing for itself and taking itself as a center. To proclaim on the other hand, that it is an exalted state is to start from the inverse notion that the proper function of the subject is to emerge from itself and realize itself primarily in the gift of oneself and in the various forms of creativity.

Of course, the refusal to admire someone has various nuances of meaning; it is not always based on jealousy or resentment. It is quite conceivable that admiration or enthusiasm can be condemned or considered as suspect by the critical intelligence on the ground that they abolish our self-control.

Reflection can easily show, however, that the primary role of critical intelligence is on the level of understanding; if it governs those activities which permit us to discriminate the facts we subsequently appraise, it is quite impossible to ascribe to intelligence a function comparable to appreciation. It is completely meaningless to assume that critical intelligence will help us to decide whether a work is or is not worthy of admiration. In this context it can only play a negative though salutary role, i.e. it may compel me to ask myself, for example, whether my admiration for a certain work doesn't really involve a spirit of contradiction,—or conversely, an anxiety to persuade myself that I am vibrating in harmony with those who set the style in the little group to which I belong—or again, the desire to be different, etc. . . .

The inability to admire, the incapacity to feel admiration, raises some slightly different yet related problems in connection with what may be called inner inertia, or better, spiritual asthenia.

To clarify this would require careful reflection on the meaning of the word *responsive*. The English word *response* provides some positive indications of what is meant since it expresses better than the French term *réponse* that vital reaction which is lacking in the being who is internally inert or asthenic.

Someone asks me a question I cannot answer; this means that I do not have whatever it is that is necessary to respond; material analogies almost inevitable come to mind in this context. I am treated as a record file—a file which could think of itself and is simultaneously its own filing clerk; there is no file inside of me which corresponds to the question asked. Here we are on the level of *having,* or more accurately, our experience at first seems to us as though it could only be represented in terms of having; but on reflection this image proves false since it is inconceivable that there can be juxtaposed elements of knowledge inside of me among which the requisite element must be found. It is clear, however, that I can have the ardent desire to satisfy the person who questions me without being able to do so; in this case, it really seems as though I collided with a material obstacle.

We may envisage next, a case which is entirely different from the above. Somebody appeals to my sympathy in a given situation. Here again I must furnish a response but it will be of a completely different kind; it could turn out that this response which involves my feeling is not within my power to draw out of myself. I do not succeed in summoning forth the sympathy which is entreated. I would have wished it to be otherwise and it is painful to deceive my questioner, but what can I do? I can only utter certain formulas I have in mind which are part of my repertory and seem to suit the present circumstances; perhaps I even find it possible to give them a sympathetic intonation, but in any case I am only reading something out of a catalogue; this reaction is relevant only to having as in the case of the file, above; it has nothing in common with that positive human sympathy to which the other person appeals and which I really do not feel. The suffering of the other person is alien to me and I do not succeed in making it my own. Why is this so? It of course may be that I have certain personal preoccupations which are too absorbing to leave any room for this feeling. We must not be misled, however, by a false atomism. It can easily happen that, in general, I feel opaque, non-permeable, and this state can be attributed to a number of different causes (fatigue, moral deterioration, the habit of concentrating on myself too much; intimacy with oneself, like any other relation or liaison, can degenerate and become vicious).

However, it may also turn out that submerging oneself suddenly in the life of another person and being forced to see things through his eyes, is the only way of eliminating the self-obsession from which one has sought to free oneself. Alone, one cannot succeed in this, but the presence of the other person accomplishes this miracle, provided one gives one's consent to it and does not treat it as a simple intrusion—but as a reality. Nothing is more free in the true sense of this term, than this acceptance and consent; and there is nothing which is less compatible with the sort of antecedent deliberation which an obsolescent psychology holds as the necessary condition of the free act. The truth is that as long as one is captive of the category of causality, so difficult to apply to the spiritual life, one will not be able to distinguish between coercion and appeal, or between the distinctive modalities of response each of these evokes from us. In my opinion, the word "response" should be reserved for the wholly inner reaction evoked by an appeal.

The individual who tries to coerce us, forgets or pretends to forget, that we are men; insofar as we give in to him, we cease to be present to ourselves, for he alienates us from ourselves; it might be said that he puts us in a state of somnambulism; our experience of what is taking place in a number of European countries confirms this view. Appeal, on the other hand, mysteriously restores us to ourselves. Not inevitably, of course, since we can refuse to give ourselves to it. For our response to be free, however, we do not have to be completely aware of the possibility of refusal; it is free, it might be said, whenever it is liberative. It is here that we may find a way of removing the obstacles a dreary and quarrelsome philosophy seemed to have enjoyed raising for unsettled minds over a period of two centuries.

We all carry a burden, a load which at critical moments becomes literally insupportable; first of all, the weight of our past, what we wanted to do and did not do, what we wanted to be and are not. As I have said before, I think an act is free when it is liberative, i.e., when it lightens the weight on our shoulders which is set to grind our face one day into the earth. Here the importance of the attitude we adopt to what is irrevocable cannot be emphasized too strongly. Insofar as the latter is viewed as an object, and therefore immovable, it has the power of destroying by petrifying, a power ascribed by the ancients to the face of the Gorgon. What must be understood, however, is that the more the past is immobilized, the more the future seems already to have elapsed before its actual advent; the contamination of the future by the past, is one of the sources of fatalism. We do not live in the full sense of this term, however, unless we deny this fatalism at every moment; if we are unfortunate enough to have reached the point where we not only sanction it verbally, (which has little significance), but sanction it in our hearts, i.e. believe in it, then life itself stops. Life may be compared to sailing; sailing implies a dual motion, of water and of air, and this may be transferred to the temporal order. Psychopathology shows how life can be literally halted, paralyzed by an image which immobilizes the past and future for the obsessive. Contrary to a popular belief which finds its support in what we may call the current philosophy, it is not true to say that the past is immutable; for we cannot legitimately distinguish between material events which are fixed, and an illumination which varies according to its source, a source which is the experienced present itself. The sort of past I am criticizing is not to be identified with the past it is or becomes when I reconcile myself to it.

We can now reveal the origins of indisposability which is

identifiable with the inner inertia I discussed in connection with admiration.

I believe that the problem becomes clear once it is understood that disposability and creativity are related ideas. An objection may be raised, however: isn't it true that a creative person is often indisposable in the moral sense of the term, i.e., is too occupied with his own work to spare any positive sympathy for others? But it is necessary to distinguish the work to be done from the work which is already done. From the moment that I constrict my interest to the form of my finished work and it becomes the center of the world for me; from the moment I judge the words of others in terms of it or judge others according to whether I approve or disapprove of their mode of appreciation of it, it is transformed into a having on which my thought anxiously dotes, something clutched in a dead hand. Thus I pass into a state of radical indisposability. This state must be shattered if I am to be free. The main difference between this state of sterile indisposability and the state of gestation of the creative individual, who is concentrated on a work he wants to bring to fruition and to which he gives his entire substance, is clear; the work to be accomplished is the embodiment of his vocation, and that vocation is related to others and to the world. It is his way of giving himself. Hence it is due only to a misunderstanding which is also a betrayal, that this creative modality, this sacrifice—since it is a sacrifice in the true sense of the term—is construed as a thing. It is just because the work has yet to be realized that we cannot treat it as a having. It should be observed that this situation can be transposed to a plane which is not that of the work of art but rather the plane on which I consider *myself* as something which must be realized or created. A contrast analogous to that between the finished work and the work yet to be realized, is one between myself as a given set of properties and myself as a continuous creation. To be sure, we must examine the conditions in which this attention to what I want to be and should be, is justified. It may be not only sterile but harmful and ultimately destructive as well, if what is involved is the realization of an inner state of perfection, rather than the initiation of some form of relationship with God or my fellow-man, in short, the rendering of aid or the production of some work.

In pursuing this line of thought, we end up, I should think, with the following formulation: I tend to treat myself as indisposable just so far as I construe my life or being as a having which is somehow quantifiable, hence as something capable of being wasted, exhausted or dissipated. Indeed where having is concerned, I find that I am in the state of chronic anxiety of the man hanging over the void, who has a small sum of money which must last as long as possible since when it is spent he will have nothing left. This anxiety is *concern,* the corrosive, paralyzing element which discourages every *élan,* every worthy initiative. We must note that anxiety or concern can be reabsorbed into a state of inner inertia in which the world is experienced as stagnation and putrescence. The word *unhope* coined by Thomas Hardy in one of his poems which Charles Du Bos translated by a neologism, *inespoir,* admirably renders that state of soul apprehended in terms of what may be called its positive negativity. Unhope which is opposed to hope as fear is opposed to desire, is truly a death in life, a death anticipated. No problem is more important or more difficult than that of determining how we can overcome it—for it seems to occur outside the zone of possible conflict, and in a zone of bleak desolation. It yawns before us as an abyss at certain moments and we are swallowed up by it as in a morass from which we do not possess the courage even of the most elementary kind to will our escape.

It is obvious that there is no infallible technique which will permit us to free ourselves; but it is no less clear that we cannot be satisfied with a fatalism which would condemn us to remain captives of this attitude until some unpredicted external event occurred to free us.

From the philosophical point of view, salvation here lies only in reflection, but it must be understood at the same time that this reflection is not separable from the freedom it embodies. We must be careful about how we express our meaning in this context; in particular, we must guard against the following type of reassuring formulation: "everyone has, or you will always have the alternative of. . . ." in this context we are not concerned with having such means at our disposal as obtaining a sedative at the pharmacy or buying a revolver at the gunsmith for the simple reason that it is not somebody else but ourself as subject who is involved. We are here in the presence of the central mystery of our being. *Because we are identified with our freedom, our freedom sometimes seems unrealizable.* Yes, everything happens as though a narrow, yet unbridgeable chasm separated us from it, as though we could not reach it. It is plain that we again find here what I tried to point out with respect to belonging to oneself and the society of individuals of which I am composed. We touch now on the most intimate aspect of being and freedom. Reflection discloses the closest yet most paradoxical relation between the fact or act of being, on the one hand, and the permanent possibility of being separated or cut off from that which makes or constitutes us as beings, on the other hand. This basic situation which is but inadequately called our own since it is that which makes possible what we call ourselves, such a situation, I must emphasize, is one we shall always be tempted to construe in objective terms which denature it; from the moment that we have given up thinking of that freedom which is somehow the soul of our soul, as a faculty with which we are equipped or, if one likes, an attribute, (a view which is in all likelihood meaningless), we are in danger of converting into a fancied power outside of us, which sometimes lends itself to us, sometimes withdraws, depending on its caprices; this, however, is clearly a contradictory image; assuming for a moment that the term freedom can be applied to such a power, it would no longer be our freedom. What may be inferred from this? how can we resolve this hopeless dilemma? only on condition that the variable and, so to speak, dramatic relation I hold to myself is acknowledged as inconceivable; that it cannot be an object of thought in the same way as is a relation relating terms which designate sensible or intelligible data—which kind is inconsequential. With this, we are in the presence of what I have elsewhere called the *metaproblematic*.

In conclusion, then, I should like to return again to the meaning of the metaproblematic or of mystery, which I continue to regard as fundamental, and which if improperly construed, will give rise to the most harmful interpretations. There is always a danger of interpreting a mystery as a problem to which the mind arbitrarily attaches the tag, *no thoroughfare;* if so, we are returning to the shallow agnosticism of the end of the nineteenth century. My entire work, my dramatic as well as philosophical writings, is opposed, I believe, to this interpretation. I am tempted to reproduce here some parts of Father Fessard's essay which appeared as the introduction to my play, *La Soif*,[3] if citing one's own commentator wasn't so ludicrous. To do justice to my accusation, however, it might suffice to remind the reader that from my point of view a mystery gives off a certain light which is not that of the understanding, but which in a metaphysical sense, encourages the bourgeoning of the understanding as the sun encourages the growth of a tree or the blooming of a flower. "The metaproblematic, I maintained, is a participation on which my reality as a subject is based."[4] On reflection, however, such a definition seems to lead us into an impasse. Whenever I use an objective terminology, I fall into the worst possible contradictions—those very contradictions so clearly manifested in modern idealism. These are based on the fact that if I construe participation as my insertion into a web of objective relations, I adopt with respect to the latter the presumptuous status of a pure intelligence which claims to survey the universe from above. But the detachment of the spectator is opposed to that of the saint or hero which is realized instead within being itself. It is evident that the saint does not detach himself from things or from a preoccupation with them unless it is for the purpose of participating more directly in the creative intention, *voluntas tua,* which is at the core of every life. Perhaps one of the basic tragedies of the modern world consists in a confusion between these two kinds of detachment.

However shocking such an affirmation may seem to be, it is clear that the more I actually participate in being, the less I am capable of knowing or of saying in what it is that I participate, or more precisely, the less such a question has any meaning for me;

and the essential meaning of negative theology consists in reaching, by successive, concentric exclusions, the heart of that central affirmation which becomes so much a part of the one who utters it that he eventually becomes incapable of uttering it.

It would appear that we are remote from the sphere of concrete analysis from which we first started; but I do not believe that this is really the case. On the contrary, the metaphysical affirmations I have just presented can be transcribed in terms of lived experience and indeed assume their full meaning only when they refer to such experience.

NOTES

1 [There does not seem to be any single word in English which adequately renders the French *disponibilité*. The term is generally translatable as availability—*spiritual* availability in this context, i.e. openness to the other, readiness to respond, forthrightness, etc. Transl. note].
2 Consider the words of a connoisseur at an exposition: "That's very good . . . very good, Ah! that's really *good.*"
3 (Paris: Desclée de Brouwer, 1938).
4 *Etre et Avoir,* (Paris: Aubier, 1935), p. 165.

III

An outline of a concrete philosophy

The ideas developed in the present chapter are not only difficult to grasp but are virtually incapable of exposition in any strict sense. Few ideas, I should think, are as ill-adapted to a didactic exposition; and in any case, I should like to avoid a didactic approach. This, however, is not the only difficulty: the title of the chapter which I chose without previous reflection, introduces a further complication into an already complex situation. The title was chosen because of its generality, for I did not wish to become involved in details I could not cope with before I knew how to present my theme. At the present time it seems to me that the title is overly ambitious, inadequate, and to a certain extent, misleading. Thus the reader may infer that I wanted to enter a plea in behalf of a particular philosophical doctrine. This is not quite true. To be sure, I shall describe a certain kind of reaction to the official philosophy which, while chiefly a personal one, is not peculiar to me. But putting aside all modesty which would be inappropriate in the present context, I shall from the outset speak exclusively for myself, not knowing to what extent other philosophers with whom I am in general agreement would accept what I propound. The reader will readily note that I become more directly and more personally involved as I go along; some readers will find this shocking, but I do not believe that such readers can be useful or even understanding adepts of a concrete philosophy as I conceive it.

After explaining in what I admit to be a highly polemical and eristic fashion what I mean by a concrete philosophy, I shall indicate—and this will be the most difficult section—my own main points of view. After this I shall try to lead you via a number of rather precipitous detours to vantage points from which it will be possible to survey certain characteristic spiritual landscapes as I should like to call them. A friend once told me in connection with *Etre et Avoir* that the book had given him an unsurpassed feeling for the developing movement of thought. Nothing, I believe, has greater significance than this, but I am afraid that it is infinitely more difficult to convey such a feeling when one must do it in expository form. If I have any success in this connection, I will not be as disappointed as I first anticipated.

The first question which may occur to the reader is: "Do you believe that the concrete philosophy to which you refer is a philosophy which has existed in the past? Where and at what period do you place it?" It is absolutely impossible to reply to this question. Or, rather, the most that can be said with respect to the past is that there have been places and times where and when concrete philosophical thought has blossomed; but this thought has always or almost always tended to degenerate either into a scholasticism or into a series of devitalized commentaries which fatally tended to sterilize and blind the really deep and fresh intuition about which they proliferated. Expend, restore: these two verbs which express the two successive but related moments of every living process of becoming, can also be applied here. Here, expenditure is also exploitation; but a mysterious event occurs on the level of philosophical thought which is contrary to what occurs on the technical or practical level: the exploitation of a thought tends to obnubilate, alter and degrade it. This is what I venture to call the peculiar danger of "isms." Cartesianism versus Descartes, kantism versus Kant, bergsonism versus Bergson, are so many possible themes for a historian of thought. There is a lot of material for reflection here, the details of which I cannot now enter into. What I should simply like to indicate is, that if the expression "concrete philosophy" has any meaning, it is primarily because it embodies a rejection in principle of all "isms," including a certain kind of academicism.

On reflection, it seems to me that the form of my philosophical thought has been shaped in response to the demands of such refusal; it is a form which has been imposed on me—since I cannot truthfully say that I willed it. From the outset before the war, my plan had rather been to write a work which would be traditional in form; while unlike Hamelin's *Essai* which had always repelled me because of its rigorously systematic character, it would hopefully be similar to the *Contingence des Lois de la Nature*,[1] for example. From the start, the *Journal Metaphysique* was destined to be a series of notes taken down day by day, which could be developed at some time or other into an organic whole. It was curious to see how, as my ideas became clearer, or rather, as my mind apprehended more directly the concrete nature of its contents, I perceived more clearly the difficulty of moving from the first to the second level; furthermore, this insight was progressively accompanied by a more critical reflection on the very notion of a system. I do not think it is an exaggeration to say that the revulsion evoked in me by the idea of a system, which I was able to formulate more clearly as time went on, has played a considerable role in this context. This point should be elaborated somewhat. What we are concerned with at present is the idea of *my* system; hence the relation signified by this expression between the system and the person who considers himself its inventor and patent-holder. It has become increasingly evident to me that the claim to "encapsule the universe" in a set of formulas which are more or less rigorously related, is absurd. And doubtless, this has been the source of the extraordinary annoyance I have always felt whenever certain amiable individuals, animated by the very best intentions, ask me questions about *my* philosophy. The attempt to imprison me in this sort of shell which I am supposed to have secreted, is, I think, all that is required to make me find it uninhabitable. Philosophy has increasingly appeared to me an open inquiry; here the possessive index is divested of a meaning which when construed in terms of results, of what is already acquired, seems to me intolerable or inconceivable; I understand very well why people should ask me about my research since it is indeed my own; however, insofar as I admit that it is completed, it on the contrary no longer belongs to me. "There is nothing less patentable than philosophy, nothing more difficult to appropriate." I have affirmed as much on a previous occasion. The philosopher is just the opposite of a property owner, which does not imply that he feels no temptation to claim certain privileges; but he should recognize the temptation for what it is. The same can be said of the artist, but here the problem is somewhat different.

Under these circumstances it is clear why the *Journal Metaphysique* increasingly became an instrument of research and even an integral part of that research. This is why I often took the opportunity to write: "We must investigate, search, continue on;" in the same way as the adventurer indicates a path to follow, the explorer the trails he has not been able to take. I believe that my concern has never been and that it never will be, self-exploitation.

What does it mean to philosophize concretely? This question does not at all imply a return to empiricism; this point is extremely important: the most pernicious and dehumanized philosophies such as Spencerism, together with the speculation associated with it, have been based to my mind on empirical foundations.

We are nearer to the truth if we say that it is to philosophize *hic et nunc*. I want to clarify what I mean by this, but I can only do so in a polemical manner, i.e., by opposing a certain official philosophy or pseudo-philosophy. First of all, with respect to the attitude with which one approaches the history of philosophy: we witness today, and have witnessed for more than twenty years—fortunately a reaction is taking place—the resignation of philosophy in behalf of the history of philosophy, a resignation which threatens to have the most dangerous repercussions on history itself. When confronted with a certain problem, for example, one first tries to determine how it appeared in history, in such or such a system; that is, the problem is treated as an entity which has evolved in a certain way; when one has reluctantly reached the final chapter or rather, epilogue, and is compelled to ask the fatal question: *Quid nunc?*—and now what? —the temptation is to let the problem evaporate, or reduce it to ashes. The crematorium is a more or less faithful image of such a conclusion. There is no task which would be of greater use nor any more delicate, than that of a phenomenological analysis of that *we others,* expressed in epilogues with an apparent modesty mingled with the extraordinary presumption typical of those who plume themselves on their scientific attitude. It is undeniable that the ideal for the majority of such philosophers (I use the term "philosopher" reluctantly), consists in a kind of general elimination of problems. We presumably pay the necessary respect to them in studying their historical development, but we must substitute for them the positive inquiries typical of the empirical sciences such as psychology or sociology. However, we must examine the significance of this attempt to absorb the former. No theme is more crucial to our inquiry.

We can now introduce the subject of what is scientifically verifiable, where team-work is required. The extent to which the image of the factory and the laboratory have obsessed philosophers is difficult to assess. A number of connected themes should be examined. The inferiority complex of the philosopher, say, when he compares himself to the scientist—but of the philosopher who betrays himself. The philosopher of integrity is not converted. This gives rise to still further questions. We must understand the cause of the betrayal; the weakness which leads to a disownment. A number of related factors intervene, beginning with the development of democratic superstitions (as Scheler has demonstrated, it is likely that this development itself has its source in an inferiority complex). Take the democratic notion of value: the "I think" which is degraded into thought in general, and thought in general which in turn is degraded to the rank of the impersonally democratic "one."

What I have called concrete philosophy must adopt a position which is completely opposed to this attitude.

First, with respect to the history of philosophy. Of course, a philosopher should "know" the history of philosophy, but to my mind he should know it more or less in the sense in which a composer knows harmony; that is, possessing the tools of harmony without ever becoming their slave. From the moment he is their slave, he is no longer a creator or an artist. Similarly, the philosopher who has surrendered to the history of philosophy is, to that extent, not a philosopher. It should be added—and this implies an important distinction—that whoever has not lived a philosophical problem, who has not been gripped by it, cannot understand what this problem meant for those who lived before him; roles are reversed in this respect, and the history of philosophy presupposes philosophy and not conversely.

However, an objection may arise: how can the philosopher be compared to the musician? The latter invents, the former claims to understand. Are not the values inspiring artistic creation and philosophical inquiry irreducibly distinct? This is a large problem which I can only touch on here. I should simply like to affirm that the two do converge despite their differences.

Separate out certain structures: one finds that there is a limiting zone of invention and discovery which is not to be identified with production. If I am not mistaken, it was Paul Valéry who wrote that "Artistic genius acts like those extremely high temperatures which have the power to dissociate combinations of atoms and regroup them in accordance with a completely different order of another type."

Nobody would care to deny that the function of the philosopher is similar, and even those who are located at the antipodes of what I have called concrete philosophy, Bertrand Russell, for example, have understood this.

However, there is another factor or aspect of the situation which seems to me just as important. Whoever philosophizes *hic et nunc*, is, it may be said, a prey of reality; he will never become completely accustomed to the fact of existing; existence is inseparable from a certain astonishment. The child, in this sense, is close to existence; we all know children who have asked extremely metaphysical questions at the age of six; but this astonishment usually disappears, the surprise dies away. The majority of licensed philosophers who are known—I will not cite any names—do not show the least trace of it. There is room for extended analysis here too. A reader of Mr. Piaget or Mr. Levy-Bruhl will not fail to relate metaphysical astonishment to heaven knows what prelogical mentality, and melancholically deplore its survival in certain backward contemporaries. However, we must closely examine the nature of this habituation to reality which is considered typical of the adult attitude. Habituation to reality, but actually, the word "reality" is inappropriate in this context. Whatever our level of approach, there can be no apprehension of reality which is not accompanied by a certain shock. Doubtless such a shock can only be felt intermittently by definition. Only the habituated mind, or more accurately, the mind which is established in its daily routine, cannot feel it any more, or else finds some way of eliminating the memory it has of it—whereas a metaphysical mind never wholly resigns itself to this routine, viewing it as a state of sleep. This is not merely a minor difference: for it implies an absolute incompatibility in the mode of evaluation.

Personally, I am inclined to deny that any work is philosophical if we cannot discern in it what may be called the sting of reality. I may add that in the development of any philosophy, there is always a point, unfortunately, at which the dialectical instrument tends to operate all by itself in a vacuum. Any philosopher who makes judgments or otherwise functions in his capacity as philosopher, cannot be distrusted enough. For he makes a distinction with respect to his own reality which mutilates it and which irremediably tends to falsify his thought; I believe that the role of the most vivifying philosophical minds of the last century, of a Kierkegaard perhaps, but certainly of a Schopenhauer or a Neitzsche, has properly consisted in revealing, directly or indirectly, that dialectic whereby the philosopher may be led to surpass himself as a simple *Fachmensch,* as a simple specialist.

It may be said in this respect that no concrete philosophy is possible without a constantly renewed yet creative tension between the I and those depths of our being in and by which we are; nor without the most stringent and rigorous reflection, directed on our most intensely lived experience.

I just mentioned the *I:* I do not believe that I, anymore than Mr. Le Senne, can dispense with this word which has been so philosophically discredited up to the present time. However, it must be understood that I do not mean by this the ideal subject of knowledge. In general, the *cogito* in its idealist interpretation—I shall not decide whether it can be taken in any other sense—does not seem to me a likely point of departure for a possible metaphysics.

In a footnote to *Etre et Avoir,* I affirmed: "The Incarnation, central datum of metaphysics. The incarnation, situation of a being which appeared to itself as tied to a body . . . A fundamental situation which cannot strictly speaking be disposed of, surmounted or analyzed. Properly speaking, it is not a fact but rather the datum with respect to which a fact becomes possible." [2] Whereas between the *cogito* and any fact, there is a hiatus which it is probably impossible to fill.

One of the axes of my philosophical inquiries, beginning with the second part of the *Journal Metaphysique,* undoubtedly passes through this point; in returning to this passage, I was surprised to find that in 1928 I used the same expressions Jaspers later used in his own system. A pure coincidence, but one based on the very character of this kind of philosophy. The importance of the terms *situation* and *commitment* which appeared in a note written at the same period, cannot be overstressed. I have always strongly emphasized the fact that a philosophy which begins with the *cogito,* i.e. with non-commitment even if construed as an act, runs the risk of never getting back to being. "The incarnation is the datum with respect to which a fact becomes a possible"; it is not a form, and it cannot be maintained that it is a pure and simple relation. It is a datum which is not transparent to itself. The truth is that the seductiveness of the *cogito* for philosophers lies precisely in its apparent transparency. It is always appropriate to ask, however, whether this isn't a false supposition of transparency. This, I believe, creates a dilemma: either this supposition of transparency is false, and there is, as I believe, in the *cogito* itself, an element of obscurity which cannot be elucidated—or, if the *cogito* is really transparent to itself, we can never infer existence from it no matter what logical procedure we use.

At this point opacity and the conditions which cause it should become the object of our reflections. I have been increasingly compelled to adopt the paradoxical thesis that it is always the self which creates its own obscurity, its opacity deriving from the fact that the self places itself between the I and the other. "The obscurity of the external world is a function of my own obscurity; the world has no intrinsic obscurity." [3] This observation will crop up again shortly. But we must first return to the other term of that tension which to my mind is the very source of a concrete philosophy. What are we to understand by "these depths of being in and by which we are?"

I want to maintain that there is something which is inexhaustibly concrete at the heart of reality or of human destiny the understanding of which does not proceed by successive stages as in the case of the empirical sciences. Each of us gains access to this inexhaustible reality only through the purest and most unblemished part of himself. The obstacles in the way are enormous. Indeed experience reveals that those pure parts of oneself which alone can make contact with being are concealed from the outset by a mass of accretions and encrustations; it is only through a long and painful task of cleansing, or more accurately, of purification, and by a painful self-discipline, that we succeed in ridding ourselves of them; while this is being accomplished, the dialectical instrument which is an integral part of philosophical thought, and which that thought should always control, is being forged. Here we touch on a central but highly difficult theme which has priority over all the others. I have to cite one of the passages in my book which I believe is essential although I am afraid it is not the most obvious, for it will give me the chance to lay bare what I believe is the hinge on which metaphysics turns. I am afraid that this passage will give you an extremely vague impression of what I mean. However, it will be clarified in the sequel where I take the detours I mentioned earlier, and where, I believe, you will be able to grasp somewhat better the meaning and implication of this extremely abstract passage:

"Reflection on the question: *What am I?* and its implications. When I reflect on the implications of the question *what am I?*, considered in its comprehensive sense, I understand it to mean: what qualifications do I have to answer this question? hence any answer to this question *which comes from me,* should be mistrusted.

Can somebody else supply me with the answer, however? At once an objection arises: it is I who discern the qualifications the other person has to answer me, the final validity of his statements; but what qualifications do I have which would allow me to exercise this discrimination? If I wish to avoid self-contradiction I must rely on an absolute judgment which is more private to me than my own judgment; indeed, so far as I construe that judgment as something external to me, I necessarily reopen the question of whether it is valid, of how it is to be appraised. Hence the question as such cannot really be asked and is converted instead into an appeal. Insofar as I become aware of this *appeal qua appeal,* however, I come to understand that it is possible only because there is something deep within me besides my own self, something more private to me than myself, and as soon as this occurs, the significance of the appeal is altered.

There will be an objection: this appeal, taken in the first of the above senses, need not have any real object; it can be lost in the dark, so to speak. What, however, is the import of this objection? that I haven't perceived any answer to this "question," i.e., that "someone else hasn't answered." In this case I remain on the level of the assertion or non-assertion of a fact; but I am thereby restricted to the circle of the problematic (i.e. of what is placed *before* me)." [4]

I will add to this passage another note written two months later, but with the same orientation:

"In no circumstances can an assertion ever appear to generate the reality of that which it asserts. The proper formulation here is:

I assert it because it is. Now this expresses the results of a previous reflection, but at this stage, the *this is* seems to be external to the assertion and prior to it; the assertion refers to something given. A secondary reflection, however, immediately follows. By reflecting itself, the assertion encroaches on the hallowed ground reserved to the *this is*. Hence I must infer: *this is* itself presupposes an assertion. An infinite regress therefore follows unless I am willing to lay down the affirmation itself as origin, but we will not press the point. Let us admit that being has beseiged the self, as it were; and by *self*, I mean in this context, the subject who affirms. Such a subject still mediates between being and the assertion; hence the problem I raised in my notes of January 19, is raised again; for I am compelled to question the ontological status of this self with respect to the being which besieges it. Is the self submerged by it, or does the self somehow govern it instead? If it governs it, however, what confers this power on it, and what exactly is its significance?" [5]

This brings us to a distinction which I regard as fundamental, and which at the present time seems a presupposition of my entire philosophical thought, although it was not explicitly formulated until October 1932:

"The distinction between the mysterious and the problematic." A problem is something which one runs up against, which bars the way. It is before me in its entirety. A mystery, however, is something in which I find myself involved, whose essence therefore, is not to be completely before me. On this level it seems as though the distinction between the *in me* and the *before me* loses its meaning." [6]

Considered in these terms, many metaphysical problems appear as degraded mysteries. The clearest example of this degradation is the problem of evil as it has been traditionally formulated; we are asked to consider evil as the malfunctioning of a certain mechanism, the universe itself, which is to be examined from the outside just as a mechanic takes apart a motorcycle which doesn't run. In so doing, I consider myself not only immune to its illness or infirmity, but also external to a universe which I claim mentally at least to be able to reconstruct in its totality. Hence I adopt a position which is completely false and which is incompatible with my real situation. What is inappropriately called the problem of freedom provides us with another example. I have defined a mystery as "a problem which encroaches on its own immanent conditions of possibility," and this encroachment is particularly obvious in the case of freedom. For freedom is a ground of that very thought which tries to conceive it.

What is more, I can say without hesitation that the act of thought itself must be acknowledged a mystery; for it is the function of thought to show that any objective representation, abstract schema, or symbolical process, is inadequate. This is the answer that we can make to the objection that the non-problematizable cannot really be thought. For this objection is based on a postulate which must be rejected, and which consists in holding that there is an essential commensurability between thought and its object.

Before going any further into the question of what I have called the inexhaustibly concrete, I should like to make one more preliminary remark.

Ultimately, any attempt to problematize implies the notion of a certain continuity of experience which must be preserved. But the experience which concerns us in this context, whatever scientific interpretation we give it, is really *my* experience, *my* system, the extension however remote, of an original datum which in the final analysis, is my body. In the case of a mystery, however, I am by definition led beyond any "system for me." I am involved *in concreto* in an order which by definition can never become an order or a system for me, but only for a mind which transcends and includes me, and with which I cannot even ideally identify myself. The terms *beyond, transcendence,* here take on their full meaning. I might add in passing that this is the main point of disagreement between Mr. Le Senne and myself.

If we now consider being as something inexhaustibly concrete, we will note first that it cannot function as a datum, properly speaking, that it cannot be observed but only acknowledged—I am even tempted to say, if the term did not have a foreign ring to the philosophical ear—not so much acknowledged as greeted.

The given is always presented to us as something which in principle can be catalogued, something which some procedure or other can fully account for; doubtless there is a further implication that this composite of qualities must have been built up by a process of addition and juxtaposition, and that I can mentally reproduce the procedure whereby that addition or juxtaposition actually occurred. Viewing it in this way, however, clearly involves a kind of manipulation which allows me to exercise control over something which I may to that extent consider as inert; and it is undeniable that a certain joy morally accompanies the exercise of this control.

Why, then, did I write: "Whatever can be catalogued is an occasion for despair?" an observation which I believe is very important since in it may be discerned the root of what I had been led to call the tragedy of having. The explanation of this paradox seems to me to lie in the fact that this power or control which is in principle infinite, is applied to something that surpasses it in every respect: more concretely, it is here we shall find what I am tempted to call a feeling of anguished expectation, a hanging over the void. At this point we must offer by way of illustration a number of particular experiences which will at first seem rather rudimentary.

For some time I have been in a place whose resources at first seemed to me to be inexhaustible; bit by bit, however, I have gone through all the streets, seen all the "places of interest;" and now I am overcome with a certain impatience, boredom, and distaste. I feel as if I were in prison. The place where I was staying was one where a certain number of experiences were to be had, and these experiences have already transpired. Moreover, I cannot communicate my state of mind to anyone who has lived there for a number of years, anyone who participates in its life and in what it contains of what is inexpressible and therefore impossible to exhaust. It is quite clear that a certain living relationship has grown up between him and this place, this region, which I should like to call a creative interchange; as far as I am concerned, however, nothing of this sort occurs; I have come there only to increase what I have with a certain number of additional properties.

I realize that the above is only a schema, but it is one to which I attach all the more significance because I have to admit against my will that I too have tended to behave during my life like a collector. Why? What is the reason for this impatience? It is clear that at the root of this avarice there is chiefly an awareness of time which passes, of the irrevocable; life is short, first this and then that, must be obtained. However, when I reflect at the same time on the value of this accumulation, it seems to me absurd: what weight can what I was able to know or annex to myself have, when compared with what I have not seen or assimilated? Once again despair overcomes me, hems me in, so to speak; again it is as though I were a prisoner.

If we investigate this further I think we shall find that wherever there is a creative interchange with its implication of genuine rootedness, the term "datum" tends to lose its meaning, and the sphere of the problematic is at the same time transcended. Perhaps this connection between the datum and the problematic will emerge more clearly if we take another example, one relating this time to the experience we have of others.

It is clear that I can consider a certain person as a mineral from which I can extract a certain amount of usable metal. The rest is waste matter; I reject it. The criterion of interest that is used is essential to the situation, although this expression need not be interpreted necessarily in a strictly utilitarian sense. The proliferation of inquiries and interviews has certainly contributed to the false belief that a being has value to the extent that he is "interesting."

Here again the notion of a collection is the heart of the matter. With or within myself I establish a sort of library or museum in which the interesting elements that I have been able to extract from my conversation with the other, are to be incorporated. A conversation to which I contribute nothing, where I confide nothing—except whatever is required to evoke the responses I want. This is tantamount to saying that my interlocutor is not treated as a being in this context; in fact, he is not even an other, since in such a non-lived, fictional relationship, I myself do not intervene as a being, as someone real.

"The other as other exists for me only insofar as I am open to him (insofar as he is a thou), but I am only open to him insofar as I cease to form a circle with myself within which I somehow place the other, or rather, the idea of the other; for in so doing, the other becomes the idea of the other, and the idea of the other is no longer the other as such, but the other *qua* related to me, as fragmented, as parceled out or in the process of being parceled out." [7]

At the moment when communication is established between me and the other, however, we pass from one world into another; we emerge into a region where one is not merely one among others, where transcendence takes on the aspect of love. The category of the given is transcended; "never enough, always more, always closer"; these are the simple expressions which clearly indicate the change of perspective I am trying to evoke; the change involved is only partial, moreover. However, there is a sense in which the thou is given to me—and here we remain in the sphere of the problematic with all that it implies of uncertainty, doubt, jealousy—a degraded state which is based on the fact that the thou is not maintained as a thou. There is a sense, however, in which it cannot be (*Albertine Disparue* for example, should be read, in the light of these relations between the given and the problematic. For Proust, the thou is instantly coverted into an it. The immanent structure of experience, moreover, ruthlessly tends to favor such a conversion) —Absence and death play a crucial role in this context.

Certain readers will be surprised at the role played by death, suicide, betrayal, in all of my writings; I do not think we can ever ascribe enough importance to these, and any philosophy which tries to elude them or conjure them away, is guilty of the worst possible kind of betrayal; it is, moreover, inevitably punished for it, in that it loses its footholds, to borrow an analogy from mountain climbing. We can push the analogy still further, but an important difference should be emphasized. For while dizziness is an obstacle to the climber, it is a positive condition of any metaphysical thought which is worthy of its name. Indeed, a certain awareness of, or attraction for, the void is perhaps necessary if being in all its plenitude is to be forcefully affirmed.

Absence, death, are construed as tests in both *Etre et Avoir* and the *Mystere Ontologique*. The notion of a test is fundamental in this context [8]—and I should like to indicate its meaning—particularly because a certain kind of religious preaching has perhaps unknowingly tended to obliterate it. Mr. Le Senne, in his *Obstacle et Valeur,* has returned to the idea of a test; I believe that I agree with him in large part, but the agreement cannot be extended to an identity of views. I do not propose to start here with a definition since this should rather be the goal of our inquiry. Here I ascribe to the word "test" the meaning it has *grosso modo* in expressions such as "submit a work or feeling to the test of time." I shall follow my customary procedure here, i.e. analyze some example which is as concretely expressed as possible. Two young people are in love, but are not certain of the sincerity of their feelings; actually such uncertainty is rather intimated by the people who form their circle of acquaintants; but this is not of any importance in the present case. They decide (or someone decides for them) that they will live apart from each other for a while so that time and the separation can have their effects; if their love endures this test, they will conclude—(or someone will conclude for them)—that they can now reasonably be married. Time and the separation are not merely obstacles, resistant to their purposes, here; rather what resists them is used, and a functional value is conferred on it; such value consists in making possible what we may call an inner confrontation. The feelings of the two young people had been established as an absolute; but reflection (whether theirs' or their parents') has intervened to give a hypothetical character to that absolute: aren't you deceived? aren't you misled with respect to the nature and *real* power of your feelings? *Real;* this word must be stressed. The question of reality, identified with value or sincerity in the present context, is raised; and it is to this question that the test provides a response. We must not be taken in by words; time in itself, or separation, do not by themselves, decide the issue; but they do clarify our awareness and help to guide it in its relations with itself; the young people meet a year later; they recognize one another. . . .

This analysis, I believe, will help to advance our inquiry. We discover that the test implies a challenge to immediate experience; a conditional challenge at least, I would maintain: of course, it seems as though I am completely involved in my feelings at this moment; but this could be an illusion; I am not in a position to decide on the answer; I succeed however in detaching myself from my immediate feeling to ask the question. The proper function of the trial is to make a reflective judgment possible which would let us modify as to its reality the affirmation of immediacy made at the beginning. Something else of fundamental importance should also be noted, namely that in this context everything is a function of freedom and freedom alone. It is an essential characteristic of the test that it is possible to be unaware of it as such; perhaps our two young people, because of obstinacy or the simple play of vanity, refuse to acknowledge that their feelings have not withstood the test, assert that nothing has changed, and that they will get married whatever anyone thinks.

Here we are on a level where the data are relatively simple; for in the example chosen, we can confidently identify duration and reality. The test of time enables us to discern whether the feeling was or was not a durable one.

This subject, however, is open to indefinite exploration. If we wish to apply the notion of a test to suffering or to death, new data are introduced—and here certain precautions have to be taken which have occasionally been ignored by indiscrete apologists. Take an invalid who has been confined to his bed for a number of years, and who can only forsee death as the end of his suffering. A priest with the best intentions in the world, comes to his bedside and says: "Thank God for the grace he has bestowed on you. This suffering has been laid on you to give you the opportunity to merit the heavenly beatitude." I am afraid that assurances which are presented in this manner will only develop an attitude of revolt and negation in the invalid. Let us forget for the moment that we are concerned with "someone else." Put yourself in the state of mind of the invalid: what sort of God is this who tortures me for my own benefit? What right has he? And what of yourself? What right do you have to be the interpreter of such a cruel and hypocritical God?

The only reason you can do so is because you cannot imagine my suffering, because it is not yours—and you have the right to say what you did only if you suffered as I do, with me. . . .

I should now like to elucidate this in terms of what I have called concrete philosophy. First of all, we have to overcome this exteriority; the philosopher must sympathize with the invalid to the extent that he *becomes* the invalid; the latter must hear his words as if they came from the depths of his own consciousness. Thought in this context can assume only a personal form, that of meditation. To be sure, I can abandon myself purely and simply to my suffering, identify myself with it, and this too, is a terrible temptation. I can reconcile myself to my suffering which I proclaim to be completely meaningless; however, since it is the center of my world, the world itself, centered on something meaningless, also becomes absolutely meaningless. This is not just an abstract possibility but a temptation which at times is almost irresistible; however limited the sphere of my action may be, my affirmation is no less one of universal meaninglessness, and it is my role to prolong, extend, verify or confirm it; to help impose it even on those who had not at first consented to it. It is clear that I have the ability to effectively increase the share of meaninglessness in the world. We can go even further: we should acknowledge that the world accepts this condemnation of itself and lends itself to it; in a sense it even invokes it insofar as it seems justified. Is this the inevitable result of my situation? I do not find this conclusion tenable. A choice, however indistinct it may be, seems to be open to me; to be sure, nobody can force me to assign a meaning to my suffering, I cannot be *taught* that it has meaning; it has been observed that such a pretension to teach it always threatens to release a corrosive spirit of contradiction. However, I myself can try to understand or create that meaningfulness within myself. I am using the words "understand" and "create" indistinguishably since their meanings coincide in the present case. One thing should be understood at the outset if I am to accomplish this: strictly speaking, I cannot affirm that my suffering is meaningless; a meaning is not something that can be affirmed; hence the absence of meaning cannot be affirmed either; a meaning can only be recreated by an act of mind. Hence to say: my suffering is meaningless, is really to refuse to admit to oneself that it has meaning; more precisely, it is to show one's inadequacy in a situation where something was in the process of being created. We can make this clearer to a certain extent if we consider a situation where suffering exposes me to others; it can then be an occasion for stiffening or contracting, for focussing my attention on myself, or it can, on the contrary, open my eyes to the suffering of others which I was unable to imagine before. Here the meaning of test becomes obvious. Our concern here is one of creative interpretation. I can refuse, once again, to treat suffering as a test, to subject my reality to the test of suffering. I can do so. But at what price? We must not be taken in by words. In the case of such a refusal, I affirm myself, but what qualities does this self possess? I set myself up as an innocent source of protest against a world which is cruel and meaningless. Reflection discloses, however, that it is rather my situation itself that is meaningless. Every protest presupposes a remedy to which it is directed; here the remedy is inconceivable and the protest is immediately canceled in the same way as a protest made by someone who thought he was addressing somebody else, is stifled, when he perceives that he is alone.

At this point someone will be inclined, I should think, to raise an objection. It will be maintained that the test so understood, is only conceivable under extreme circumstances which, if they are not compelling, nevertheless encourage me to ask myself what I am; and here we have a concrete example of the dialectic I described at the beginning of my exposition. For does not our life go on under average, normal conditions, without being in such jeopardy?

I believe that our reply must first of all be—but we should not be satisfied with the reply—that on reflection, the opposition between normal and extreme conditions is untenable. The extreme circumstance, *par excellence,* is the immediate nearness of death, and nobody can be really sure that his death is not imminent. If, as we must concede, the point of view of the philosopher coincides with that of the man who is fully alert to his state, we can then hold that he should view the world in the light of that threat, for the normal state is an extreme state. To be sure this is only a part, an aspect of the truth, so to speak; and it is no less true and perhaps even more essential for us to affirm that we should live and work every moment as though we had an eternity before us. This represents an antinomy for which there is no dearth of examples and which is connected with the mysterious relation between my being and my life. At this point I should like to say a few words about one of the most significant yet hidden of all the relationships I have tried to illuminate in my work.

The person who gives up his life for a cause is aware of giving all, of making a *total* sacrifice; but even if he is going to a certain death, his act is not a suicide, and there is, metaphysically speaking, a gap between the act of sacrificing his life and that of killing himself. Why? Here we must introduce the notions of disposability and indisposability. Doubtless, the person who gives up his life gives up everything, but he does it for something else that he asserts means more, that is worth more; he puts his life at the disposal of that higher reality; he extends to the ultimate that disposability which is exemplified in the fact of dedicating oneself to a person, to a cause. In so doing, he has, if I may say so, proved that he has placed or situated his being beyond life. There is not and cannot be any sacrifice without hope, and hope is suspended in the ontological realm. Suicide, on the other hand, is basically negation. If there is any exclamation which signifies the intention of the suicide, it is the word: enough! If killing oneself does not mean the deliberate desire to make oneself indisposable, it in any case means that one does not care whether he remains disposable for others. Suicide is essentially a refusal; it is a resignation. Sacrifice is essentially attachment (and every secular critic of asceticism has ignored this characteristic and thereby failed in his purpose).

To be sure, these observations are phenomenological, but they clear the way for a hyperphenomenological reflection which is identical with metaphysics itself. Whether or not he actually believes in eternal life, the person who sacrifices himself acts as if he believed; the suicide acts as if he did not believe. The philosopher, however, cannot be satisfied with the use of the expression "as if" in this context. Whatever Vahinger may have thought, every philosophy of the "as if" is self-contradictory; every authentic philosophy is the active negation of the "as if." In this connection a preliminary reflection will be of help. Nothing is less able to illuminate a being for us, less able to show his worth or what he is, than knowing what his opinions are; opinions do not count, and if I had the time, I would be glad to demonstrate this in detail, and to exhibit what is entailed by such a demonstration, particularly in connection with those implications of a political complexion. The question which then arises is whether, contrary to the atheistic, unmeaning justifications that the nonbeliever offers or claims to offer of his sacrifice, the latter does not actually confirm the truth of that which the nonbeliever denies. Consider the passage of Proust in *Le Prisonnière,* which I will cite in an abridged form: "All these obligations which have not their sanction in our present life, seem to belong to a different world . . . , a world entirely different from this which we leave in order to be born into this world, before perhaps returning to the other to live once again beneath the sway of those unknown laws which we have obeyed because we bore their precepts in our hearts, knowing not whose hand had traced them there—those laws to which every profound work of the intellect brings us nearer and which are invisible only—and still!—to fools. So that the idea that Bergotte was not wholly and permanently dead is by no means improbable." [9] Here we have one of those Platonic intuitions—so rare in Proust's work—which contradicts the general tenor of his work.

If such a hyperphenomenological reflection is possible, however, it is because we penetrate here into the zone of the metaproblematic. The views I have expressed in *Etre et Avoir* on fidelity, faith, hope, are completely unintelligible if the distinction between a problem and a mystery is not understood. A philosopher friend once said to me with respect to this book: "It is more moving, more compressed than the *Journal Metaphysique,* but it seems to me to be less positive." I shall ignore everything involving the emotions evoked by the book since this is clearly not for me to judge; however, I can say that if the reader does not see that this is the most positive book he can find, the essence of it has entirely eluded him. To be truthful, I see clearly what the reply will be; and this will afford me the opportunity of explaining myself with respect to a particularly delicate point insofar as it is possible to do so. Somebody will maintain: "This book is positive to the extent that it is obviously written by a catholic; but those who do not participate in your faith will be brought by your reflection up against a wall which for them is unsurmountable. In this sense your friend was right. And generally, the anguished question in the minds of those who read your book is the relation between a concrete philosophy and a christian philosophy. Is it your view that one passes imperceptibly from one to the other? How is this possible, however, without sophistry? Moreover, from the christian point of view, wouldn't this imply a kind of rationalization or naturalization of the supernatural? Even the use of the term 'mystery' is misleading."

This question in its own right deserves to be developed in much greater detail. I can only reply in a general way.

First of all, two things are clear.

It is plain that an adept of concrete philosophy as I conceive it, is not necessarily a christian; strictly speaking, it cannot even be said that he is embarked on a path which should logically lead him to christianity; on the other hand, I believe that the christian who is also a philosopher and can dig under the scholastic formulas on which he is frequently nourished, would almost inevitably rediscover the fundamental data of what I have called concrete philosophy (whereas he will certainly never find the idealism of Brunschvicg nor doubtless even that of Hamelin). Such an answer, however, is still beside the point.

In the first place, I must say that at least to my mind, a concrete philosophy cannot fail to be magnetically attracted to the data of christianity, perhaps without knowing it. And I do not think that this fact should shock anyone. For the christian, there is an essential agreement between christianity and human nature. Hence the more deeply one penetrates into human nature, the more one finds oneself situated on the axes of the great truths of christianity. An objection will be raised: You affirm this as a christian, not as a philosopher. Here, I can only repeat what I said at the beginning: the philosopher who compels himself to think only as a philosopher, places himself on the hither side of experience in an infrahuman realm; but philosophy implies an exaltation of experience, not a castration of it.

With respect to the ambiguity of the word "mystery", I can only say this: insofar as it seems a disturbing fact to me that one should grant that the mysteries of faith are superimposed on a completely problematizable world, hence one stripped of ontological thickness; on a world penetrable to reason as a crystal is to light; so it seems to me if not rational, then at least reasonable to think that this world is itself rooted in being, hence that it transcends in every way those localized problems with their similarly localized solutions which permit the insertion of the technical into things. I have referred to the incarnation in a purely philosophical sense; this incarnation, mine and yours, is to that other Incarnation, to the dogma of the Incarnation, as philosophical mysteries are to revealed mysteries.

"Doubtless, the recognition of the ontological mystery which I perceive as the main bastion of metaphysics, is only possible through the fructifying radiation of revelation itself, which can also be realized in the depths of those souls for whom every positive religion is alien; this recognition, which occurs in certain higher modes of human experience, does not imply any adhesion to a determinate religion, but it does permit the person who rises up to it, to forsee the possibility of a revelation quite differently from someone who, never having passed beyond the boundaries of the problematizable, remains on the hither side of the line where the mystery of being can be perceived and proclaimed. An irresistible movement impels such a philosophy towards an encounter with a light of which it already has a presentiment and whose hidden stimulus and future energy it already feels in its heart." [10]

NOTES

1 [Émile Boutroux, 1874. Transl. note.]
2 p. 11.
3 *Etre et Avoir*, p. 13.

4 *Ibid.,* pp. 180-182.
5 *Ibid.,* pp. 203-204.
6 *Ibid.,* p. 145.
7 *Ibid.,* p. 155.
8 [An alternate translation is *trial.* The French term is *épreuve.* Transl. note.]
9 Marcel Proust, *The Captive,* Part I, *Remembrance of Things Past,* Transl. C. K. Scott Moncrieff (N. Y.: Random House, 1927), vol II, p. 150.
10 *Le Monde cassé,* (Paris: Desclée de Brouwer, 1933), p. 301.

IV

Phenomenological notes on being in a situation

In a recent lecture,[1] Mr. Minkowski was prompted to clarify the very unconventional conception he had formed of the *cosmos*. Ignoring the Greek connotation of the term, he understands by *cosmos* a primitive dynamism, or again, the *Breath* which penetrates us and gives us life. It is clear that the cosmos so conceived, cannot really be contemplated; it is not displayed before us as a spectacle, as some monumental arrangement of things. It is equally clear, on the other hand, that our awareness of this "primitive dynamism" is not equally lively or intense at every moment of our time. And the philosopher has to ascertain why this intermittancy. However, it is no less clear to Mr. Minkowski that any one of us can suddenly have an intuition of the cosmos, and that some of us, the poets among us, are far better endowed with this unique talent than others. In adopting a phenomenological point of view, we of course are not concerned with justifying the view that intuition or poetic awareness is not a part of the realm of knowledge.

This may be clearly understood if we bear in mind the fact that man is not only a part of nature, but also that "every movement of his soul shows that it has a deep and entirely natural foundation in the world and thereby reveals a primordial quality of the structure of the universe." [2] The author concludes from this that "this structural solidarity of the world and the soul is one of the guarantees of the objectivity of the poetic aspect of life." For my part, I confess that I have to cavil somewhat at his terminology which seems loose and capable of giving rise to misunderstandings. To my mind there is little sense in speaking of the objectivity of the poetic side of life precisely because the idea of an anthropocosmic relation can only be established beyond the opposition of subject and object; what is more, we should ask whether such an expression as "structural solidarity" is not misleading. It is indeed necessary to examine the implications of the idea of structure. I do not think this expression can be used unless the mutual externality of contemplator and thing contemplated, hence of subject and object, is first re-established, at least implicitly; it is just this dualism, however, that is supposed to be transcended. It is useless to urge against this that Idealist philosophy has been busy determining the structure of the subject; isn't it plain that in so doing, it has by the same token converted the latter into an object? Furthermore, there is hardly any relation between the *situations* that Mr. Minkowski tries to designate and describe, and the *categories* of traditional philosophy. The term "situation" as used in this context is quite adequate, and its meaning is unambiguous. Can we not say that anthropology is oriented in a cosmological direction whenever it is understood that *the essence of man is to be in a situation*—and that this is remote from treating the situation as something contingently related to or an epiphenomenon of a particular subject capable of being understood and defined in itself?

Hence I believe that what is requisite at the start of an inquiry such as that of Mr. Minkowski's, is the most rigorous reflection possible on this datum which, to be sure is not opaque, but is imperfectly translucent, and which constitutes "the fact of being in a situation." The words we use here, however, instantly betray us. It would be better not to use the term "fact." One should be able to resort to but a single neuter article preceding the verb as in the case of German and Greek, but unfortunately, this is just what the structure of our own language does not allow.

Mr. Minkowski, in the lecture I have referred to above, has underlined as have many others, the equivocal, and even in a sense, fallacious nature of the expression "inner life" while observing that his own meaning is perfectly clear to us if not strictly definable. I believe that if we thoroughly examined being-in-a-situation, we should find not so much a synthesis as a juncture of externality and internality. A determinate place is located by certain landmarks external to it: yes, this is no doubt true, but it must be added that these marks, these coordinates, are part of the expression which is used to specify the place. The use of the personal pronoun in this context is indeed sufficient to set up what may be called a reflective situation or something like a potential inwardness. I have once more chosen an extreme case where the situation only involves spatial position. It is quite clear that when we say it is characteristic of man to be in a situation, we do not exclusively nor even mainly envisage the fact that he occupies a position in space; however, it is of advantage to proceed here by gradual steps, showing how certain properties which seem to be purely spatial are capable of being qualified in an increasingly inward manner. I shall take as an example the meaning expressed by the preposition *between:* A glade between the trees, a valley between some mountains; living in this glade, in this valley is to be aware of being in a situation or even at a juncture of situations of which the word *between,* despite appearances, already gives us an, if not dynamic, at any rate, pre-dynamic schema. If I live in a valley which separates two chains of mountains, I may be vaguely aware of being crushed in a vise and may feel an instinctive need to separate these masses which will crush me if they draw together. But it is also possible that the intermediate position I occupy is felt as mediatory, that I view myself as a link between powers whose communication with one another is my responsibility.

This is open to a host of applications, of which only the point of departure is spatial; I am thinking of the self-awareness of a buffer state like Belgium in recent years, for example, or that of modern Switzerland, or less abstractly, the enlightened citizen of such nations. Analogous analyses are applicable to situations which are expressed by the locutions *at the end of, along, above,* etc. . . . In all such cases, we must be systematically alert against that sterilizing abstraction which treats place as a simple determination, and must recognize how it becomes an inwardly qualified situation.

It will be correctly pointed out that this description or meaning applies to such relationships only with respect to what is living as such. It is quite clear that the examples cited above are only meaningful on this condition. We must note, however, that this living being, the fact that it lives, and the dynamic scheme which expresses its situation, can be separated only at the price of a vicious abstraction. In reality the two are strictly inseparable.

It is at this point that we again encounter—perhaps even go beyond—the penetrating observations of Mr. Minkowski on the dynamic and vital category of *reverberation*. He shows that while we are led at first to reserve the use of this term for auditory phenomena, it really has a far more extended meaning. If we restrict ourselves to the auditory level, it is "as though there were a spring inside a sealed vase, and as though its waters, lapping repeatedly against the walls of the vase, filled it with a sonority; or as though the echos spread in every direction by the sound of a hunting horn, made the smallest leaf or bit of moss tremble in the same motion, filling the forest to its boundaries and transforming the entire forest into a sonorous and vibrant world. . . ." "Let us assume that these factors were missing. I think that in this case we would see the world become animated and filled, apart from any agency, any physical property, with deep and penetrating waves which, although not sonorous in the sensory meaning of the term, would nevertheless be harmonious, resonant, capable of determining the whole tonality of life. Moreover, this life will itself reverberate in the deepest depths of its being when in contact with these waves which are at once sonorous and silent, will mingle with them, vibrate in unison with them, will live their life, joining with them into a unified whole." [3] This is the very essence of the phenomenon of reverberation.

The fact is, it seems to me, that Mr. Minkowski shifts from something which is specifiable purely and simply in sensory terms, to something else which is undifferentiated from the sensory point of view. To my mind it is even more important to succeed in defining the metaphysical significance of reverberation; and here again our reflection should be focussed on being in a situation. As a start, we can begin again with the spatial point of view. Take, for example, a badly situated hotel. What is the meaning of this expression which unites in such a paradoxical fashion a spatial determination and a value judgment? At bottom we find an objective affirmation in the strictest sense of the term: the hotel for example, is near a tannery or a boiler-factory. On the other hand, however, a hotel cannot be considered apart from a certain purpose; its function is to take in travelers. When I affirm that the hotel is badly situated, I mean that those who live there are exposed just because of their spatial situation to noises or odors everybody considers disagreeable. If we assume that the hotel is deserted, abandoned for some time, we shall still say: the explanation is that it is badly situated. Here, however, we always allude to past or to possible travelers. Consider now a man whose situation, we say, is good. In this case we are no longer dealing with space. Certain objective data are nevertheless presupposed: this man earns so much per year, has some money saved up, etc. . . . All this is supposed to put him in a certain inner state of equilibrium —even though the relationship between the two is not a necessary one: we will say: although such a person is in a good situation, he doesn't seem happy.

In both of the foregoing examples, certain relationships which we at first tend to construe as purely external, are internalized, hence qualified, while these in turn qualify a certain mode of being or of feeling.

In general, it is accurate to say that the moment one is involved

in the order of the living being, to be situated is to be exposed to.
. . . What generic term should we use to fill the ellipsis? Personally I am tempted here to rehabilitate in a measure the discredited
term "influence." The meager and rather obscure information that
Mr. Le Senne[4] gives us about this scarcely satisfies me, and I, at
least, find it impossible to subscribe to the definition according to
which influence is "the passage from the existent to existence."
Here, as is often the case, the actual structure of the word enlightens
us more than its really debased use does. If the living being is
exposed to influences because it is in a situation, this really means
that it is to a certain extent *permeable* to them. But this again must
be further analyzed. We shall better understand the meaning of
permeability if we identify it more specifically with porosity. Something filters through a sieve or through a piece of material. But a
metaphor of this kind is obviously inapplicable here. Perhaps we
can make some progress by observing that permeability, in the
broadest sense of the term, is doubtless related to a certain lack of
cohesion, or if one prefers, of density. We can say, it seems, that a
being is more exposed to influences insofar as he has less density.
We may add that these possible influences will be all the more
numerous or diverse insofar as the nature of this relatively in-
cohesive being itself implies a greater multiplicity of elements.

If the views I have just outlined are correct, we can assume that
the fact of being in a situation, i.e. of being exposed to (influences),
is inseparable from a certain in-cohesion. We should not attempt to
discover a causal relation here. It would be better to say that we are
confronted with two aspects of the same reality. Indeed, there is
reason to suppose that however it may look, the term "incohesion"
really refers to something which has positive characteristics; and
inversely, cohesion, construed here in terms of its contrary, can be
considered as a negative quality; indeed, isn't it that very thing
which offers no foothold to the other? It is true that we may be
tempted to see in this the expression of a self-sufficiency which has
generally been considered by philosophers to be the distinctive
sign of whatever is highest in the ontological hierarchy. We should,
however, be alert against confusing two opposite limits of the same

series. Here we are in fact concerned with something which, because of an inner need, is on the hither side of any possible foot-hold. We must not identify this hypothetical πρώτη ὕλη [primary matter; matter without form] with an absolute which is protected against the possibility of assaults by the other only because it has first integrated the other into itself.

It should be noted, however, that if we take this well-trodden path, we stand no chance of reaching our goal, and that at the end we are even in danger of losing contact with the concrete data from which we started.

If I were to try to summarize and to internalize the conclusions which have been reached, I would be led, I think, to express myself more or less in the following terms:

When I reflect on the fact that I occupy a certain place in the world, when I try to uncover what it is that masks my *ecceity,* I am led to recognize that my condition as a living being admittedly subjects me not only to objectively describable properties, but also exposes me to, or better, opens me up to, a reality with which I somehow communicate.

A new perspective is opened to us here. On what conditions can I communicate with this other reality? I now put aside the fact that to understand another person, I have to use a language common to both of us which will allow us to understand one another. I confine myself in this context to stressing the following preliminary condition: I must somehow make room for the other in myself; if I am completely absorbed in myself, concentrated on my sensations, feelings, anxieties, it will obviously be impossible for me to receive, to incorporate in myself, the message of the other. What I called in-cohesion a moment ago here assumes the form of disposability; thus we are indirectly brought to the question whether there is not a basis for granting the existence of a fundamental analogy between the sensory receptivity of a living being exposed to the solicitations of his surroundings and the disposability of a consciousness capable of caring for another person.

If this analogy is not altogether arbitrary, we may carefully try to illuminate the inferior in terms of the superior and to examine whether the positive aspect of disposability is not already preformed or prefigured somehow in pure receptivity. Exactly what does it mean to *receive?* Here, as in many other like cases, we must start from the richest and fullest acceptation of the term, not from the most impoverished and most debased. To receive is not merely to undergo; nor is it exactly to welcome, although receiving borders on welcoming in a way which we cannot ignore. The term "receive" has an application which is the more obvious to the degree that it has to do with a reality possessing a specific form. I am aware that people talk about "receiving an imprint," referring thereby to a piece of wax or to some plastic substance. Here, however, "receiving" is not used in its proper sense, but instead becomes synonymous with "undergoing." I hold in principle, that reception, hence receptivity, can only be considered in connection with a certain readiness or pre-ordination. A person receives others in a room in a house, if necessary, in a garden; not on unknown ground or in a forest. Here we might supply further nuances of meaning and introduce in addition to the relation of inherence, the rather subtle and almost inexplicable relation embodied in the expression *being at home.* The latter hardly seems to have attracted the attention of philosophers up to now. *Being at home* is only relative to a *self* which moreover, can be that of another person, and I understand by *self* some one who says or who presumably can say, *I,* who can posit himself or be posited as an *I.* Further, this *self* must not only possess in the sense of legal ownership a certain domain, but must also experience it as his own: the English word *area,* it seems to me, is more appropriate in this context. There are good reasons for stressing the second aspect over the first. I believe it can be said that legal meanings are here altogether unimportant and only deserve to be retained to the extent that they hide what I shall tentatively call a *having which is felt.* We are concerned exclusively with the experience which is expressed by the words *being at home*—or better, its living reference. It may very well be the case that in living among the objects which belong to me, in a house I have bought or inherited, I do not have the feeling of "being at home." This means that the framework within which I live is alien to me; I do not apprehend myself in it, I seem to be placed there. It can also occur that one of my relations or fellow-boarders, because of the fact that he is living with me, dispossesses me of that awareness of being at home which I should apparently have. Doubtless I could explain this fact by saying that the other person does not know his place. Here it is the indiscretion of the other which intervenes between me and my possessions and separates me from them, breaking the vital connections between me and them that I am trying to describe. The term "possession," however, is quite inadequate; here again the English term (belongings) seems clearly preferable.

We must notice the difficulty of expressing in rational terms the subtle relations I am considering here. There is no doubt that the relation expressed by the words *being at home* or *being at another's home* would be denatured if we tried to express it in terms of a power the other has over me or I have over myself; in that case we would be apprehending it from the outside and would at the same moment tend to destroy it. It seems to me much more accurate to acknowledge, although we shall find ourselves here on a rather mysterious path, that the self, more or less consciously, seems to endue with a certain quality of its own the surroundings which it makes its own: hence a kind of harmony between the two which renders the surroundings habitable to it. Reflection along these lines would be appropriate with respect to the almost inexpressible meaning of the words *heimlich* and *unheimlich,* on the one hand, and with the more easily grasped connections linking having (*habere*), inhabit, and even dress-habit, on the other. The distress felt by a child during a trip or change of residence, the nameless sadness we have all experienced in certain hotel rooms where we had the feeling of not being in *anybody's home*—all such experiences which philosophers considered unworthy of attention until lately, assume an importance and an unsuspected meaning when viewed in this light. In a manner, they help reflection to reach the vital and even religious element concealed in a phrase which is otherwise insignificant.

We must admit that the act of receiving takes on new meaning when viewed in this way. To receive is to admit someone from the outside to one's own home, to introduce him into that qualified area I evoked above. I shall not risk stating this categorically, but it is perhaps the case that an historico-sociological inquiry into hospitality could only be fully meaningful if it were based on these phenomenological data which are so difficult to specify. There are grounds for assuming that even social protocol which still exists in a tattered state in our disjointed world, is ultimately related to certain fundamental experiences which are part of our *condition*. I believe that this latter term should be increasingly substituted for that of "nature" in philosophical anthropology. I repeat that whoever would again take up Hume's task today, should entitle his work *On the Human Condition*.[5] We may deplore the fact that Andre Malraux has pre-empted this title for a book which is magnificent in many respects but which nevertheless does not fulfill in some ways what it seems to promise.

Following this line of thought, we will be led to acknowledge that the term "receptivity" really refers to a spectrum of meanings extending between limits which are remote from one another. One of these is *undergoing* which I referred to when I spoke of the imprint received by a piece of soft wax; the other is really a *gift,* and in the final analysis, even a gift of *self,* of the person who is involved in the act of hospitality. Actually we are not concerned here with filling up some empty space with an alien presence, but of having the other person participate in a certain reality, in a certain plenitude. To provide hospitality is truly to communicate something of oneself to the other.

We might inquire as to whether these same considerations do not in a way indirectly illuminate the receptive nature of knowledge itself. No one, I believe, can subscribe any longer to Condillac's thesis concerning the sensible. To be sure, I do not have being, or at any rate, I can only grasp myself as being- on condition that I feel; and it can also be conceded that to feel is to receive; but it must be pointed out at once that to receive in this context is to open myself to, hence to give myself, rather than to undergo an external action. We already encounter at this level the paradox which is at the core of creation itself, but it can perhaps be more easily discerned in the case of the artist than in cases involving the expansion of the understanding where pragmatism in its various guises succeeds in obscuring the original mystery, the "dawning of reality" at its unfathomable source. The artist seems to be nourished by the very thing he seeks to incarnate; hence the identification of receiving and giving is ultimately realized in him. This, however, can be accomplished only in his own sphere, which on this level corresponds to the zone I evoked in my analysis of *being at home*. There is reason to believe that there is a difference only in power and not in nature between the ability to feel and the ability to create; both presuppose the existence not only of a self, but also of a world where the self can recognize itself, act, expand; a world intermediate between the closed and the open, between having and being, of which my body necessarily seems the symbol or materialized nucleus. However, we may assume that we are deceived by the most obvious appearances when we hypostatize, treat as a self-enclosed, independent reality what is perhaps only the land of a certain undefinable realm whose submerged areas and underwater outcroppings can only be identified by accident or by sudden illumination. Doesn't the very fact of living, in the full sense we give the word when we refer to our life, human life, imply for anyone who considers the matter carefully, the existence of a kind of metaphysical *Atlantis,* incapable by nature of being explored but whose presence actually confers on our experience its body, meaning and mysterious density?

"Is not my life," as I noted some weeks ago in my *Journal,* "related to time as my body is related to space? We therefore have to consider it in terms of density and organicism—and this will doubtless have important repercussions on the metaphysical level." One of the great services rendered by the work of imagination, the drama or the novel, by their very existence, is to help us to clearly perceive in the privileged milieu which they offer, a type of unity of which our immediate experience gives us only a dim and but occasional intimation. I may readily add, although there is a risk here of shocking people, that astrology, whatever may ultimately be thought of its methods and the results it has actually obtained, has had on an entirely different level the major attraction of drawing our attention to the notion of a form, a pattern of individual destiny. We live, on the other hand, in a period when the most heterogeneous forces seem to conspire to abolish any distinct awareness we might have of this fundamental cohesion. Idealism, in its modern versions, has contributed to the acceptance of a complete divorce between myself and my life, my life appearing as a particular group of phenomena falling within the province of the natural sciences, perhaps of sociology too, but deprived of its characteristic intelligibility; the cessation of or rupture in this life possesses no intrinsic meaning, no metaphysical significance, for a self which identifies itself with the very act of thought. Such a philosophy denies the truth of an exigence which is so deeply rooted in the depths of ourselves that we succeed only with difficulty in expressing it distinctly—and we are doubtless far from having properly weighed the ravages of a scientific civilization which systematically ignores it. Thus by an anomaly which reflection illuminates, it turns out that Idealism plays the same game as an essentially materialist philosophy which tends to identify living and subsisting; indeed, it too, deliberately eliminates that aura of diffused confidence and hope which recently seemed to accompany the awareness the *homo religiosus* had of his destiny. Of course, what is common to both idealism and materialism here, is their radical rejection of the pivotal-datum of the incarnation.

I should note in passing that a sort of oscillation seems to be set up, a mutual contamination takes place, between the idea that contemporary man forms of life, or more accurately, his refusal to think of it as a spiritual reality—and the image he tends to have of death, or more correctly, his refusal to treat it as a positive test. If the fact of living appears to me to consist in maintaining as best one can a complicated set of mechanisms subordinated to ends which are themselves problematic, then I would be naturally inclined to admit that death is reducible to the rupture of these very mechanisms, to the casting aside of an apparatus. Conversely, if for motives of a basically religious nature or rather for motives which express an inverted sense of religion, I proclaim that there is no life after death, I shall almost inevitably be led to depreciate or devaluate an existence which is bound to eventuate in the absolutely meaningless fact of dissolution: which, in any case, is at the mercy of the total meaninglessness of pure chance. Here we should emphasize a paradox which is rich in significance: theoretically, those who plume themselves on having "turned out the lights" constantly exalt by their words this mundane life; but these words mean nothing; for it is an undeniable fact that human life has never been so universally treated as a vile and perishable commodity than during our own era of massive impiety.

The parallelism I tried to establish between my body and my life should be examined again from this point of view. The more fixed the reduction of living to subsisting becomes for me, the less I shall be tempted to assign, I need not say a dignity, but merely a positive meaning to the expression: "my life." Everything occurs as though a certain anonymous quality of social life progressively invaded me to the point where it ultimately abolished in me any temptation to see in my destiny a line of development, particular characteristics, a visage. In the final analysis, we acknowledge little more than pleasure and pain as being able to resist this depersonalization of an existence which has become internally collectivized: but there is no reason to think that this kind of resistance can be effective in the long run. There is such a thing as gregarious pleasure which is only an adjunct to the standardized gratifications of the eating hall. We can conceive of a type of society in which all personal pleasure was considered a form of masturbation, hence perverse. As to pain, it is clear that in such a world it would be increasingly treated as the evidence of a simple inadaptability or as a functional defect, hence as falling within the province of a technique which could eliminate it or of improved analgesics which could deaden it. In any case, I would not have to devote to my body an attention any different from the attention I give to the tools society places in my hands, tools which I have to handle so as to get the best possible output from them.

Following this line of thought, we can see that my body or my life, treated as subsistent entities, are situated in an area of experience, in an intermediate phase of history, as it were, between a world in which the individual is still the bearer of certain mysterious energies, cosmic or spiritual, and whose transcendent nature it vaguely feels—and a socialized world, one might even say an urbanized world, possibly, in which the meaning of this original world is increasingly obliterated, in which the accent is rather placed more heavily on the function we must fulfill in a certain economy which is at once abstract and tyrannical.

Belonging to God; belonging to oneself; belonging to the state: such are the moments of this kind of dialectic which we are perhaps not yet capable of fathoming, and within which there is a progressive degradation of a complex, ambiguous and infinitely dilutable relation.

"The phenomenon *I belong to,*" Mr. Minkowski writes,[6] "in no way signifies certain forms of social life. It is nonetheless their common basis and is what renders their existence plausible. As such, it is narrowly related to an ethical *élan* . . . *I belong to* has a more static quality, is less exceptional, hence more material and more stable than this élan; it is compatible with institutions, hence is an echelon below the élan, but of all the phenomena in this echelon, it is the nearest to such an élan and appears as its natural support as soon as we shift our attention to the more palpable features of existence."

What is so striking to my mind, and I am sure that I do not disagree here with Mr. Minkowski, is the fact that this relation—the term is inadequate—is capable of exhibiting variant signs of inwardness. When I say: I belong to a nation or a people which has always practiced thrift, I restrict myself to the utterance of a fact; I refer both to information which is listed in the official records, and also to an observation which has a banal, yet objective character. If, on the contrary, I declare that I belong to my country or my family, my affirmation is on a wholly different plane, and has an altogether different ring. We are no longer on the level of assertion but on that of engagement or adhesion: I may add that here to *say* is to *seal*. I shall make no comment on the relation linking the adhesion which is proclaimed, to the institutional phenomenon, properly speaking.

These observations necessarily reflect back on the idea we have to form of the dialectic evoked above. Where Mr. Minkowski speaks of élan, I prefer to speak of religion. Moreover, it is very important to emphasize the role which is played here by what I may call the category of the *threatened*. A certain revolutionary fervor (which is expressed by *I belong to the Cause*) does not seem to me to be in any way separable from a feeling, both acute and intense, of the opposing forces which threaten to destroy the work one has dedicated oneself to. This *I belong to,* in its strongest acceptation, involving an optimal significance and inner density, implies the awareness of a contest which is engaged, which can therefore be lost, and for the sake of which one completely exposes oneself, not an attitude of detachment or reserve. If this is so, we must say that the *I belong to* is degraded just to the extent that the reality to which it subordinates itself is consolidated, stabilized, hence becomes like a machine of which I am a gear. I may mention in illustration that strange soviet play *Rust* where the phenomenon to which I refer was expressed with great intensity.

In bergsonian terms, the *I belong to* in a closed society can thus be opposed to the *I belong to* in an open one, and it can be shown that only the latter is capable of a positive justification. This, I believe, allows us to glimpse the solution of a number of obscure problems raised in connection with the claim made by the self that it "belongs to itself." The more I identify myself with a certain closed system of determinate interests, the more hollow and the more illusory this formula is shown to be; basically, it can be reduced to a protest against certain intrusions which are disturbing to my peace. It is quite different when the self affirms itself as a creative power, as freedom, or what amounts to the same thing, as a thinking being. At bottom, I can validly assert that *I belong to myself* only insofar as I create, as I create myself; i.e., where, metaphysically speaking, it must be admitted that I do not belong to myself.

This can also be expressed in terms of the distinction between being and having which I have emphasized on a number of occasions. However paradoxical such an assertion may seem, I really belong first of all to what I have. But the whole meaning of spiritual evolution consists in making me aware of an opposed belonging: belonging to what I am, ontological belonging. I can just as well say, however: creative belonging; and for me, the two expressions have exactly the same meaning. The second has the sole advantage of eliminating the factor of an implicit restriction which at first seems to burden the term belonging, a factor which, however it is played down, threatens to evoke in the mind the notion of a servile dependence. The more one reflects on it, the more one is convinced, I believe, that the passage from constraint to freedom is accomplished in belonging. This, however, opens up a vast field for meditation. How indeed shall we judge the modern anarchical notion of freedom which implies precisely the fact of not belonging to anybody or anything? Analysis discloses that what is here presented as a plenitude may be after all only a void. We should closely examine, however, the historical relation between this anarchical individualism and a socialism which at first sight seems to be opposed to it in every respect, since they have not only developed concurrently, but have even at times encroached on one another; as though, by a clearly marked dialectic, the unity without content of a self which belongs to nobody gave birth to the false plenitude of a social idolatry to fill or absorb it.

I should like to point out here on a somewhat different level of thought, the curious incongruity, phenomenological rather than logical, between the statement *I belong to you* and its counterpart or rejoinder: *you belong to me*. The latter implies a claim, the former a commitment. The most important characteristic of these statements would be lost if we considered either one as an assertion although at the limit they are reducible to this. The fundamental philosophical problem here, however, consists in asking in what sense either the commitment or the claim is valid. I shall focus my attention here on the claim.

Let us assume that there is a point of view from which it can be validly determined whether the claim on you is legitimate: what would this point of view be? We can envisage three possibilities. The point of view in question can be:

(a) that of the affirming subject;

(b) that of yourself;

(c) that of a third party who mediates between the two.

(a) It is at once clear that the first alternative is not universally acceptable; here the subject is both judge and judged; which means: It is I who can determine whether my claim on you is valid. Reflection discloses that the more such a *thou* is treated as external to the subject, the more this new claim, bearing on the judgment itself, is unacceptable; in fact, it is equivalent to a radical despotism.

(b) The second alternative at first seems more acceptable. "You belong to me: it is for you and you alone to decide if you are right in granting me this adhesion." This solution, however, is not free from ambiguity: exactly what does this "it is for you to decide" mean? Does it mean: I leave you free to decide whether . . . ? But doesn't this ultimately imply my acknowledgment that you do not belong to me? The exact formulation would be: it is up to you to decide whether you belong to me. Unless we can conceive of a limiting case where to say you "belong to me" means precisely: insofar as you decide (to belong to me or to refuse to do so) you belong to me; in other words, insofar as you are free you belong to me.

(c) The third alternative, that of mediation by a third party, is only conceivable if the I and the thou are treated as radically external to one another, and in this case it is questionable whether the belonging of one to the other is even thinkable.

All of the above can be illustrated in the most concrete and most varied ways. To take a specific example, we may envisage what takes place between two lovers. A woman says to a man: you belong to me. It is clear that this affirmation may be classified as either a claim or an assertion. Only the first of these two possibilities, however, concerns us here. The man who is the object of the claim is degraded by it to the rank of a slave (Samson), unless it is inwardly compensated for somehow by a "but I on the other hand belong to you," i.e., by a commitment. Taken by itself, the claim is despotic. I can do what I want with you, whatever I please. If it is inwardly compensated for, its meaning, its virulence, are attenuated. Since I belong to you as you belong to me, I cannot wish to make you anything other than what you wish yourself; my caprice as such does not enter. From that moment on, I cannot even decide whether it would not be better for you not to belong to me. To be more accurate, since I cease to belong to myself, it is not literally true to say that you belong to me; we transcend one another in the very heart of *our love*. The doubt which threatens to infiltrate each of us is thus abolished to make room for a superior certainty which transcends us. Here the very thought of a third party and of mediation is eliminated; it becomes a pure absurdity; reference to the other is here eliminated of itself; the other can exist in relation to me, in relation to you, not in relation to our love. No one has the ability to even understand it, much less to judge it: with what could it be compared? Whatever the principle of comparison may be, our love rejects it. I should note in passing that here and only here is it perhaps possible to confer a concrete meaning on the notion of an absolute taken in the strict sense of the term.

Thus we can conclude that if the statement *you belong to me* is in danger of becoming ambiguous or offensive to the thou when considered apart from a concrete context, it is so no longer the moment reflection reveals certain counterpart meanings which however, are not necessarily implied by the statement. Here I should like to point out a particularly important corollary to the foregoing. On reading certain spiritual or even mystical works so called, in which Christ addresses the believer precisely in order to signify to him that He has absolute right over him, that he belongs to Him from all eternity, I have personally experienced an acute annoyance amounting to an inner refusal. In the light of the above remarks, it is possible to justify in part this recoil as well as to control it by opposing to it a contrary course of action realized on a different level.

On the one hand, the fact that His word is transcribed, that it is addressed to me by means of the written word, threatens to degrade it to the level of a tyrannical injunction addressed to me by someone in particular and against whom it is after all quite comprehensible why I should revolt: what right has *someone else* to claim that I belong to him? How could such a claim, when made, fail to arouse in me a claim which may be described as essentially Cornelian?

On the other hand, however, reflection promptly does justice to these false appearances: it is precisely because He is not someone else that He can arrogate to himself this right over me, but only to the extent that He becomes more internal to me than myself. It is not in terms of power but in terms of love that this right can be understood. There is a very profound metaphysical reason why, in the heart of Christ, an infinite weakness is conjoined with a sovereign strength; the weakness is an essential moment which cannot be wholly eliminated if a Christocentrism is not to be converted into a heteronomy that is incompatible with the radical exigence of our freedom. It may also be said in somewhat different terms, more acceptable to the philosopher but also more ambiguous, that absolute inwardness is here inseparable from the only concrete universal we are able to attain, although we are unable to appropriate it.

Hence I shall refrain from supporting the strictly rebellious claim that the *you belong to me* evoked in the depths of my being. But it must be clearly noted that it is the meaning rather than the logical possibility of the claim which is at issue. "Indeed, who am I to pretend that I do not belong to You? The point really is that if I belong to You, this doesn't mean: I am Your possession; this mysterious relation does not exist on the level of having as would be the case if You were an infinite power. Not only are You freedom, but You also will me, You arouse me too as freedom, You invite me to create myself, You are this very invitation. And if I reject it, i.e. Thou, if I persist in maintaining that I belong only to myself, it is as though I walled myself up; as though I strove to strangle with my own hands that reality in whose name I believed I was resisting You.

If this is so, to know that I belong to You, to Thou, is to know that I belong to myself only on this condition—what is more, that this belonging is identical to and confused with the only complete and authentic freedom to which I can lay claim: this freedom is a gift; yet it is necessary for me to accept it; the power granted me to accept *or refuse it* is not separable from this gift, and there is a way of claiming this freedom which is tantamount to a refusal, and this refusal, addressed to the very thing which makes it possible, possesses the distinctive traits of a betrayal.

What I have said above entails a number of different conclusions: among the most important are those which cannot be said so much to refer to my body, as to the relation linking me to my body. Whatever the great majority of philosophers of the various schools have thought, this relation is not a datum which is definable in an objective, univocal way, as it would be if it were reducible to a causal relation, or to a parallelism, or again as it would be on a monist, materialist, or spiritualist hypothesis. However paradoxical and even self-contradictory such an affirmation at first seems to be, there is reason to believe that the mode of liaison uniting me to my body depends in some way on me: if *to be* means *to affirm oneself, I am,* depending on the way in which I respond to what was originally only a question, or, more adequately, to something which can only be treated as a question by a reflection which operates retrospectively on the conditions of my own development in time.

Just as it is part of my essence as a living being to be in a situation, so it is of the essence of my body as mine to be the substance of a test which is literally constitutive of myself, since at the end, I either will or will not be. We must, however, guard against oversimplification: What I have just said is valid only for self-reflection, and I must always ask myself within what limits I have the right to treat the other as a prolongation of myself. If I adopt a point of view which is no longer reflective but prospective, if I ask, for example, about the future destiny of a new-born child, there is no sense in envisaging in its regard the existence of a presently existing freedom of which his body would be a test. This freedom is yet to *be,* and is remote from a datum; and foresight is only effective and not a dream if it is an active love and is transformed into the continuous creative act of the teacher. A new dialectic begins here, moreover, for the time will come when, in order to awaken freedom, we must pretend to believe in it, i.e. presuppose its existence.

What reply can be given, then, to the question of how I can know whether my body belongs to me or instead, whether I belong to my body? As I have observed, my condition is such that the problem does not entail an objective solution. I mean a solution which is given as soon as the terms of the problem are themselves specified. I can orient or direct my life in such a way that it will become increasingly true to say: I belong to my body. But this isn't final: the path is open to me to treat my body as my absolute property, which, appearances to the contrary, results in my becoming its slave. Couldn't it be said that in this sense, prostitution is to love what suicide is to death? Contrary to what one may believe, this does not embody an authentic freedom just because it implies one's own disposition of oneself, but is an inverted counterfeit of this freedom. When Kirillov in *The Possessed* believes that he has found in suicide the only absolutely free act that the creature can accomplish, he is thereby a victim of the most tragic illusion of all, for he confuses freedom with its inverted counterfeit. Everything encourages us to believe that a metaphysically satisfying relation between my body and me, i.e. a relation which safeguards a freedom always in danger of being compromised because of the manner in which it conceives itself, can only be established on the basis of the ontological or creative belonging which I have discussed above. In more concrete terms, my body can only fulfill its function of *servant* to me, if I have an active as well as theoretical awareness of non-belonging to myself; failing this, I establish the falsest of all autarchies and create that sort of monumental prison for myself which a facile association of images can always convince me is the impregnable fortress of my personal sovereignty.

NOTES

1 Lecture delivered Jan. 21, 1937 to the *Groupe d'études philosophiques et scientifiques pour l'examen des tendences nouvelles.*

2 Eugène Minkowski, *Vers une cosmologie* (Paris: Aubier, 1936), p. 169.
3 *Loc. cit.,* p. 101 ff.
4 René Le Senne, *Obstacle et Valeur* (Paris: Aubier, 1931), p. 172.
5 Mr. Georges Bastide published a book of this title in June 1939. [See p. 33. Transl. Note].
6 E. Minkowski, *Le Temps Vécu* (Paris: *Collection de l'Evolution Psychiatrique,* 1933), p. 119.

V

Observations on the notions of the act and the person

We are not likely to find any terms which have been used as indiscriminately as the above during the past few years. This is particularly true of the idea of the *act*. One explanation for the abuse of the term lies in the fact that the idea of the act has trailed in the wake of the idea of revolution. And this idea is, I think, essentially impure from the philosophical point of view, and infects every idea in its vicinity.

I believe that by and large, as soon as we resort to capital letters, something is irretrievably lost, and this is just what has happened in the present case. Instead of speaking of *an* act, *a* revolution, we speak of the Act, the Revolution, possibly without realizing that we are hypostatizing certain dialectical transitions or moments.

While reflecting these past few weeks on the *act* and the *person,* I have discovered for myself, on the heels of a number of other discoveries which were quite analogous, that in the last analysis, "we don't really know much about the matter," and that we have been wasting our time in an effort to plug up gaps of unintelligibility

with words. I want to adopt the simplest and most concrete procedure possible in this regard, re-examining those ideas which
lie ready at hand and considering them from the start in terms of
their rootedness in our living experience. From a personal point of
view, I categorically deny to the philosopher any dictatorial power
over these ideas; to say as does Mr. Denis de Rougemont, that the
person is a creative *vocation,* is in the first place to accomplish a
sort of *coup d'état,* and in the second place, it implies a fundamental disregard for the meaning of words.

In attempting to define the act—a task which is impossible in
all likelihood, and we shall see why presently—in any case, to
approximate to a definition, I first of all want to present a few
specific cases where the word "act" is used in the strongest and
most distinctive acceptation of the term.

Ordinarily, we first of all compare the act to desire; we say of a
certain person: when will he stop being satisfied with desires;
when will he begin to act? Begin to act—let us keep this expression in mind.

In a quite analogous sense we say, for example, of a politician:
we have had enough words, we want action.

Let us consider these elementary data; it is clear that desire is
opposed to the act in the sense that it is at once indeterminate and
impotent; on the one hand, the person who desires does not succeed in deciding and he remains basically divided, hesitant, fear-
ful; on the other hand, he is incapable of biting into reality, of
effectively modifying it. Everything remains static. The same thing
occurs with respect to talk which is no more than talk. We admit
first of all, that the word is not inscribed in reality, that it does not
even adhere to it, that it passes over it like the wind, that it does not
subsist and hence has no effective influence on things. This postulate has to be closely examined, however, and will have to be con-
siderably modified.

At the moment, therefore, we can see that it is the essence of the
act to effectively change—change what? a certain situation to
which it is applied and which it is possible the agent cannot completely take in at a glance. Nevertheless, he must perceive it in

part, at least. It is evident that a change is not a sufficient condition of an act. And here we make further inroads into the nature of the act. When I say of a crime, for example: this is the gesture of a madman, this expression implies a negative counterpart; if it is a gesture it can't be an act; I postulate a difference here. However, the gesture in question can, and in fact inevitably does, transform a certain situation—and it does it in a way which, we grant, is indeterminate and somehow inscrutable.

Rightly or wrongly, the gesture seems to us to be assimilable to an accident in the strong sense of this term (an illness, a catastrophe)—*quod accidit*. Hence there is something more in the act besides the fact of occurring.

It will be maintained: the act is voluntary. Doubtless this is true, but to my mind not very illuminating; for whenever the term "will" is used there is a danger of getting lost in endless psychological analyses.

My conclusion is more or less the following:

On the one hand, the act is essentially such and such, it has certain contours (today we too often have a tendency to lose sight of this). We have to be able to reply *yes* or *no* to any question relating to it. The transition to the act is precisely the fact of crossing the threshold separating the region which is on the hither side of the yes and no or even the region where the yes and no are confused with one another—and that region where they are distinct from and opposed to one another. Consider the crudest possible example: somebody takes care of an invalid whom he detests; the invalid dies; someone asks: did you desire the death of this invalid? It is possible, perhaps inescapable, that the reply will be yes and no at the same time, which amounts to saying that one cannot reply, that the question does not imply a response. On the other hand, there is a single, determinate and univocal response to the question: did you administer poison? We may note by the way that these two are limits between which there are degrees. Let us assume that I have miscounted the number of drops of laudanum that I gave to the invalid; this mistake can give rise to an infinite number of questions to which it is not certain there is a univocal answer. In a case such as this, there is a sort of indefinite inner obscurity which we must not lose sight of later on.

On the other hand, it is clear that the reality of the act is by no means exhausted in the apparent accomplishment of a *doing*. Another complementary, and in a manner antinomic consideration, enters here. I shall tentatively describe it by saying that the essence of the act is to commit the agent.

The notion of commitment, however, must be carefully developed: do we mean by this that the agent implicitly accepts the consequences of his act whatever they may be?

Now it should be observed that the latter is a pure abstraction; these consequences, being indefinite, are unforseeable, and it may be added that the complicity of causes is such that I shall always be justified in imputing those consequences which are contrary to my desires, to some related cause.

When I say that my act commits me, it seems to me that it means just this: what is characteristic of my act is that it can later be claimed by me as mine; at bottom, it is as though I signed a confession in advance: when the day comes when I will be confronted by my act, whether through my own agency or that of another—the distinction here is of no consequence—I must say: yes, it is I who acted in this way, *ego sum qui fecit;* what is more: I acknowledge in advance that if I try to escape, I am guilty of a disownment. Let us take a specific example. The clearest, the most impressive example, is doubtless that of promising, to the extent that promising is an act and not "mere words," just words. I promise someone that I will help him if he gets into difficulty. This amounts to saying: "I acknowledge in advance that if I try to escape when these circumstances occur, in thereby disavowing myself I create a cleavage within myself which is destructive of my own reality." This is obvious, and is equally applicable to any act whatever, even a wrong one, a theft, for example: to say that a theft is an act as opposed to the gesture of a kleptomaniac or a somnambulist, is to say that later, when confronted with the theft, I shall be forced to acknowledge that it was I who did it, and not some malignant power or other who possessed me and who somehow hypnotized me inwardly. In other words, there is no act without responsibility; and it immediately follows from this that the expression *gratuitous act* is actually self-contradictory. A gratuitous act is not an act, or nullifies itself as act; this pseudo-idea is only the result of a confusion, possibly voluntary, between certain categories which are irreducible to one another.

If I lie, for example, I *ipso facto* commit myself to acknowledge later on that it was I who lied; any act which implies a kind of anticipated retrospection is an act which is as though assumed in advance. Otherwise, it was not I who lied, I nullify myself as subject, as person. To express this somewhat differently, it may be said that there is a solidarity between me and my act, as if we were both members of a certain inner community, a certain clan. And it should be observed that this assuming of responsibility is impossible without an appraisal or evaluation; hence it may be that I applaud my act, or on the contrary, that I regret it, or even that I do not know whether to regret it or congratulate myself on it. In any case, however, it seems to me that the act is qualified: it is good or bad. The closer it comes to indifference, the less it is an act.

Does the above discussion provide us with the elements of a definition of the act? Truthfully speaking, I think not. To clarify what I have just said, it should be noted that it is of the essence of the act that it is not objectively verifiable nor perceivable; it is not conceivable without a personal reference, a reference to an "it is I who. . . ." This is tantamount to saying that the act only presents its character of act to the agent or to whomever mentally adopts, through sympathy, the point of view of the agent. Hence it must be understood that to really think the act, is not and cannot be to objectify it, since in objectifying it, I tend to consider it as non-act.

Certain important consequences follow from the above remarks.

Our tendency to objectify is such that we inevitably tend to represent the act to ourselves as an effect, and to ask about its source, who caused it. Analysis leads us to discern in this connection an ambiguity in the *ego sum qui fecit*. If I may say so, we are tempted to give a local interpretation of it: "It is I" means: it is this very hand, this very mouth. This description, however, is really devoid of any meaningful content. It may be that I have to impute the act, the words of another person to myself. It is not this mouth, not this hand, yet it is I. But "I" does not mean anybody: anybody is by definition someone else. In a way, the I is the very opposite of anybody, and in this case I am in the absolute. This, however, is only a dialectical moment: for the other, for Peter or John, I am somebody; my act is that of someone determinate; on the other hand, I have the power of apprehending Peter and John as agents, i.e. of seeing through their eyes, of seeing myself as they see me, hence as someone—as someone else. I thus cease to be identified with myself, and it is as though my own reality was sundered. This is the inevitably illusory result of introspection. Let us take a concrete case. I have performed a specific act in certain given conditions. Let us assume, for example, that I have intervened to protect a child against an adult who was abusing him; there is no doubt that it is within my power to detach myself from this act, to treat it as no longer mine, but as the act instead of someone whom I am observing, at the performance of which I am present; from that moment on, I can dismember it, so to speak, and denature it to the point where it becomes unrecognizable. This act will imperceptibly cease to be my *act,* hence ceased to be *an* act, and becomes a kind of gesture. We may observe that the more the act is *mine,* i.e. the more it is incorporated into the totality of what I am—the less I am capable of succumbing to a temptation of this kind. This is very significant—because there is a criterion here on the basis of which we can establish a hierarchy of acts as such. An act, I shall maintain, is more an act to the degree that it is impossible to repudiate it without completely denying oneself; and this again shows us the radical impossibility of a gratuitous act. It may be said that the more a life is paid out, i.e. divided into discontinuous phases, the less will it involve acts, the less will it be assimilable to an act. Inversely, the less it is paid out, the more it is consecrated, in the deep sense of this term, the more it tends to assume in its totality the form of a unique act.

It is in the light of these reflections, that I should like to consider the idea of the person.

I want to proceed here as I did in connection with the act, i.e. by means of concrete approaches which are as specific as possible.

It seems to me at least, that we cannot succeed in positing the person by starting with the notion of something opposed to the individual (I have not mentioned the word "define"; for the task of defining raises perhaps unsurmountable difficulties). To a certain extent I find it equally repugnant to consider it in terms of the opposition between person and thing, although we shall certainly encounter this opposition again in the course of our discussion and will have to justify it. I believe that the person is first posited in opposition to the *man*,[1] the *one*. Further, we should observe that the *one* itself is not definable, strictly speaking. Yet its distinctive characteristics are self-evident. In the first place, it is by definition, anonymous, without a face. In a way it cannot be apprehended; I have no direct hold on it, it escapes me, it is by nature irresponsible. In a certain sense, it is the very contrary of an agent. Its nature- does it possess a nature?- has something self-contradictory about it, like that of a phantom. It affirms itself as an absolute and is the very opposite of an absolute. There is nothing more dangerous and yet more difficult to avoid, than our confusing it with impersonal thought.[2] Actually, the *one* is a thought that has regressed, a non-thought, the shadow of a thought. But I perceive that this phantom is on the horizon of my awareness and clouds it; it hems me in, it threatens to hem me in on all sides (I shall not lay too much stress on such an obvious point, particularly in a world like our own which is contaminated by the press). Further, reflection shows me that the *one* is not only all around me; it is insufficient to say that it surrounds me; it penetrates into me, it expresses itself in me; I spend my time mirroring it. Most of the time my opinions are only a reproduction of this *one* by an *I* which does not even know that it is reproducing it. To the extent that I reflect the opinions of my newspaper without even realizing that it is my newspaper I am reflecting, I participate in the *one*, I retail it, I market it (this is expressed by naïve phrases like "everybody knows," it cannot be doubted," etc.).

The mind here conjures up a pseudo-problem. How can we find

room for the person between the surrounding *one* and the *one* which is penetrated? How can we localize it? If the problem is presented in these terms, it has no solution and is devoid of meaning. Any pretension to localize the person somehow rests on a confusion. The fact itself is evident although its acceptance raises serious difficulties.

What characterizes the person as opposed to the *one* which is anonymous, incapable of being apprehended, irresponsible?

We can start at the very heart of the question and affirm that to *confront* is what is characteristic of the person. We can maintain, from this point of view, that courage is the dominant virtue of the person—while the *one* seems on the contrary to be the locus of every flight and every evasion. Nothing is more typical in this respect than the mental procedure of someone who, not daring to adopt a position, hides behind this kind of shield: one claims that . . . one guarantees that. . . . Anyone who talks in this manner does not even identify himself with this *one,* but literally hides himself behind it.

It does not suffice to say that the person confronts the *one:* in the very fact of confronting it, he destroys it; to someone who tells me: "It has been claimed that the King of Belgium killed himself," I reply or should reply: "Who claims that?" The question, shifted to the plane of the *who,* exists outside of the realm of the *one;* by confronting the enemy, I force him to declare himself; the *one* is *qua* one, what never declares itself. But what does "declare itself" mean in this context? It means to specify itself. In this sense the person is an active negation of the *one;* I cannot acknowledge the *one,* i.e. ascribe the simplest rudiments of positivity to it, without becoming its accomplice, i.e. without introducing it into myself.

We must now analyze the act of confronting itself and consider its implications: some of these are intellectual. To confront is in a sense to envisage. What does one envisage? Primarily and essentially a situation. It is appropriate at this point to define as clearly as possible the nature of those intellectual operations whereby we grasp and master a situation. It seems clear that the simple fact of envisaging a situation instead of merely undergoing it—i.e., in short, incidentally apprehending certain aspects of it—already implies the kind of inner development which becomes prolonged into the act of confronting; but this still implies too much of a distinction and separation. In some respects, to envisage is already to confront.

This conclusion, however, must be developed in at least two directions. First, it is plain that to envisage is, in more than one sense, to *evaluate*. Here again, I believe, we must return to the situation.

First of all, a situation is in its very essence, something which is not altogether clear; because of the fact that we exist in time, we are required to live in the non-resolvable. Hence there is a certain indeterminateness. And here the traditional problem of knowing whether this indeterminateness is or is not real loses any interest it may have. This indeterminateness exists, is even the essential datum for the consciousness which envisages and confronts. It therefore forces me to reckon together chances, probabilities, risks—which already involve an elementary form of evaluation; on the other hand, it is eminently true that to envisage a situation is at the same time to appraise it. Without a preliminary appraisal, I cannot confront. For to confront is to expose myself, i.e. to orient myself in a certain way, in a determinate direction, and only an appraisal can fix this direction. It would be worthwhile at this point to consider a detailed example.

Let us consider a newspaper story: most of the time we submit to the news that is given us; from the moment we venture to criticize it, the "person" intervenes—this way of expressing it is very inadequate and we will have the occasion to return to it. Most of the time a kind of invisible partition separates us from the thing referred to. Images parade before us as in the cinema; our attitude is that of the spectator; we do not have the slightest idea that the situation might have something to do with us. At this point the question of our confronting, envisaging, or of appraising, in the most personal sense of these terms, does not arise; we passively adopt the "system of values" of the editor—which amounts to saying that we are not evaluating, for to evaluate effectively, is to evaluate in one's own name, to commit oneself. Let us now assume that a specific detail in the story attracts our attention; we get a certain shock; at a certain, specified moment, we no longer have the impression of just a story related in the newspaper which does not concern us; we are possessed with a feeling of reality. What is especially noteworthy, is that *ipso facto* the invisible barrier I mentioned above, disappears. My indifference was linked to an implicit judgment of unreality (this may be expressed in somewhat different terms as: to a basic non-belief). Now everything has changed. This story takes place in my universe; it is no longer possible for me not to adopt a position with respect to it. We can shed more light on this, specify it in more detail: let us imagine, for example, that the detail which has "attracted" me has induced me to doubt the accuracy of the interpretation given by the newspaper; to believe, for example, in the possible good faith of the individual who was portrayed as nothing more than a thief. It is then possible, though by no means inevitable, that by adopting in conscience a position in favor of this person, I can no longer be satisfied with revising my own opinion; I feel constrained to go further, to communicate my new way of seeing things to others; hence I commit myself more and more, I expose myself; I confront the current opinion which blindly reflects that of the press, etc. . . . I can thus be led to a personal course of action in behalf of someone whom I consider an innocent person who has been slandered; I thereby progress towards the act, I *assume* responsibility for it. And here we have a phrase which is no less essential than the previous ones: what is characteristic of the person is not only envisaging, appraising, confronting; it is also assuming. It is possible that here is where the fusion between the act as we have described it, and what has just been said about the person, is most perfectly realized. The act, we said, is something to assume; i.e. the person must apprehend himself in it; but in itself it is only an act to the extent that it makes possible this later course of action of the person; hence it is interposed between the person and himself. It is in the act that the nexus whereby the person is unified with himself is realized; but it must be immediately added that the person does not exist apart from that unification. A being who is not unified with himself is in the strict sense of the term alienated—and hence incapable of acting.

Now it would be worthwhile to bring out more adequately the fundamental unity of the various moments which I have had to distinguish from one another for the sake of analytical clarity. In particular, it can be shown that to assume is in a sense to confront, but, curiously enough, to confront one's own past: i.e. something which is already behind one. This is a paradox whose metaphysical significance seems to me to be incalculable. I can only indicate this here. If assuming means confronting one's past, it may be said on the other hand, that confronting a situation means in a sense assuming it as one assumes the responsibility for one's own act, treating it as one's own.

If we consider it from this point of view a number of perspectives are opened up.

In the first place, we can now understand the true meaning of the distinction between the individual and the person. It can be readily said that the individual *is the one in the fragmented state.* The individual is only a statistical factor—and conversely, a statistic is a possibility only on the level of the *one.* It may also be said that the individual is without a visage, without eyes. It is a specimen, a scrap.

In the second place, by characterizing the person in this way, we can catch a glimpse of what the absolute person might be, without, however, being able in any way to determine whether or not this is anything more than a metaphysical fiction. For the absolute person, the already fragile distinction between the relatively passive act of confronting and the active one of assuming is completely abolished; the absolute person tends to posit itself as wholly responsible for history. The *one,* diffused around it and absorbed within it, disappears in the complete specificity of its glance.

Yet I find it impossible to end this account with such a complete congruency, such a metaphysical apotheosis. I have to acknowledge that while the analyses whose outlines I have sketched seem to me completely accurate, I still have the impression that it is extremely dangerous to pretend to extract from them the elements of a positive philosophy. To expose my reasons for this, I believe, on the one hand, that the person is not and cannot be an essence, and on the other hand, that any metaphysics which is somehow established apart from, or protected from essences, is in danger of collapsing like a house of cards. I want only to mention this fact, because it really is something of a shock and disappointment to me. However, if we take up again at this time the problem of the relations between the individual and the person, I am afraid that we shall witness the resurgence of almost unsurmountable difficulties.

In a word: the person can be neither a variation of, nor an improvement on, the individual; but what then is it? what is its metaphysical status? isn't it ultimately something which, as a correlative of the *one,* possesses no more metaphysical density than the latter? And wouldn't it be better to establish a concrete philosophy on altogether different grounds?

We have to recognize first of all that there is a temptation to establish a direct relation between the person and the individual; but what relation in fact?

It is at once clear that the person is not a species or variety of individual; that there is absolutely no sense whatever in asking oneself in the presence of a given being: is this or is this not a person? It is a waste of time to stress this.

Shall we say that it is an improvement on the individual? This, however, raises insoluble difficulties. The fact is that we can neither grant that this improvement is universal, nor that it is not. The whole of democratic philosophy, however, is built, if I am not mistaken, on such a pseudo-idea; it implies a dogmatic which, as Scheler among others has seen, is only explicable in terms of the vestigal presence of a sort of degraded theology which one continues to cling to even while not believing in it any more, or more precisely, while believing that one does not believe it any more. If we should try to bring out what is still valid in the postulates on which such a philosophy is based, it seems to me that we shall have to acknowledge the following:

We have seen that in confronting the *one,* the person tends to reduce it, specify it, hence eliminate it as such. Now this is applicable in a way to the individual, if it is true as I have maintained that the individual is the *one* in a fragmented state. By confronting the individual, the person tends to assimilate it to itself; i.e. to treat it, think it, will it as a person. We can express this by saying that the person is luminescent, and it is solely because of this that justice is possible, justice in the sense of a will for justice, not as a static order, as a transposition of an abstract equality. From this point of view, justice does not refer to a less essential aspect of the person than does courage or sincerity.

Nevertheless, as soon as we try to express all of this in metaphysical terms, i.e., by taking reality itself for our axis, we encounter serious difficulties which however, should have been anticipated from our analysis of the act; indeed, we have seen that we cannot contemplate the act as spectator without negating it. But this fact has obvious repercussions on the person. Let us examine this more closely. What is characteristic of the person, we said, is to evaluate, confront, assume. How can we resist the temptation to hypostatize the person, question oneself about the nature of this principle which confronts, evaluates, assumes? I am afraid, however, that in so doing, we shall find ourselves in a labyrinth. We shall in fact be led to construct a sort of entity endowed with a certain number of abstract properties, and we shall then be compelled to ask what sort of couple this entity can possibly form with the individual itself. This is the cul-de-sac I indicated a little while ago. How shall we escape it? probably by perceiving that it involves two inverse yet complementary perspectives, and that we are always in danger of confusing them.

We will become aware of this, I believe, if we reflect that we cannot in fact treat the person either as a datum, or perhaps even as an existent. At bottom, our formula: *the characteristic of the person is to confront,* reveals its inadequacy insofar as it cuts off, at least implicitly, the person from the act in which the former realizes himself—and every theory of the person is in danger of somehow exploiting this unwarranted cleavage.

Shouldn't we raise the question how we can conceive of the connection which links two successive acts, and whether the person is not the synthetic unity making this connection possible? Here, however, we must guard against the fact that the question we claim to resolve by positing the person as a unifying principle is itself of a *theoretical* nature; it is a question which arises for someone who is on the outside and who converts these acts into determinate events, hence who tends to deny their individuality. In general, we in fact clearly tend to define the person as subject of the act as such; to the question: "Who is the author of the act as such?" We reply: it is the "person." On the other hand, however, we know that this question has the least justification for being asked, or better, is the most senseless in the measure that we are more directly in the presence of an act apprehended as act. The question can only be asked when we shift to another meaning and the act is envisaged as an operation; for wherever there is an operation we are naturally entitled to ask who the operator is. This shifting over is in fact altogether inevitable: we are in the realm of the fragmented, we are individuals, we are exposed on all sides to the impersonal *one;* it may be added that we are a *prey of history.* The contradictions I have indicated are therefore really inscribed in our very condition; it is certain that only through an agonizing effort of thought which is practically impossible to sustain, can we succeed in transcending these contradictions, and even here our victory is but a precarious one.

Two diametrically opposed metaphysical conclusions are entailed by the above, according to where we are inclined to center the idea of the person.

On the one hand, we can ask whether the idea of the person is not to a certain extent a fiction. Possibly there is no human person in the strongest sense of the term "person," nor can there be any; thus the person can become a reality only in God. For the rest of us, the person is perhaps but a point of view which is always in danger of degenerating into an attitude or into a palpitating anticipation, an appearance which can be degraded at any moment, can harden into a disguise, or can by some unholy masquerade, become a parody of itself.

Philosophical thought, however, can take another direction. Indeed, it can instead be maintained that the person is correlative with that anonymous or disguised factor which it confronts to the very end, and that in God, in whom this factor disappears, the person is abolished, simply because it is here that it fully emerges into the light.

It would be worthwhile to examine closely these two alternatives and to ask whether the opposition here between the two is not more verbal than real.

It should be noted that the most dangerous complications are introduced into the problem of the person because we perhaps have a tendency to confuse person and personality, on the one hand, and act and creation, on the other.

I simply wish to point out here that if we construe the personality as a stamp, as an individual imprint, as *Pragung,* it would not seem that a direct relation has necessarily been established between the personality in this sense and the person in the sense I have tried not so much to define as to evoke. Of course, we can argue here over the use of terms, but what is important to my mind is to understand that we are presented here with two aspects or two completely distinct levels of thought. The personality insofar as it is *Pragung,* is inwardness; it is given to us if not immediately, at any rate through certain media which are as mysteriously transparent as the voice or the glance—whereas in the act where it seemed that the person was focussed, we can say that abstraction has been made of any kind of inwardness, of any rootedness. In these circumstances, however, is there not a danger that a philosophy based on the person rather than on the personality will almost ineluctably tend towards formalism?

Now in this connection we have the expedient of recalling the fact that the person, as I have said, confronts his past. Next, we can try to maintain that what is involved is the personality assuming itself, inwardness receiving its consecration from itself. However, it is not altogether certain that this solution is intelligible, and in any case, it would be impossible to remove the qualifications attached to this conclusion, for we know quite well that there are cases in which the person only succeeds in affirming himself by a kind of *coup d'état* whereby he strangles whatever inwardness exists within him.

As to the danger of formalism, it is clear that contemporary advocates of the person claim to restore at least in some measure the particular characteristics of which kantism made a clean sweep. It may however be asked whether this does not thereby issue in an unintelligible syncretism.

My conclusions with respect to creation are no different; and here I encounter again what I have said elsewhere about the opposition between a mystery and a problem. There is surely no creativity aside from a certain mystery which envelops and reverberates through the creator; so that what we call creation is basically a mediation at the core of which passivity and activity, as the romantics have observed, are united and fused with one another. If this view of creativity is adopted, however, will not the nobility of the person lie in a certain ontological impoverishment? We could thus explain how it is that the creator so often seems to us to be at once both more and less than a person.

NOTES

1 [That is, the impersonal pronoun in German. Transl. note.]
2 And it is easy to show that democratic rationalism is entirely based on this confusion; as though there could be the least contact between the democratic *one,* the *one* of universal suffrage, and the kind of reason operative in science.

VI

From opinion to faith

Those who are acquainted with my work know that the paramount task of philosophy as I conceive it lies in the analysis of certain spiritual situations; these situations must first be circumscribed as carefully as possible and reflection must be induced to revive them for our inner inspection. I wish to adopt this same procedure in approaching the problem which is raised by the coexistence in our society of believers and non-believers.

It is not difficult to see why this problem has remained and will continue to remain in the forefront of my interests. I came to the catholic faith at a late date; my deepest sentiments still ally me with the non-believer; I can understand his difficulties better than others. Hence a personal and somewhat incongruous situation which is fraught with difficulties, but which at least serves to stimulate reflection.

I shall begin with an observation that I owe perhaps to my friend Father Fessard—although I am not altogether sure of this —, one which he has in any case admirably developed in one of his recent works.[1] We shall understand nothing of the relation between the believer and the non-believer and there is danger of giving the most harmfully pharisaic interpretation of it if we fail to perceive something else which is even more mysterious, namely the symbiosis of belief and disbelief in the same soul. If the believer has any duty at all, it is to became aware of all that is within him of the non-believer.

This observation actually occurred to my mind in an anguished form during the past few months when the pressure of external events had become almost intolerable; I sensed the approach of a disaster in which everything we loved would founder; I said to myself: there is no reason why our worst presentiments should not be realized. Then I took to asking myself: what is becoming of my faith? I did not possess it any longer; to me it seemed devitalized to the point of degenerating into a certain *opinion* that I recognized as part of my mental furniture, nothing more. I debated with myself: I still cannot blind myself to the facts, I said; there is a kind of facile optimism which I cannot compel myself to adopt; God's purposes are inscrutable, there is no guarantee that everything I love will not be destroyed. At that period I had some conversations with a catholic friend of mine who had an extremely lucid mind which did not overlook any of the dangers of the present time. His calm at first irritated me; I was inclined to take his composure for indifference; then I suddenly thought: this is a real faith because it brings peace. Peace and faith are inseparable. I shall revert to this relationship later; it seems to me to be of central importance. I also realized at the same moment that if I was able to recognize his faith for what it was, it was because such faith inhabited me as well; this reflection was a source of encouragement. But the memory of this inner crisis has not left me—in particular, the awareness of the unbridgeable gulf between opinion and faith.

As a matter of fact, I should like to draw the attention of the reader to something which requires considerable development in its own right: it seems clear to me that certain developments in contemporary thought exhibit a tendency to confuse belief with opinion. To someone who does not share my belief, it in fact tends to appear as an opinion; through a commonly known optical illusion, I myself tend to consider it from the point of view of the other person, hence to treat it in turn as an opinion. Thus a strange, disturbing dualism is established within me; to the extent that I in fact live my belief, it is in no way an opinion; to the extent that I describe it to myself, I espouse the point of view of the person who represents it to his mind but does not live it; it then becomes external to me—and, to that degree, I cease to understand myself.

The fact is that if we wish to understand this clearly, we must pay particular attention to the question of what is—and above all what is not—an opinion.

Needless to say, a large part of the following reflections are directly related to the analyses of Plato which are still unrivaled; I note this here to avoid reverting to it again in what follows. My own orientation, however, will be somewhat different; for I am particularly concerned with describing the relation of opinion to belief and faith, not to science; confusion is most to be feared in this connection.

Let us put aside those opinions which are conjectures bearing on some undetermined fact; these will teach us nothing; it may be immediately noted, however, that the proposition with which we shall begin our analysis is perfectly applicable to these "conjectures." This proposition is as follows.

In general, we only have an opinion of what we do not know; but this lack of knowledge is not discerned, is not avowed. Here, the best example we can take is an opinion of a person. It should be noted at once that we do not have an opinion, strictly speaking, of those beings with whom we are intimately acquainted; this observation is also applicable to artistic works, etc. If someone asks me my opinion about Mozart or Wagner, I do not know what to reply; it is as though my experience were too dense, my cohabitation with Mozart or Wagner too close. I think it can be confirmed in every instance that an opinion can only be established from a certain distance, that it is essentially far-sighted. It remains to be seen whether this far-sightedness is not myopic in certain respects. These metaphors, of course, are always faulty. Nevertheless it is always the case that to the extent that an experience is enriched, perfected, it tends to eliminate those elements of opinion at first hidden within it which were merely stop-gaps.

Let us turn now to the structure of opinion; this in fact is essentially fluctuating; for basically, opinion always glides—in essence—between two limits, one of which is an impression, the other an affirmation; when it is nothing more than an impression, however, it is not really an opinion. In a case of this kind everybody will say when asked: "I only have an impression of him, not an opinion." (To be sure an uncritical mind is sometimes unable to make this distinction). To my mind, opinion, properly speaking, invariably involves a certain implicit reference for which I cannot find a name in french, a reference to a part of the sentence that is understood: *I maintain that.* . . . However, it can, and in fact generally does, happen, that the latter remains implicit. Opinions are expressed in propositions which refer to a reality whose roots remain buried; it is just these roots that reflection must expose. It must explain the expression, "I maintain that . . . ." The best way to exasperate a discussant is to supply such an explanation as is implied in the simple remark: "You are the one who said so." In general, when someone spontaneously affirms of his own opinion: "That is my opinion, I give it to you for what it is worth," this is a proof of the fact that he does not have too much confidence in it. Language here is wonderfully expressive: "hold," "maintain." The manner in which one adheres to something and the manner in which one upholds something are interdependent. To maintain an opinion is to maintain it before someone else, even if this someone be oneself; an opinion which is not maintained or is not capable of being so, on the other hand, is not really an opinion. Personally, I am convinced that opinion is impossible without a reference to another. There is an imperceptible transition from "maintain" to "claim," and I am not using "claim" in its pejorative sense, although here too there is or can be a continuous transition in meaning.

Thus we arrive at another proposition which this time is a definition: in general, an opinion is *an appearing to be which tends to change into a claim;* and it should be at once added that this occurs because of an absence of reflection; to put it differently, the initial appearing to be is not understood as such—and it is because of this that it can be mobilized into an opinion. Examples of this are plentiful: I might take as a favorite example the sort of opinion which refers to nationalities of which most of us have only the barest outlines of an experience. "The English are hypocrites, the Russians unreliable." The implied reference is immediately understood: "I maintain to you that the English are hypocrites, etc." If we take the trouble to ask ourselves what its, so to speak, gold-backing may be when we have uttered an opinion of this kind, what its cash value is, we would be horrified. Suppose that I have made two or three statements each of which, taken alone, has clearly not been confirmed; let us assume moreover, that no inferences have been drawn from any of them; everything takes place basically on the affective level, the level of impressions; and it is at this moment that the "change" has taken place, that I have converted the impression into an opinion. I have given my opinion, and it is strengthened in the utterance, just as a muscle is strengthened by being exercised. We have to consider what sort of life it will lead in the future, however. It will tend to nourish itself on everything that is capable of making it stronger. The extent to which we can talk here of a mental biology and of a biology of opinion in particular, is never adequately appreciated. Opinion tends to behave like an autonomous organism which admits into itself whatever is able to strengthen it and which avoids whatever threatens to weaken it.

Up to now we have merely scratched the surface, however; and the reason for this is that we have proceeeded in a completely abstract way, as though the subject was isolated, as though it had only its own experience to deal with. Unfortunately, this is not so. Each of us is *immersed*—and opinion can be understood only if we take account of such *immersion.* If reflection concentrates on the implicit reference, it will observe how it changes its form. The fact is that in the great majority of cases, it is not I who "maintains that. . . ." If someone presses me when I have just uttered an opinion, I will usually resort to flight, sheltering myself behind "it is said that" or "everyone says." "Everyone knows that the English are a nation of hypocrites." Here again we must pause, for a very important feature comes to light. I am afraid that opinion usually has a false basis. I treat something which is not mine as though it were mine, something that I have somehow inhaled without realizing it. We are dealing with a reality which is of an even greater complexity than this, however. The more an opinion is offered as an evaluation, the more we find inextricably mixed in with it both the factor I have just described and another of a different sort that we should now try to grasp.

In these critical years[2] when people are so badly divided in their convictions, it is impossible to avoid being not only preoccupied with, but really haunted by the hybrid mystery concealed behind the word "opinion." I was recently prompted to say a few words to an audience composed entirely of communists or at least persons inspired by communism. I found it possible to refrain from uttering any words which would offend the audience. But while I also felt a certain *basic sympathy* for my audience, I at the same time recognized how completely impossible it was to reach them on the level of opinion. Now it is precisely here that we find this complex of factors which are in fact indissociable, but which we must nevertheless analyze with the greatest care. I accept it as a fact that if we try to understand what an adherent of the popular front (evidently assumed to be sincere) thinks, we will find for the most part an acute awareness of certain injustices together with the fundamental evaluations presupposed by this awareness. This does not have the character of an opinion; the injustices are perceived, are flagrant, even if the individual who denounces them has not personally been a victim of them, and particularly so in his case, perhaps. Every assertion of the form: *such-and-such cannot be condoned* to my mind transcends the plane of opinion. On the other hand, however, as soon as a judgment is uttered on "those really responsible" for this state of affairs, all the observations I have made above, hold; with what authority do I assert that such-and-such a person or even such-and-such a corporation is responsible?

What I am doing here is mirroring something else. This involves a transition from "I maintain that" to "Everybody knows"—meaning here "my newspaper said"—without my being able to discern the roots of the statement. Generally, we can say that for the man in the street, "my paper" is something that can no more be transcended than can "my consciousness" for the idealist; in fact, it is not an exaggeration to say that from a certain point of view "my consciousness" *is* "my paper." Yet this is a somewhat unwarranted simplification, because in the first place, I have chosen my paper. A great deal can be said about the meaning and implications of this choice, but it is particularly necessary that "my paper" conforms to a certain mute exigence within me which finds its satisfaction in the paper and which ratifies *a posteriori* the latter's statements; and this mute exigence is the basic and irreducible element in my way of evaluating. Here again, however, we have to guard against excessive simplification. We do not have to do with a single exigence, but with a bundle, a skein of exigences. Only a rigorous examination of consciousness can enlighten us in this respect; we must indeed begin with ourselves if we are to discern the role played in our opinion by our own personal interest or by some emotional bias for or against someone. Here again, we shall discover a spectrum of meanings. At the one extreme, opinion is only the expression of a desire or aversion, or of a complex of factors in which desire and aversion are indissolubly mixed; at the opposite extreme, opinion implies inversely, a kind of ideal claim having value in itself, which disregards the interests of the empirical subject who expresses it. The significant point about this, however, is that hypocrisy too often enters in, and allows me to express in terms of an ideal and impersonal claim what in fact is only an appetite—but one which does not dare reveal itself in all its nudity. We have to recognize, nevertheless, that opinion is located just between the two, in this penumbra receptive to mirages and phantoms. Indeed how can we speak of opinion when appetite reveals itself without disguise? Where an intrinsic value is defended, on the other hand, we are in the realm of what I shall call the *hyperdoxical*.

It follows from the above that if we wish to consider the value of an opinion, a political opinion, for example, a series of preliminary distinctions are required.

First of all we may ask about the meaning or import of the experience underlying an opinion although we cannot establish any equivalence or measure between the two.

On the other hand, and on a wholly different level, we must assign to any opinion whatever, a certain existential significance, insofar as an opinion expresses, whether adequately or not, a set of needs from which we cannot abstract.

Finally, the ideal and depersonalized claim which can be concealed in an opinion is a factor which must be treated separately. What must be clearly granted, however, is that the coexistence of such distinct and irreducible factors at the core of opinion compels us to proclaim its essential lack of reality. The mode of relation established by consciousness between these diverse elements will in fact always remain unverifiable.

We must now closely examine the "religious opinions" of the free thinker in the light of the foregoing observations. We shall have hardly any difficulty in rediscovering here the incongruous elements I just now attempted to catalogue. The simplest approach is to consider the case of the atheist who candidly affirms his atheism. The characteristic feature of opinion as such is nowhere more in evidence then here: "I maintain that" God does not exist. Atheism, on the other hand, is something that is affirmed essentially before another, or before oneself insofar as one is another. It is not and cannot be lived as faith. It is essentially a riposte—or what amounts to the same thing, an objection. That this *I* now conceals a *one*, that it inevitably refers to a "general opinion" conveyed by conversation, the press, books, is so obvious that I believe it unnecessary to pursue the subject any further. What is here of greater moment is to discern the respective contributions made by experience, the existential affirmation, and the ideal claim. To make such a discrimination, moreover, is much more difficult; and nuances of meaning which I cannot introduce here have to be presented.

First of all, the empirical contribution; the "I maintain that" of the atheist implies a "my experience shows me that." Here an important observation should be made. It seems to me that the atheist claims to conjoin two kinds of observations: one is negative, the other positive (or one he believes to be so—wrongly, in all likelihood).

On the one hand he asserts that he has had no experience of God. "If God existed, I would have experienced him." This is more or less what a person who occupied an important position in the state system of education once affirmed to me.

There is, however, a complement to the above: "On the other hand, I have experienced certain facts which would not have occurred if God existed." There is absolutely no doubt that the stumbling block of evil in all its guises is one of the bases of atheism. However, we have to analyze this judgment of inconsistency. In fact, if we examine it closely, we will find a paradox. When in talking about a certain person, I say: "if she had been there, such a thing would not have happened," I base my remark on an exact knowledge or on a knowledge I claim is exact, of the person in question; for example, she would have prevented the child from playing with the matches. This means: she is prudent, careful, good: hence she would not have allowed the child to play with the matches. However, this assumes not only that the person exists, but also that we know his manner of existing. But we can see at once that we are dealing with something different in the case of God. The atheist bases his view on a certain idea of God (not on an experience, clearly). If God existed, he would have such-and-such properties; possessing these properties, he would not allow that . . . etc. . . . . The judgment of inconsistency is based on a judgment involving an implication. Possibly the term "implication" is not strong enough. What is really meant is that to think of God is not to think of anything at all, to limit oneself to the mere utterance of the word "God," if our affirmation does not involve the existence of a being who is sovereignly good and sovereignly powerful. Now this is justified. But in all likelihood the transition to the conclusion is not justified. Let us consider the example I took from the finite or created order. If Jane had been there she would not have allowed the child to play with the matches. The ground for my statement is either certain analogous cases in which Jane has in fact demonstrated her prudence, or, if such cases have not occurred, the consciousness of what I would have done in her place. Is this applicable to the case where we claim to reason about the behavior of God? Clearly not. If I base myself on the consideration of what in fact has been the action of God in such or such a particular circumstance, I put myself in a position where it is impossible to arrive at an atheistic conclusion. Is the second alternative more acceptable? Can I put myself in God's place in order to affirm that in such-and-such a case I would have acted in such a way, would or would not have allowed such an event to take place, etc.? Something odd takes place here. Whenever we are dealing with an influential person who is responsible for taking the initiative in a difficult situation, we readily recognize that we cannot put ourselves "in his place," that we do not know ourselves what we would do if we were "in his place." The politician, however, always seems to be at grips with a situation he has not created, but which he should nevertheless try to control. On the other hand, it can be conceded that God, being thought of as a creator, does not confront an infinitely complex series of data; he is rather viewed as a privileged being who has only to will that things be so,—so that the atheist does not have the least hesitation or scruple in pronouncing what we may call a verdict of non-existence.

Now it is here that the characteristic features of opinion appear in all their nakedness, in particular, the externality of opinion relative to the very thing to which it refers. The more a state of affairs concerns me, the less I can say in the strict sense of the term that I have an opinion about it. Hence the justice of the remark which is wholly negative but still helps advance our inquiry, that commitment and opinion are mutually exclusive. This entails the metaphysical conclusion that I have an opinion about the universe only to the extent that I actually disengage myself from it (where I withdraw from the venture without loss). The pessimism of a modern disciple of Voltaire or of an Anatole France, for example, lies precisely in this: he is tied to a non-participation—to be sure we must note that this is not true of all pessimisms, and is not true of the pessimism of Schopenhauer, for example, to the extent that *it is lived*.

Atheism, however, can be based not so much on an experience or the lack of an experience as on a claim, or more precisely, on a willing. A number of variable relations between this will and this experience or non-experience can be established.

"God," writes Maritain,[3] "is completely rejected in principle, as the result of an absolute metaphysical dogmatism . . . in the name of the social community, the collective or collectivised man. . . . The social communist ideal shows up as the conclusion of an initial atheism which has been postulated in principle." I believe this to be quite true. But wouldn't it be well to note that a kind of identity of attitude is realized here—paradoxically—between the collectivised man and the anarchist as Stirner, for example, has conceived him? It may be said by the way that we are touching here at the root of a paradox in which anarchism and communism tend to become identified in the minds of many people today. Here and there we encounter the same affirmation that man can only realize his full stature in a world devoid of God; and this, too, is why the idea or pseudo-idea of a communist humanism today tends to attract the attention of many minds whose principal talent, moreover, does not appear to be the gift of reflection. As I have indicated, it is clear that this humanism is based not on an experience but on a claim. The hyperdoxical characteristic which we tried to exhibit earlier, fully reveals itself here. The more it grows, however, the more it becomes aware of itself—the more we tend to pass from the sphere of opinion into the sphere of faith.

However, someone may inquire whether it would not be appropriate to intercalate between opinion and faith an intermediate link, namely conviction.

Here again we have to make a careful examination of certain realities that ordinary language—which is so loose—tends to conceal. "I have paraded my convictions right and left," a vaudeville character once said; "and they have remained unshakeable." In this case there is no doubt that opinion and conviction coincide. On the other hand, consider the case of a man who has arrived at a conviction on a specific question after patient effort and persistent inquiry: Scheurer-Kestner or Zola arriving at the conviction that Dreyfus was innocent. Conviction here refers to a limit, an end, a bar that has been drawn. My investigations can reveal nothing more. This means: the cause is known to me; it is useless to talk about it further. Thus conviction in principle refers to the past; if it does refer to the future, it is an anticipated future, hence a future treated as though it were already past; there is in this respect a fundamental and also extremely subtle difference between conviction and prophetic certitude. Can we apply this observation to political or religious conviction? I believe we can. The person who professes his republican convictions thereby affirms that he has attained something which for him has a definitive character. The curious thing about this which is worth notice, however, is that the affirmation referring to the invariability of an inner disposition inevitably tends to become converted into a judgment asserting the immutability of its object. If I have republican convictions, I shall not be satisfied to say: "I shall always be convinced that a republic is the most rational political form"; I will go further and affirm: "a republic will always fulfill the desires of the most rational minds." This is actually an irrational and unjustified inference, the psychological mechanism of which, however, instantly leaps to the eye.

Here I wish to strongly emphasize the word "definitive," which I have just used. It is a word which embodies a claim to arrest time. Whatever you may say, whatever happens, my conviction is unshakeable. It is worth the trouble to reflect a moment on the extravagant nature of this *pretension,* for it *is* one and eminently so. The individual does not confine himself to saying in effect: "Starting now, I am going to close my eyes and stop up my ears": this would be a decision, not a pretension. No; what is affirmed is that "Whatever happens or whatever may be said cannot alter what I think." Now we have either one of two alternatives:

either I want to affirm by this that I have already anticipated in detail and refuted all the objections my questioners or the events themselves might confront me with;

or I affirm that these objections, whatever they may be—and this is tantamount to saying that I have *not* anticipated them, have *not* examined them in detail—cannot shake my conviction.

Let us consider the first alternative; it involves an absurdity. How can I be sure that I have anticipated all objections? The cases in which all the possibilities are enumerable are infinitely rare; one scarcely finds them except in pure logic or mathematics; and when I refer particularly to events which are by nature unpredictable, such an enumeration seems strictly inconceivable.

We must therefore fall back on the second alternative. Whatever objections there may be—I do not claim to predict them all in detail—I am determined not to take them into account. We fall from the level of pretension to that of decision. It is not certain, however, that we can remain there. I indicated that I am determined not to take them into account; but can I actually do this? Isn't there a part of myself which is in danger of being influenced in certain ways, which surrenders to a certain pressure? a part of myself which is relatively refractory to the power of control or domination that my will claims to exercise over the totality of myself? At the moment when I profess my unshakeable conviction, a concord, a harmony happens to be realized between the different parts of myself; will this harmony continue? it is impossible for me to affirm that it will in good faith; I cannot be responsible for what my state of feeling will be tomorrow. What then? If I were fully aware of these possibilities, these perils, I would say:

either: my conviction is unshakeable—except for the change in those parts of myself for which I cannot truly say I am responsible because they are in an immediate contact with the event; which is tantamount to saying that my conviction is *not* unshakeable, that I cannot sincerely state that it is so;

or: my conviction is unshakeable, whatever the changes that might occur in those areas of my inner realm which are not completely submissive; I decide once and for all that if inconsistencies should occur, they will have no repercussions on my conviction itself. However, the justification or the validity of this attitude is extremely doubtful. To be sure, if only my subsequent acts were involved, I could say: "Whatever happens, I will act as if. . . ." But the zone of conviction is intermediary between that of feeling and that of action: and it is quite clear that between it and the zone of feeling there neither is nor can be any precise boundary. I must guard against the fact that at the moment I affirm my conviction, basing it on the harmony now realized within me, I cannot really envisage a different feeling, or better, dissonance, which I will experience tomorrow; I only have an abstract idea of it which I can juggle. Nothing more.

These reflections lead to the inference that the apposition of the terms *definitive* or *unshakeable* with the utterance of a conviction always implies a claim at the basis of which we can discern either a delusion or the consent to an inner lie. All I really have the right to say is: "given the constellation of my present inner dispositions and the set of events of which I am now cognizant, I am inclined to think that. . . ." Moreover, I should guard against affirming the immutability of this constellation of factors on which my conviction is based, one which therefore seems to me to be essentially capable of being modified.

Doubtless this relativism will seem singularly cold to many readers, particularly prudent and timorous, and therefore incapable of giving that tonus, *élan,* or dynamic value to life in which we set so much store. What has happened all this time to belief? it will be asked. Isn't it, too, infected by relativism? I do not think that it is, but the greatest care must be taken in showing this.

For the sake of clarifying the following remarks, I can say that the temporal orientation of belief is, in a way, the inverse of that of conviction. The latter refers to an arrest, to a bar that has been drawn; it implies a kind of inner closure. With belief, just the inverse is true. I am convinced that the bergsonian opposition between the open and the closed has a significantly novel application here.

However, we must guard against the pitfalls of language. The word *believe* is often used with the most fluctuating meanings; it sometimes means quite simply: "I assume that," or even, "it seems to me that." I do not believe we will succeed in extricating its essential characteristic unless we resolutely put to one side what is expressed by *believing that*. (although there are some rare cases where this expression can be preserved). I shall concentrate first of all on what is implied in the act of belief *in* or *about* something or someone.

I think that the notion of *credit* can guide us in this context. To give, or better yet, open a credit account to someone. . . . This to my mind is the most essential and constitutive aspect of belief. We have to uncover its meaning. We must not be misled by the fact that to agree to extend credit is to place at the disposal of someone else a certain sum, a certain quantity of something, with the expectation that it will be returned to us together with an additional sum, a certain profit. We must unburden the meaning of extending credit of this material weight. I am in no way separable from *that which* I place at the disposal of this X (whose nature we must explore later). Actually, the credit that I extend is, in a way, myself. I lend myself to X. We should note at once that this is an essentially mysterious act.

To be sure, conviction, too, refers to something which is external to me; but it implies no commitment on my part towards this X. My conviction refers to X; I indicate my position with respect to X; I do not bind myself to X. I acknowledge that this is a very subtle difference, but it is a very important one to my mind. Believing means, to begin with, following a certain course, but only to the extent that following in no way means *undergoing*, but rather *giving oneself, rallying to*. The image evoked by *rallying* is possibly as instructive as that of credit; it connotes even more adequately the kind of inner gathering together presupposed by belief. It is interesting to note that this gathering together is the more effective to the extent that the belief is *stronger*. It is here that the analyses of Bergson are most clearly applicable. The strongest or most vital belief is one which brings all the powers of our being most completely into play—which does not mean that we can measure it exactly in terms of the consequences it implies on the plane of action. The human situation is infinitely more complex, and here as elsewhere, pragmatism proves to be inadequate.

Let us now consider this X to which we extend credit, to which we rally. What are its characteristics? I am prompted to say that it always is either a personal or a supra-personal reality; but the idea of a supra-personal reality raises difficulties which I can only touch upon. Whatever is on the hither side of the person always participates in *thingness*. But how can I put my trust in a thing—which is inert by definition, i.e., incapable of responding? This is only possible if I personalize this thing, if I make a fetish of it, a talisman, i.e., the incarnation of powers which are in reality those of the person himself. To believe in someone, is to put one's trust in him, i.e.: "I am sure you will not let me down, that you will instead fullfill my expectations, that you will realize them." I expressly use the second person here. One can only trust a "thou," a reality capable of fulfilling the function of a "thou," of being invoked, of becoming something I can fall back on. And it seems to me that this is of the utmost importance. It is clear, however, that this assurance is not a conviction in the sense I have described above; it goes beyond what is given, what I can experience, for it is an extrapolation, a leap, a bet, which like all bets, can be lost. The stakes involved are difficult to define—for the reason that it is I who am the credit which I extend to the other. I am convinced that in this context all our habitual categories of thought are inadequate. In a concrete philosophy we must almost invariably confront the drama concealed by the problem. As long as we think in terms of a problem we will see nothing, understand nothing; in terms of the drama or of mystery, however, the case may be somewhat different: as is so often true, it is negative experience, the experience of disappointment or defeat which is here the most revealing. I have placed my trust in a certain individual; he betrays me; if I had not established a completely inward relationship with him, or more precisely, with what I took to be him, this disappointment could not have touched me in the strict sense of the term; the fact is, however, that I *am* affected by it. This could result in a collapse for me, in a real uprooting of my being. What then has happened? that I have identified myself with this X and that I became partly alienated from myself because of him. (We must not forget the extending of credit). The result is that his failure is in a way my own. I find it impossible in this connection to adopt the detached attitude of the person who regrets what has happened but whom it "does not concern" in the final analysis. My disappointment is in a way a partial destruction of myself.

How was it possible to be disappointed, however? because my reliance on X had a conditional character. I counted on him to fulfill a certain task, for example: this task, as it happens, he did not fulfill; I ascribed a certain determinate quality to him; the event seems to demonstrate to me that he did not possess it. In sum, I had formed an idea of him which has now been contradicted and, as it were, nullified. In the light of my previous remarks, however, isn't it plain that this vulnerability of my belief is linked to the residue of opinion still left in it? Here there are two boundary-cases which we must consider.

However strange it may seem to our minds, it is possible for there to be an unconditional love of creature for creature—a gift which will not be revoked. Whatever may occur, whatever disappointment experience inflicts on our hypotheses, our cherished hopes, this love will remain constant, this credit intact. Perhaps it is on data of this sort that the philosopher should first base his meditations when he tries to reflect on the absolute; for the most part these data are hardly ever taken into account. Examples like these, however, involve an anomaly which somehow seems to be suspended in a reality frequently unperceived by those very souls in which it blossoms. . . .

The other boundary-case is this: love is faith itself, an invincible assurance based on Being itself. It is here and here alone that we reach not only an unconditioned fact but a rational unconditional as well; namely that of the absolute Thou, that which is expressed in the *Fiat voluntas tua* of the Lord's Prayer.

I shall not inquire here into the obscure, subterranean relation linking pure *Faith* in its ontological fullness with the unconditional love of creature for creature mentioned above. I deeply believe, however, that this link exists; and that this love is only conceivable, only possible, for a being who is capable of such faith, but a being in whom it has not yet been aroused; such a love is perhaps like a prenatal palpitation of faith.

There is, however, a further point on which I should like to make some concluding remarks; what are we to think of the secularized expressions of faith of so many of our contemporaries? faith in justice, faith in science, faith in progress, etc.?

Here we enter the realm of the supra-personal; yet in all cases such as these we are in fact clearly concerned with an order which can only be established by persons, and which, while above them in certain respects, nevertheless depends on their good faith.

Consider more specifically what "faith in science" means. I confess to some difficulty in determining what this can be.

The word "science" seems at the very outset to be stamped with a formidable ambiguity. Does the word designate a certain body of truths? If this is the case, it is really meaningless to refer to a faith in science. It is an abuse of language to apply the word "faith" to the mind's adherence to a demonstrated truth. The fact is that those who have faith in science have faith *in the influence exercised* by those who have mastered a science. It is conceded that minds which are completely penetrated by scientific truth cannot but illuminate those other minds in which they in turn instill these truths. Hence if we do not want the sort of dictatorship of scientists as Renan, for example, conceived it, it seems clear that our hope must rest on the idea of an educational science, i.e. one which is endowed with the marvelous power of purifying those whom it illuminates.

I am very much afraid, however, that no worthwhile empirical or rational justification can be offered for this view. If a scientist can exercise a personal influence—this, moreover, is a pleonasm: what act is not personal?—this is not because of the truths that he disseminates, but because of the power of disinterestedness which animates him, or in other words, because he himself leads an exemplary life. It is an arbitrary distortion of meaning to imagine that

the truths discovered by a patient and persevering inquiry somehow preserve a trace of these virtues, that the latter remain embodied in them; *nothing of the sort occurs.* Any truth, whatever it
may be, considered apart from the fervor of the person who discovers it, is something ethically neutral, ethically inert. And this
is more so to the extent that such a truth has a more positive nature,
i.e., to the extent that it is presented to us as more radically independent of those values it is the task of the mind to recognize and
acknowledge.

Thus if we concentrate on the analysis of the meaning of this
"faith in science" which our rationalists at the Sorbonne and elsewhere profess—and this is an extremely important task—we shall
discover within it the most disparate elements.

As the basis of it we can discover a trace, an indistinct survival,
as it were, of what another era apprehended as the attributes of
Being and their mutual implications: for it is a plane on which the
transcendentals are interconnected, where the True is inseparable
from both the Good and the Beautiful. This plane, however, can by
no means be identified with that of positive science; it is rather like
an Atlantis of the mind—a submerged Atlantis.

If we want to describe the psychological mechanisms which
make this "faith in science" not only possible but effective, however, we have to turn to opinion and to opinion alone. In general,
opinion, as we have noted, is defined as an *appearing to be* which
tends to become converted into a *claiming* through an absence of
reflection. Indeed I firmly believe that such a shift occurs in the
present case. "Faith in science" is only explicable in terms of the
phenomenon of prestige, and of an extrapolated prestige, if I may
say so. It is appropriate to introduce here some reflections or observations borrowed from the concrete history of ideas. I do not
believe that we can separate this scientific prestige which is envisaged by the imagination—not conceived—as liberative, from
the corresponding representation of religion as a principle of spiritual slavery—as obscurantism. I do not believe I am mistaken in
saying that the more weakened anticlericalism becomes the less we

will be led to view science itself as a power of promethean emancipation.

I shall conclude my observations at this point; for it is not my purpose to continue with an examination of pure Faith. Again, as at the beginning of our discussion, I suggest that we view the foregoing as an indispensable introduction to the act of reflection, permitting us to discern at the core of our own beliefs what part is the truly incorruptible gold of Faith, and what part we must view, whatever the cost, as an unusable mass of slag, the dead weight opinion throws into the infinitely delicate scale of our spiritual acts.

NOTES

1 *Le dialogue catholique-communiste est-il possible?* (Paris: Grasset, 1937).
2 1936.
3 "Le Sens de l'Athéisme Marxiste," *Esprit* (Oct., 1935), p. 93.

VII

The transcendent as metaproblematic[1]

At any given moment I am free to detach myself sufficiently from life in order to view it as a succession of lottery drawings. A certain number of these drawings have already been made. I note that such-and-such numbers of mine have already come up so that I can say that I had certain lucky chances, certain unlucky ones. Other numbers have still to come up; further, I am completely ignorant of how long the drawing will take. Will I have time to finish my present work? to go to Greece next year? to attend my son's marriage? All this is problematic: from the moment I have been allowed to participate in this lottery—and this participation has begun the day of my conception—a ticket has been issued to me on which a sentence of death is inscribed; the place, date, the how of the execution are blanks.

If, breaking somewhat with my original attitude of detachment, I consider more closely the consecutive drawings which have been made, it is clear that I cannot treat them as simple, juxtaposable elements making up a collection. The lucky and unlucky drawings react on one another, color one another, interpenetrate. I cannot even assign fixed values to the drawings already made; these values vary, as I am aware, with the drawings I have still to make. Further, I note that the very manner in which I am prepared to accept these results can likewise seem like a certain lottery to me; my tendency to revolt is one of these, my capacity for resignation, another. I notice at the same time, however, that if what I am is something already dealt out, something settled, my representation of life as a lottery tends to lose its meaning. There is of course no justification in saying that I accept unless I grant that I am before I accept; but can I be without being something or someone? Similarly, it is clear that I have no hope of tracing out an objectively determinate boundary line between my nature and the blessings or afflictions which have been parceled out to me, by whom or by whose agency I moreover do not know. Surrounded by these accumulated obscurities which are somehow handed down from an unknown future to the depths of a past which is recognized less and less as something given, there is one certainty which is inescapable: I shall die. Only my death, among all the things which await me, is non-problematic. It is sufficient in this respect that it obtrude on me as a fixed star in the universal scintillation of possibilities. My death: this isn't a fact yet; is it then an idea? If it were an idea, I would be able to circumscribe it, consider it as an object; but it is impossible for me to do so. I cannot transcend it by thought or imagine it as already accomplished unless I put myself in place of someone else who will survive me and for whom what I call *my death* will be *his death*. It is possible to assimilate it to some fact or other which I represent to my mind only because of an identification realized in thought. As soon as I am aware of this mental substitution, however, the illusion disappears; and at once my death, that death which I cannot circumscribe, hangs over me, crushes me. It hangs over me because of the simple fact that it is inescapable. My situation differs in no way from that of the person who has been sentenced and who is imprisoned in a cell the walls of which draw imperceptibly closer together at every minute. Hence there is nothing in my present, and even in my past existence which cannot be eroded, pulverized by this presence of my death to myself, or rather, over myself. Furthermore, when overcome by dizziness as a result of this awareness, how can I avoid succumbing to the temptation of putting an end to this wait, to this wretched and indefinite respite, thus liberating myself from the torment of the impending?

Thus what is created for me is a metaproblematic of *no longer being* which is at the same time a systematic of despair, abolished only when it is realized in suicide. This metaproblematic can obviously seem to me to be the highest wisdom, can seem to me the expression, not so much thought as lived, of an ultimate truth from which the ordinary man cowardly averts his eyes. Embracing this truth can at the same time entail the repudiation of all the commitments binding me to my fellow-prisoners, can cut me off from a certain spiritual community, and even, it may be, from any community whatever. My suicide, which can be prefigured in my very way of life, is this same rupture, this repudiation. Indeed, it may happen that, hypnotized by an impending death, I even fulfill certain obligations contracted prior to this dark awakening; but if this is not merely the fruit of custom, mechanically prolonged into my behavior, and perhaps exaggeratedly so just in this case, then it is my affirmation of a reality or of a resistance of which I may be more or less aware, to the invasion by despair. This reality, which yet is practically incapable of expression, is the affirmation that something remains which has no need to take my impending death into account and for which the latter is of no concern. A nuclear affirmation, as it were, to which I can cling, or on which I can lean so as to contemplate my death which henceforth ceases to suck me into its center; and the consequences of this for me seems to be that I thereby succeed in attaining a certain fixity.

To be sure this cannot entail the thought that I can tear myself away from the situation expressed by the metaproblematic of "no longer being" by means of a dialectical process which is invariably successful and which operates like some sort of mechanism. Nothing of this kind is possible in the present context. The absolute despair to which my mortal condition beckons me, remains a permanent temptation, which only freedom can overcome—a freedom which is manifested in the very act of suicide, in the absolute negation of oneself. Are not our extreme possibilities of self-destruction inversely proportional to a certain positive power which ceases to be conscious of itself the moment it breaks its ties with being and challenges or problematizes it? It is therefore my responsibility as a thinking being to recognize that it is my freedom which has also created the abyss which attracts me. A strange polarity is established between consciousness—or the affirmation of this freedom —and the obsession with death. This, however, does not adequately express what is involved; for reflection immediately reveals that these do not really represent two opposed terms. My death only avails against me in collusion with a freedom which betrays itself in order to confer this reality or seeming reality on that whose petrifying fascination I indicated at the outset. It is this freedom, and it alone, which can blot out, can conceal from my eyes the unimaginable richness of the universe. How can I arrive at this view, however, without creating at the same time a positive metaproblematic of which the metaproblematic of "no longer being," of "not being," is in the final analysis only an inverted prefiguration?

If my freedom is therefore dissociated from itself, it is so on condition that its possible uses may be distinguished without this implying the establishment of any difference in objectivity or validity between the uses. There is not and there cannot be any science in whose name the refusal of being can be either absolved or condemned, and since this problem is devoid of meaning, it destroys itself as a problem. If we are to speak of an ontological counterweight to death—and, as we shall see, this is an inadequate description—this counterweight can be neither life itself, always disposed to compromise with the forces that destroy it, nor an objective truth which remains on the hither side of the existential, an ἀδιαφόρητον. [An indifferent object or thing (Stoic).] This ontological counterweight can only lie in the positive use of a freedom which becomes adhesion, i.e. love. Death, however, is at the same stroke not only counterbalanced, but transcended. The metaproblematic is the transcendent.

This, however, threatens to raise a number of difficulties. Won't

this "transcendent" ultimately be identified with an unjustified objectification of the act of transcendence, of the *sursum* wherein I
become aware of myself as freedom existing beyond the zone of the
finite and the contingent? But isn't this objection itself based on a
confusion? The *sursum* which concerns us here, cannot imply a
mere tautening of the will moving on its own axis, nor can it involve
an exaltation of the will which nullifies itself precisely to the extent
that it finds satisfaction in itself. To be sure, it is the essence of freedom to be able to find satisfaction in itself; but how can we fail to
see that such an ascetic narcissism is only despair insofar as it
implies an arrest, a contraction, the beginnings of a depreciation of
reality which is viewed as something to be vanquished and forgotten?

The act of transcendence, in the fullest sense of the term, is characterized by the fact that it is oriented; in phenomenological terms,
we can say that it entails intentionality. But while it is an exigence
and an appeal, it is not a claim; for every claim is autocentric; and
the transcendent is no doubt definable in terms of the negation of
all autocentrism. It may be conceded that this is a completely negative property; but it is a property which is only conceivable in
terms of a participation in a reality which overflows and envelopes
me, without my being able to view it in any way as external to what
I am.

But what then am I? Moreover, if it is I who ask the question,
what qualifications do I have for answering it? Even assuming—
and this may be just a series of empty words—that I possessess
such qualifications, how could I in principle know this—since experience, when it is examined with sincerity, reveals to me the fact
that I transcend myself in every way and that I only think I know
myself when I do not really know myself? In this respect I do not
have the completely social, non-metaphysical possibility of appealing to the other person: how or why should I ascribe to another the
privilege I deny to myself? I can become another for myself, the
most lucid, penetrating, and pitiless, witness and judge. Moreover,
as to the property the other possesses of revealing what I am to me,

it is still I who confers this property on him, it is I who bestows on him the privilege he has of judging me.

Hence I have to acknowledge that the question "What am I?" cannot be confronted the way in which a problem can be confronted; for the question encroaches on those same conditions which make it possible for us to raise it: who am I to question myself on what I am? and at this point I perceive the question imperceptibly changing into an appeal.

Into an appeal for whom, however? Can I be sure, have I any justification for thinking, that this appeal is understood and that there is a being—someone—who knows me and evaluates me? We must reject at the outset the postulate on which this question is based—and it is precisely here that the transcendent may be identified with the metaproblematic. In asking myself whether there is a being who hears my appeal and is capable of responding to it, I consider it as a hypothesis, a proposition which implies a possible verification. It is clear, however, that if "by a miracle," I was in a position to perform this verification—as in the case where I might try to determine whether an S.O.S. sent by a ship in distress was picked up by some wireless station located somewhere in space— it is clear, I repeat, that this Other, this empirically identifiable Receiver, neither would nor could be that absolute Recourse to which I addressed my appeal. The transcendence of the One to whom I appeal, is a transcendence of all possible experience as well as of all rational conception, which is but experience anticipated and schematized.

"Who am I? You alone really really know me and judge me; to doubt You is not to free myself but to annihilate myself. But to view Your reality as problematic would be to doubt You, and, what is more, to deny You; for a problem exists only through my agency and for me, the person who raises it, and in the present case it is I who am placed in question in that irrevocable act in which I humble my pride and yield myself."

I acknowledge the strangeness of this terminology when used in a philosophical register; isn't it more the prelude to a speech, an exordium to mysticism? But whether there is ultimately a precise boundary between metaphysics and mysticism is just what we are concerned to determine. The expressions I have used certainly do not describe an experience; they express an ultimate situation which the philosopher has to acknowledge, whatever his actual confession, whatever his personal capacity or lack of capacity for inner effusion. The latter is a contingent datum and one of which he must never become a prisoner. It is time that the metaphysician understands, if he wants once and for all to get out of the epistemological rut, that adoration can and ought to be a *terra firma* for reflection, a ground where he can find support, even though he is an empirical being and can participate in it only to the extent that his natural endowments permit.

If what I have said is true, a philosophy of transcendence must never divorce itself *even in principle* from a type of reflection which is directed on the hierarchy of the various modes of adoration, culminating not in a theory, to be sure, but rather in an understanding of saintliness; a saintliness apprehended not as a way of being, but as something given in the purest form in its *intention*. The fact is that it is here and here alone that the problematic is overcome, and that in such a life the imminent presence of death is abolished in the fullness of being itself. The fact that this saintliness, realized in some individuals, in some witnesses spread out over the centuries, is not felt to be an unnatural and outrageous anomaly by a weak humanity; that it evokes certain echos in our hearts, that it is for the indecisive mind a permanent stimulus to judge oneself and to hope—this certainly is the second datum which allows us to perceive in the saint—just as we perceive in the inspired creative individual on another level—the mediator of Him who no advance in technique, in knowledge or in what is called morality, will ever bring nearer to the individual who appeals to Him from the depths of his suffering.

NOTES

1 Paper read at the International Congress of Philosophy in August, 1937.

VIII

Creative fidelity

"It is private life that holds out the mirror to infinity; personal intercourse, and that alone, that ever hints at a personality beyond our daily vision." [1]

I was deeply moved when I recently reread these lines of the distinguished English novelist E. M. Forster which I did not remember having used as an epigraph to the second part of my *Journal Metaphysique,* and which accurately expressed one of the basic convictions inspiring my entire philosophical development.

Whenever I try to consider that development as a whole, I have to observe that it has been dominated by two interests which may at first seem contradictory; the first of these is more directly expressed in metaphysical terms, but still lies in the background at least, of almost all of my plays without exception. The latter is what I shall call the exigence of being; the first is the obsession *with beings* taken in their individuality but also affected by the mysterious relations which link them together. Clearly the paramount problem was to find some means whereby these two different inquiries could meet, although they at first seemed oriented in opposite directions; indeed, aren't we inclined to assume that the more the mind concentrates on being in its unity, in its transcendence, the more it is led to abstract from the diversity of beings, to view the latter as of trivial importance, as insignificant? and inversely, the more our attention is concentrated on that diversity, the more we tend, it seems, to view being in itself as a fiction, or at the very least, as a completely abstract postulate having no real referent. I think I can say without any exaggeration that I have always rejected this dilemma, even if I have not done so explicitly, and that instead, I have started from the *act of faith* which provides an *a priori* solution to it. It seems to me that I accepted the view *a priori,* long before I was able to justify it to my own satisfaction, that the more we are able to know the individual being, the more we shall be oriented, and as it were directed towards, a grasp of being as such. I expressly use terms which are vague and I think, even somewhat inappropriate, in order to characterize the compelling though vague assurance which seems to have guided me through the narrow, tortuous paths in which I have so often been in danger of losing my way.

The whole first part of the *Journal Metaphysique* is a reflection on the act of faith considered in its purity, on those conditions which allow it to remain an act of faith even while it reflects on itself; at the same time it is a partly desperate attempt to escape fideism and subjectivism in all its various forms. Faith, I maintained, cannot be transcended; it is not to be confused with the imperfect approximations characteristic of empirical knowledge; but it is an integral part of the realities in which it is suspended; to say that it would otherwise be mutilated is insufficient; we deny its very essence if we claim to sunder it from these realities. At that time I called them mental realities; and this qualification clearly brings home to me now the danger of my position then. I should add, however, that the relation to God, the status of the Divine transcendence, are what allow us to conceive individuality; this does not mean merely that the individual realizes himself as such by granting that he is a creature, but also that those who remain dominated by what Claudel has called the spirit of the earth, can, through the mediation of the believer, gradually develop individuality. It is possible that I caught a glimpse here of an essential truth; but it is clear that I did not have the equipment to justify it or to understand it in all its fullness.

To over-simplify the question without, however, distorting the essentials, I will say that faith on the one hand became clear to me from the moment I thought directly about fidelity; while fidelity, on the other hand, was clarified beginning with the *thou*, with presence itself construed as a function of the *thou*.

I apologize for this somewhat disorganized preamble; I have no intention of giving the history of my reflections on this question, (a feat which is perhaps impossible in principle), but only of attracting attention to the truly central position occupied by fidelity in the general economy of my thought.

Before entering into a somewhat detailed analysis of fidelity, I want to make some comments on a play which anticipates my later development in several ways, and whose importance first Edmond Jaloux and then Father Fessard have rightly emphasized; I refer to the *Iconoclast*. Not only was it not produced, but when it was published by Stock in a short-lived series, no critic, I believe, took any notice of it. As you may observe, the *Iconoclast* is precisely the tragedy of fidelity. Here is how I described the problem about which the play revolved in the *Remarques* which were published at the same time as the play:[2]

"How can an active and even militant fidelity towards a lost loved one be reconciled with the laws of life? or to put it more adequately; how can a true and stable relation be established between the dead and the living? Let me explain: whatever opinion we may have on what we vaguely and confusedly call survival, it is clear that the dead person whom we have known and loved remains a *being* for us; he is not reducible to a simple "idea" we may have; he remains attached to our own personal reality; he continues in any event to live in us, although it is impossible, given the rudimentary state of our psychology and metaphysics, to clearly describe the meaning of this symbiosis.

"What attitude can and should we adopt to this being who is at once present and gone forever? We are inescapably led to desire the restoration of communications between ourselves and this dead person who is present; even if he is but a veiled questioner with whom we may still carry on a dialogue. It is *certain,* however, that this desire can apparently be granted in certain cases; and it is possible that this can be more than an appearance. But what is the spiritual value of such a relationship? This is supremely important, not merely from the religious point of view, but for the personal life itself; that is the problem of the *Iconoclast.*"

Abel Renaudier passionately loved Viviane, the wife of Jacques Delorme, his best and most loyal friend. But he has not expressed his love overtly; what is more, thinking that Viviane was passionately attached to Jacques, he has bent all his efforts towards finding the latter worthy of her and has remained in the background. But Viviane dies; Abel cannot entertain the idea that Jacques should remake his life; in his eyes and as a counterpart to the sacrifice he himself has made, it is as if Jacques had committed himself to the view that he would never be happy again. Hence he is really indignant to learn that Jacques is preparing to marry Madeleine Chazot; Jacques is therefore a mediocrity, and it now seems to Abel that he must avenge the woman who no longer exists. This arbiter of justice does not see clearly enough into himself to understand that he is trying to satisfy a completely personal and egoistic instinct. His vengeance takes the form of arousing Jacques' suspicions of Viviane's fidelity in retrospect: isn't Jacques unworthy of keeping a spotless image of the person he himself has betrayed? However, what happens is that at the very moment he has succeeded in kindling in Jacques a horrible anguish in retrospect, he discovers that the reason Jacques has remarried was because he believed that death itself had compelled him to do so; in his despair Jacques wanted to kill himself; but Viviane had then revealed herself to him, had urged him to live, and to marry Madeleine to provide a mother for their children. Hence what Abel had taken for a betrayal was only a mode of fidelity. It is not our part to judge what constitutes fidelity or treason in another. By uprooting Jacques' faith in Viviane, he therefore saps the faith which permitted him to live. Jacques will now doubt the validity of that communication with the beyond on which he based his existence; it will seem to him as though he were the plaything of an illusion, and he will end up by invoking the death he wished. Abel does not hesitate to tell a lie to restore to Jacques his lost faith. But his action is futile. Beings can only be in harmony in the truth, but truth is inseparable from the apprehension of that great mystery which envelops us, in which we have our being. I shall transcribe here a few lines from the final scene which anticipate thoughts I had formulated in philosophical terms at a much later date.

JACQUES   There is nothing . . . phantoms in the void: that is what we are.

ABEL   That can't be so since we suffer.

J.   Everybody lied.

A.   The mistakes, the lies, are a penalty.

J.   Words, words!

A.   The awful penalty we have to pay for our being.

J.   Nothing but words.

A.   Maybe the soul can only find itself at last by paying the price of its mistakes.

J.   The soul!

A.   The living soul, the eternal soul.

J.   Did Viviane speak to me?

A.   We were walking in the shadows, but here for a few moments, the past with all its mistakes and suffering was lighted up and I wasn't deceived. You might say that a certain order emerged from all the confusion . . . ah, not a lesson, but a harmony.

J.   There can't be any rest for me if I do not know whether she hears me.

A.   No, Jacques, even if it is true, even if she spoke to you, you will never find the certainty you thirst for in an indecisive conversation, in a dialogue as dangerous as this.

J.   To see, hear, touch her.

A.   That's a temptation which can't mislead your true self. Believe me, you won't be happy for long in a world abandoned by mystery. Man is made like that.

J.   What do you know about man?

A.   Believe me: knowledge banishes everything it thinks to grasp to infinity. Perhaps it is mystery alone that reunites. Without mystery, life could not be lived. . . .

Here we observe something basic to my whole thought, namely, that mystery is not, as it is for the agnostic, construed as a lacuna in our knowledge, as a void to be filled, but rather as a certain plenitude, and what is more, as the expression of a will, of an exigence that is so profound that it is not aware of itself and constantly betrays itself in forging false certainties; a completely illusory kind of knowledge in which the will cannot find any satisfaction, however, and which it destroys by an extension of the very *élan* it had yielded to in order to establish that knowledge in the first place. This appetite to know, this *Trieb zum Wissen* which is at the root of our greatness as well as of our misery, is transcended rather than satisfied in the apprehension of mystery.

It is also important to notice here how the problem of fidelity is linked with the problem of death.

As I had the occasion to indicate in the discussion which brought Mr. Brunschvicg and myself to grips at the Congress of Philosophy, the problem of death—is it really a problem? it is doubtful that it is, as we shall see—is only real for the loved one; it cannot be isolated from the problem, or mystery, of love. Insofar as I create a void around me, it is quite clear that I can be lured to my death and can make preparations for it as for an indefinite sleep. The situation is entirely different as soon as the *thou* manifests itself. Fidelity truly exists only when it defies absence, when it triumphs over absence, and in particular, over that absence which we hold to be —mistakenly no doubt—absolute, and which we call death.

The problem of death, however, coincides with the problem of time considered in its most acute and paradoxical form. I hope to succeed in showing you how fidelity, apprehended in its metaphysical essence, must seem to us the only means we have of effectively vanquishing time—but I also want to show that an effective fidelity can and should be a creative fidelity.

It seems to me that the question of fidelity has hardly attracted the attention of modern philosophers generally, and that there are a number of significant metaphysical reasons for this. However, if we consider the question on historical grounds, it may also be said that fidelity is tied to the feudal phase of consciousness and that in a universalist philosophy of the rationalist type, it can be thought of only with difficulty and tends to become eclipsed by other aspects of our normal life. For our contemporaries, on the other hand, and especially for all those thinkers influenced by Nietzsche, it is considered suspect and is identified with an outworn conservatism. I believe that it is in Peguy and Peguy alone, that we can find certain elements of a metaphysics of fidelity; and even here I find it difficult to locate them exactly. On the other hand, it is in a work like Scheler's—I cannot present any specific evidence here either —that we find something going beyond the Nietzschean critique which has been a source of its depreciation. In what follows I wish to present an analysis of it which will, moreover, go beyond psychology.

First of all, it seems to me important to distinguish carefully between constancy and fidelity. Constancy may be viewed as the rational skeleton of fidelity. It seems that constancy could be defined simply as perseverance in a certain goal; we can make a schematic representation out of this which identifies constancy more closely with fidelity. But this would make us lose contact with the very reality we seek to grasp. The sameness of this purpose, of this goal, must be ceaselessly affirmed by the will in opposition to everything which tends to weaken or obliterate it in me, and also to the obstacles which confront me through my dedication. Now it is precisely this will which we must succeed in describing as accurately as possible.

It may at once be observed, however, that constancy, construed as immutability, is not the only element entering into fidelity. Fidelity implies another factor which is far more difficult to grasp and which I shall call *presence;* it is here that we shall begin to observe something paradoxical; here reflection reveals at the core of fidelity something novel which dissipates the feeling of *staleness,* of *rancidity,* which threatens to overcome us whenever we focus our attention on a virtue, on the reliability of a certain value. When I assert of so-and-so: he is a faithful friend, I mean mainly: he is someone who does not fail me, someone who stands up to whatever the circumstances may bring; he does not slip away, but we find him there when we are in difficulty.

To be sure, I do not want to imply that there is an opposition between constancy and presence, for this would be absurd. But constancy, when compared with presence, exhibits a characteristic which is to some extent formal; it may even be said (and this is a more accurate description), that I am constant for myself, in my own regard, for my purpose,—whereas I am *present* for the other, and more precisely: for *thou*. I can easily imagine a man who assures me in the best of faith that his inner feelings or dispositions in my regard have not altered; to a certain extent I will believe him; but if I notice that he was not there in a certain circumstance when his friendship would have been of value to me, I would hesitate to refer to his fidelity. Of course presence is not to be construed here as externally manifesting oneself to the other, but rather as involving a quality which cannot be so easily described in objective terms, of making me feel that he is *with* me.

It should be noted that a being who is constant can make me see that he simply forces himself not to change, that he makes it a duty not to exhibit indifference on a certain occasion when he knows that I am counting on him; he can make it a point of honor to fulfill his obligations to me down to the last detail; and in such case, as I indicated earlier, his constancy is quite clearly based on an idea he has formed of himself and which he does not wish to be unworthy of. However, if his behavior really gives me the feeling that he has shown his sympathy in such-and-such a way "for conscience's sake," I shall say of him that his behavior has been beyond reproach, that he has been absolutely correct; but how could this correctness of behavior be confused with fidelity strictly speaking? the former is only a semblance of the latter. He is without reproach: it is like a diploma I feel obliged to confer on him. He is then discharged of his debt; no more is required of him; or rather—since we are not concerned with *doing* but with *being*—it is not required that he will to be any different than he is. However, I cannot with clear conscience—without emptying my words of all meaning—say of him that he has been a faithful friend to me; to be sure, "friend" and "faithful" are terms which cannot be separated in this context; fidelity is by no means a characteristic which happens to be added to the concept expressed by the word "friend."

No doubt—and here we shall observe that the problem around which these reflections revolve is becoming internalized—if I will to be constant, or if I am careful to fulfill certain obligations, I can, and almost inescapably seem to myself to be, a faithful friend of X. But how does the situation seem to X? This is what matters, "faithful friend" not being a title I can ascribe to myself. Without dwelling on it further, it can be clearly seen how shocking and how contradictory it would be for me to confer this diploma on myself. Assuming that X learns in some way or other that I have behaved towards him in a *conscientious* way, it is likely that he will release me from this obligation at least in his conscience; there is even a possibility that he will say to me with an intonation that can have infinite variations: "Don't think you are obligated to. . . ." To be sure, he knows that my conduct has been irreproachable; however, or rather because of this very thing, something has been shattered within him; we can even say that in his view a certain value has been lost and that what remains is only straw—and it is here that we see the problem of fidelity dawn, strictly speaking.

Of course it would seem normal from the rationalist or merely rational point of view for the ground of value here to lie in good will, in the constancy I have forced myself to maintain; and if I were to imagine an outside judge who gave out grades, I could indeed agree that this judge would give me a good report. It is clear, however, that this hypothesis, this commendation, is absurd. There is nothing here which can be measured by an impartial third party, nor even evaluated in the strictest sense. For fidelity as such can only be appreciated by the person to whom it is pledged if it offers an essential element of spontaneity, itself radically independent of the will.

If we reverse the relation between myself and the other, noth-

ing is essentialy changed. The absence of the element of spontaneity in the person whom I thought was my friend and in whom I
find "nothing to blame," creates an intolerable situation for me as
long as I do not explicitly release him from what he considers his
obligations to me. Why? the answer on further analysis, is clear.

I represent the other to my mind; I note that he apparently
feels obliged to have a certain consideration for me. But I have
reason to assume that there is in him—as in me—a sensitive nature
which perhaps secretly, perhaps openly, rebels against the discipline this imposes; hence a kind of struggle in him which is in
danger of being touched with rancor, who knows? of exasperation
towards me. Instead of the faithful friendship in which I believed,
therefore, I perhaps inspire a feeling of irritation in the other—
since he is in danger of feeling that he is a slave of his obligations
to me. Unless, that is, I destroy the kind of pact binding us, unless
I free him as I free myself, since we are here on a plane where each
attitude creates its own counterpart in the other.

Constancy in the pure state, with respect to interpersonal relations, is therefore in danger of being replaced by a struggle, at first
internal, then external, which can culminate in hatred and in mutual
aversion. How then can I exact from myself with regard to the
other, or from the other with regard to myself, an effective fidelity
which involves, as I have indicated, a pure spontaneity which I
cannot by definition coerce?

We must now bring out the more general import of the preceding remarks; they are by no means restricted to friendship alone.
However, it would be well here to distinguish various shades of
meaning. The more we confine ourselves to the realm of ideology,
the more obvious the identification of fidelity with constancy
seems.

I join a party; the members and the head of the party committee
only expect of me a strict and regular obedience to a certain discipline. It may be that I submit to this discipline only against my
better judgment, that something within me fiercely rebels against
my subjugation by the party; however, the committee and the
membership are only directly concerned to the extent that a secret

insubordination of this kind can lead to treason or to a future defection. It is only because of these possible consequences that somebody who divined my state of mind might be prompted to advise me to quit the party.

There is a further point which is important: it may in fact be maintained that party membership threatens either to sustain a continuous division between the words or gestures of a man and his true thoughts or feelings, or, what is no less unfortunate, to culminate in the enlistment of the soul itself, discipline becoming internalized to the point where all inner spontaneity is eliminated. The more organized the party, the more it encourages either hypocrisy or spiritual subservience; the present-day world offers us far too many ominous examples of this dilemma to make any further emphasis of this point useful.

Again, we have to show the form this problem takes with respect to the closest and perhaps most fundamental of all personal relationships—I mean the conjugal relation. We are all acquainted with marriages where one spouse is faithful to the other only out of a pure feeling of duty, where fidelity is reduced to constancy. Let us assume that the other person perceives this; this discovery can lead to an anguishing problem for him. Can he—I mean: does he have the right to reason the way in which the friend does in the example I gave above, and release his partner? It is impossible to deal in general terms with this case. Nevertheless, we can see at once that we cannot completely assimilate this case to the other. We cannot for reasons of a social nature which are clearly evident, above all if we are dealing with a family with children, since one may be concerned to safeguard a certain family unity at the cost of a partial hypocrisy, a unity which is not altogether inward, but which is still more than a mere seeming. But the decisive factor above all—and here we leave the social plane—is the way in which this conjugal union has been established, the way it was viewed when entered into; and it is here that the question of the sacrament to which I shall revert in my concluding remarks, is raised. It must be determined whether in this case, constancy, even in a situation where a certain feeling no longer exists, cannot be interpreted as a higher fidelity which is, as it were, rooted in God.

Now this can only be determined by a more detailed analysis of the conditions on which promising is based.

What does it really mean to swear fidelity? and how can such a promise be made? The question cannot be asked without giving rise to an antinomy. The promise in fact is made on the basis of some present inner disposition. However: Can I affirm that the disposition, which I have just at the moment that I commit myself, will not alter later on? No doubt there are certain states of exaltation which are associated with an awareness of their own perenniality. But don't both reflection and experience indicate that it is my duty to question the validity of this awareness, i.e., this affirmation? All I have the right to affirm is that it certainly seems to me that my feeling or inner disposition cannot change. *It certainly seems to me. . . .* But it is sufficient for me to say *it seems to me* in order to find it necessary to add as though *sottovoce*: but I can't be sure of it. It is then impossible for me to declare: I swear that my inner disposition will not change. This immutability no longer is the object of my allegiance. What is more, we may observe that the being to whom I swear fidelity can change in turn; he can become something which gives me the right to say: "This is not the man I committed myself to; he has changed so much that my promise is null and void."

But now, if my inner disposition can be changed, either because I have changed or because the other has, can I commit myself to act as though this disposition were not capable of altering? We have to be careful here with respect to the meaning of the expression *can I*. It is extremely ambiguous. The first meaning it can have is:

Can I affirm that if my inner disposition was changed, I could act all the same as though it were immutable? More specifically: there is a certain link which may be called objective although we cannot describe it completely, between what I feel and what I can do. Am I justified in affirming that, feeling differently, I can nevertheless act as though I always felt the same? In other words, does this affirmation go beyond the limits of what I have the right to affirm?

There is a second meaning, however, which is distinct from and perhaps more profound than the first, or at least more significant from a spiritual point of view: Have I the right to will that my behavior in this case remain the same as it would be if my feelings had not altered?

It is immediately obvious that there is a great difference between this point of view and the foregoing. Let us assume that it is still possible for me to act in the future towards X as though I still loved him, even though I no longer did love him; do I have the right to do so? In other words, can I consent to promise something about myself which will turn out to be a lie? And doesn't this future lie have repercussions by anticipation on the present itself, since I in effect speak as though I could maintain a disposition which I really know or should know, cannot be eternal? Must I not therefore view my commitment as conditional—introduce qualifications which conspicuously restrict its meaning?

The more difficult examples of this should not be presented straight off. So to start with, I shall take the example I gave in *Etre et Avoir,* an example, moreover, which is directly related to the first part of the present account. I am visiting an invalid; I come to see him out of pure politeness, perhaps; but I notice that my visit has given him more pleasure than I expected; on the other hand, I understand his solitude better, his suffering; succumbing to an irresistible impulse, I commit myself to come to see him regularly. It is quite clear that when I make this promise to him, my mind definitely does not dwell on the fact that my present disposition is capable of changing. But let us assume that this thought *does* flash through my mind; I dismiss it, I have the feeling I should dismiss it and that it would really be an act of cowardice to take it into account.

The moment I have committed myself, however, the situation is altered. Someone else has registered my promise and henceforth counts on me. And I know it. . . . An obstacle arises. We can ig-

nore the question which of the two forces is the most compelling
since this does not raise any real problem. Let us assume that I
have been invited to a play which I want to see and that the performance takes place precisely at the time that the invalid is ex-
pecting my visit. But I have promised, I have to keep my promise;
what helps me to do so is of course the thought of the disappointment inflicted on the invalid if I break my word, and also the idea
that I could not give him the real reason for doing so because it
would hurt him. Nevertheless, I go to his bedside unwillingly; at
the same time I reflect that if he knew the mood in which I kept my
engagement, my visit would not bring him any pleasure; it would
even be painful to him. Therefore, I have to act a part. Hence the
paradox which we have already skirted, that fidelity—or at any
rate the appearance of fidelity—in the eyes of the other, and a lie
in my own eyes, mutually imply one another and cannot be separated. The truth is that in this situation there is something which
does not depend on me; it does not rest with me not to prefer the
play to the visit which has become an irksome duty. Reflecting on
this situation which I had become involved in through an ill-con-
sidered commitment; I am led:

to acknowledge that I was wrong in making a commitment I
wasn't sure I could keep;

to ask myself whether, since I was wrong at the outset, I should
not at least have had the courage when the time came to refuse to
simulate feelings I no longer experienced, and to reveal myself
as I really was.

In other words, isn't it a serious mistake to transpose credit in
the realm of feelings and acts? Isn't it strictly more honest to live
by paying on delivery—to imitate in short those valetudinarians
whom we are all acquainted with, who never accept an invitation
categorically and who say: I can't promise anything, I'll come if
it's possible, don't count on me . . . ?

We can see at once the various consequences engendered by
such an attitude. Clearly it would tend to make social life impossible since nobody could depend on anybody; possibly a consistent
anarchism, though one which has never been practiced, could go

this far. It is of far greater interest, however, to describe the postulates on which this attitude is based:

1. The most significant of these can be expressed as follows: at a certain moment, I identify myself with the state of myself which I can apprehend at this precise moment. Everything outside this state is obscure, impenetrable, and in any case cannot be the object of any valid assertion. It may be noted that in this respect every assertion referring to my past appears unreliable, if it does not allude to facts which could be observed by others, which can therefore be viewed as external to me, as objective in the strong sense of this term. This postulate, however, is linked to a certain representation of the inner life—a representation which is in the final analysis, totally cinematic. Suppose at a certain moment I want to halt a film I am watching; it is clear that at the moment the film stops, I "will be" at a certain spot in the film which can be empirically designated. Perhaps the development of a living being, *qua* living can appropriately be identified with a film of this sort, so that I can use for this purpose snap-shots or instantaneous exposures; however, the more we are concerned with the personality considered with respect to both its complexity and its profound unity, the more logically inconceivable does this view become. This must be stressed as strongly as possible: at any moment my physical life can terminate and an autopsy can disclose the approximate state of my organs at the time that my heart stopped beating. But the notion of a mental autopsy reveals its absurdity in the measure that we are concerned with exhibiting the more fundamental modes of personal existence, with determining, for example, what feelings the defunct had for certain of his relations, or what his religious convictions were at the moment of his death. These snapshots can only capture an immediacy which has to be evaluated in terms of a larger whole which is actually indeterminate. Imagine a man, who during a perhaps trivial quarrel, declares to his wife that she is a nuisance, that he can't stand her any longer; these are his last words, for he is struck by an automobile a few minutes later. Should or can the outburst of violent emotion to which he succumbed be considered as the definitive state of his feelings for

his wife? It is impossible to say. A host of possibilities and considerations will crowd in on anyone who wished to decide the issue. Other cases are still more complex; I am thinking of the controversies surrounding the death of Jacques Rivière, of the question whether he had or had not rediscovered his faith, i.e. of the judgment we have to make on the basis of the words he uttered *in extremis*. All of this only illustrates a general truth: the personality infinitely transcends what we may call its snapshot states; which is tantamount to saying that the postulate in its present form is related to a view of its development which is as superficial as it is crude.

2. We may also distinguish another postulate of the phenomenalist or instantaneist attitude we are now examining. It holds that my future state is something which will occur (something that will happen to be) [3] the way an external event occurs, for example, the weather. I am in a good mood now, but I don't know the mood I will be in at the same time tomorrow; the sun is shining now, but who knows whether it won't rain at the end of the day? This is tantamount to denying any efficacy, any influence to the attitude I espouse with respect to the film; hence I am denied any capacity for acting on myself, for somehow creating myself. Hence for reasons of an *a priori* nature which it is therefore rather difficult to render fully conscious, certain data of private experience are impugned even though they are obvious to everyone.

The fact is that when I commit myself, I grant in principle that the commitment will not again be put in question. And it is clear that this active volition not to question something again, intervenes as an essential element in the determination of what in fact will be the case. It at once bars a certain number of possibilities, it bids me invent a certain *modus vivendi* which I would otherwise be precluded from envisaging. Here there appears in a rudimentary form what I call *creative fidelity*. My behavior will be completely colored by this act embodying the decision that the commitment will not again be questioned. The possibility which has been barred or denied will thus be demoted to the rank of a temptation.

However, we must still determine the ground of this refusal to again put something into question which is of the essence of commitment. Cannot our grounds be mistaken? But how are we to construe this possibility? Can I not decide to remain faithful to a resolution which I made unthinkingly—hence by treating something as essential which is really a pure accident, plant a lie at the center of my life? This would be but an imitation, a counterfeit of an authentic fidelity. On the other hand, however, have I ever adequate grounds for making the right decision, and doesn't commitment in any case embody a risk of which I should be aware?

In short, how can I test the initial assurance which somehow is the ground of my fidelity? But this appears to lead to a vicious circle. In principle, to commit myself I must first know myself; the fact is, however, that I really know myself only when I have committed myself. That dilatory attitude which involves sparing myself any trouble, keeping myself aloof (and thereby inwardly dissipating myself), is incompatible with any self-knowledge worthy of the name. Nothing is more puerile than the efforts made by some individuals to resolve the problem by compromise: I allude in this respect to the idea of a pre-marital trial whereby the future spouses begin by surrendering to an experience which commits them to nothing, but which is supposed to enlighten them about themselves; it is all too clear that such an experiment is immediately nullified by the very conditions under which it is performed.

This, however, seems to be a vicious circle only to the mind of the bystander who views fidelity from without. Yes, it is true that when viewed from without, all fidelity seems incomprehensible, impracticable, a wager, and scandalous too: how, it will be asked, could this man be faithful to that coarse person with the flat nose, or to that cadaverous old woman, or to that blue-stocking? What from without seems to be a vicious circle, is experienced within as growth, as a deepening or as an ascending. Here we are in a realm in which there is something that cannot be viewed as a spectacle either by oneself or by others, of something, therefore, which cannot be reflected without danger. This must be carefully examined, however: I can become a spectator of myself; what I have experienced can become, because of the utterance of a single word by another or because of some trivial episode, an object of surprise and scandal for myself. After this inner shock, relationships can become reversed; for example, I can come to view as a temptation what I used to call a duty, and conversely. I alluded to Jacques Rivière a moment ago; a reversal of this kind happened to him at a certain period of his life; this event was one of his motives for writing his last book, *Florence,* which I do not however think we should regard as his last testament, since mere chronology is not very significant.

This possibility of subversion and even destruction through reflection is embodied in the very essence of the free act; it is because we are free that we are in danger of self-betrayal, of seeking our salvation in treason of this kind; and this is the truly tragic element in our condition. This situation with all it implies is surely no less ultimate than the situation which involves me at once in both being and non-being—that of my body; and we must soon try to determine how these two situations may be described metaphysically.

At present we may note that all fidelity is based on a certain relation which is felt to be inalterable, and therefore on an assurance which cannot be fleeting. Inspiration, the bolt from the blue, are limiting-cases which are ultimately not very much more mysterious than any others; they focus the mystery of commitment on a privileged, decisive moment, that is all. But we cannot eliminate the mystery by trying to reduce fidelity to habit or to some mechanical counterpart of social constraint. Such attempts at minimizing and discrediting it were widely practiced by philosophers at the end of the 19th century, and we may wonder whether they did not thereby help to plunge the world into the chaotic state we find it in today.

Another attempt at devalorizing fidelity consists in interpreting it as a mode of affection for oneself, of human self-respect, of pride. This effort is closely related to the subjective interpretation of knowledge which denies that I can know anything except my own conscious states. I should like to transcribe here a passage from *Etre et Avoir* which exactly expresses my thought on this issue:

"Just as a philosophy which denies that I can know anything except what it calls my 'states of consciousness' is shown to be clearly false where we confront it with that spontaneous and irresistible affirmation which forms, as it were, the ground-bass of human knowledge; thus to maintain, despite appearances, that fidelity is never more than a mode of pride or self-regard, is to clearly deprive of their distinctive character what men have viewed as the loftiest experiences they have known." The link between these two kinds of undertaking cannot be overstressed. . . .

"When I assert that I cannot know anything transcending my states of consciousness, am I not indolently opposing this knowledge which is disappointing and even deceptive—since it in effect embodies an unjustifiable claim—to a knowledge which is not actually given but which is at the very least an ideal possibility, and which, unlike the first, touches on a reality existing independently of the mind? Without this axis of reference, however imaginary I may consider it, it is quite clear that the expression 'my states of consciousness' would be devoid of meaning, for it has a determinate meaning only if it remains restrictive. 'What lies within me can *only* lie within me.' [4] The whole question, therefore, is one of determining how I can conceive of a knowledge which is irreducible to the sort of knowledge I am said to enjoy on the above hypothesis, or even more significantly, of determining whether I really do have such a conception. To admit that I had no conception of it would entail the collapse of the dubious doctrine I pretended to support. But it is hardly possible for me to understand how the idea of a real knowledge, i.e. one referring to being, can emerge in a world composed of pure states of consciousness. Hence I find a secret escape passage, so to speak, in the wall below the tall keep in which I claimed to immure myself. Shouldn't this force me to acknowledge henceforth, that this same idea is in a sense the indelible mark which another realm has left upon me?

"The same is true of fidelity; the shadow of another fidelity whose existence I am able to deny only because I had first a conception of it, casts itself over the proud affection which the I lavishes on itself; but if I can conceive it to begin with, isn't this because I have experienced it however dimly in myself or in the other person? Surely it is no accident that I use those things which I affect no longer to believe in, as the models for that personal reality whose distinctive character lies in the unremitting effort of coherence and balance between its two aspects?

"Am I not, moreover, justified in mistrusting the actual nature of the step by which I claim to gather up into myself the roots or links of fidelity? How can I help seeing that such a dogged and determined contempt for evidence cannot originate in any experience however momentous or however concealed it may be. It can originate only in a prejudice, in the act of fundamental negation by which I banish the real to infinity, and then venture to usurp its place and bestow on myself those attributes I had stripped from it, thereby degrading them, of course, in the process.

"Can fidelity be preserved only at this price? It seems to me that it is far better to find in this nothing more than a survival, a lingering shadow, which should melt right away under the light of reason, than to establish such an idolatry at the center of my life." [5]

The foregoing considerations lead us to perceive the following metaphysical paradox; this paradox can be developed, in a way, from two different points of view; the first is as follows:

On the one hand, fidelity to a specific individual who is given in our experience, seems to the person who *lives* it rather than who views it from the outside, as irreducible to that feeling linking consciousness with itself or with its contents.

On the other hand, an absolute fidelity, which is therefore vowed not to a particular being, to a creature, but to God himself, is in danger of being construed today by the critical mind which is generally allied to the common sense view, as an unconscious egocentrism which ends up by hypostatizing a subjective datum.

In other words, (still considering the first aspect), it is readily granted that on the empirical level there can be a real fidelity with respect to a *thou* having an objective reality.

The fact is, however—and here we turn to the other aspect— that if I stay on the hither side of the ontological affirmation strictly speaking, I can usually call into question the reality of the bond linking me to some particular being; in this domain disappointment is always possible in principle, i.e. the separation of the idea from being; I can always be induced to recognize that it is not to this creature as she really is that I have been faithful, but to the idea I have conceived of her, an idea which experience has belied.

But on the other hand, the more my consciousness is centered on God himself, evoked—or invoked—in his real being (I imply a difference between God himself and some idol or degraded image of him), the less conceivable this disappointment will be; in any case, if it comes, it will be in my power to blame only myself for it, and to see in it only the sign of my own inadequacy.

Hence this ground of fidelity which necessarily seems precarious to us as soon as we commit ourselves to another who is unknown, seems on the other hand unshakable when it is based not, to be sure, on a distinct apprehension of God as someone other, but on a certain appeal delivered from the depths of my own insufficiency *ad summam altitudinem;* I have sometimes called this the absolute resort. This appeal presupposes a radical humility in the subject; a humility which is polarized by the very transcendence of the one it invokes. Here we are as it were, at the juncture of the most stringent commitment and the most desperate expectation. It cannot be a matter of counting on oneself, on one's own resources, to cope with this unbounded commitment; but in the act in which I commit myself, I at the same time extend an infinite credit to Him to whom I did so; Hope means nothing more than this.

As we may readily see, then, the order in which I have taken up these problems has been completely reversed. We are now concerned with determining how, beginning with that absolute fidelity which we may now call simply faith, the other fidelities become possible, how in faith and no doubt in it alone, these find their guarantee.

Pursuing this line of thought we will come to recognize the meaning and value of what should in fact be called consecration.

Only after reaching this point can we now examine the conditions under which fidelity can be creative: I shall say first of all—

and this is only a preliminary remark—that it is a real fidelity only when it is truly creative; it is justifiable to assume that if it is identified with that proud self-esteem in which we saw its shadow, it will be necessarily sterile—which does not imply, inversely, that the reality will necessarily be translated into visible consequences whereby we can know it. But it is important here to guard against the ambiguities involved in the word faith, and also, though this is not so evident, those involved in the expression "absolute fidelity". Do you understand by faith a determinate religious belief, I shall be asked, and in particular, the catholic faith? in that case you are going beyond the limits of philosophical re-flection, strictly speaking, you are smuggling contingent factors into the realm of pure thought without being able to justify or even admit the act whereby you have accomplished this. If, on the other hand, you claim to abstract from any reference to a particular religion, is it not to be feared that you are substituting for the reality of faith which is always determinate, an abstract schema lacking the vitality characteristic of faith?

The reply to this is that I am concerned with determining the place and the significance of the *I believe* in a metaphysical and spiritual economy; that in undertaking this, I am not compelled to abstract from the data provided by the existing religions. Any kind of fidelity whatever must be defined starting with the *I believe;* and the radical instantaneism which we had to introduce above, can only be understood in terms of a complete rejection of the *I believe.*

We must note at once in this context, however, the link between *I believe* and *I exist,* which does not entail that we can derive the former from the latter; I do not believe that there is any relation here which can be expressed by an *ergo.* I mean that if I assent to *I believe,* I do so as an existent being, and by no means as thought in general; i.e. as something which can formulate abstract distinctions with repect to itself, something trying to free itself from what I have called my basic situation: existing.

As you see, we have reached the point where the axes of my thought intersect. An intellectualism which claims that I can only rise to the condition of faith if I divorce myself, if only mentally, from my sensible nature is doomed to find the essential characteristic of the very thing it seeks to apprehend in its purity elude it. This, I believe, is what I glimpsed when I wrote on May 4, 1916 that faith must participate in the nature of sensation, the metaphysical problem being to rediscover both through and beyond thought a new infallibility, a new immediacy.[6] In the light of our discussion I do not pretend that this does not exhibit a certain obscurity. Although I have explicitly repudiated everything resembling or in any way connected with materialism, I would not be surprised if my complete rejection of dualism seems to some as necessarily establishing ties between man and his earthly environment which are so strong that the doors which open on the transcendent are thereby closed to him.

I believe this view is mistaken; to be sure I can be content to rest my defense on reassuring historical references, to Biran, to catholic philosophy in general, and for contemporary figures, to Peguy or Claudel. From the philosophical point of view, however, this would only be an evasion. The problem must be directly confronted: what does it mean to believe?

It seems to me that the above considerations should prepare the reader to understand that belief in the strong sense of the term —not in the sense of believing that, i.e. assuming that—is always belief in a *thou,* i.e. in a reality, whether personal or suprapersonal, which is able to be invoked, and which is as it were, situated beyond any judgment referring to an objective datum. As soon as we represent belief to our minds, however, it becomes the belief of a certain person in a certain other person, in a *him;* we then envisage it as the idea or opinion A forms of B. It must also be said that I can at any time become a stranger to myself, and I can to that extent lose contact with my belief in its being as belief. Furthermore: ordinarily, normally, I am in fact cut off from this belief with which I am identified and which is really indistinguishable from what I should in effect call my soul. This is the meaning of my often repeated statement that we ourselves do not know what we believe.

Whence the extraordinary difficulty of the problem I raised above: what is the meaning of belief? because of the very fact that we raise it, that it is a problem, we tend to intellectualize it, i.e. to falsify it; hence to see in belief an imperfect and even impure mode of knowing (to believe is to imagine that). And it seems to me that my observations on fidelity derive all their meaning from this fact. A meditation on the soul which has faith, i.e. the consecrated soul, clears the path for an authentic philosophy of belief; but there is a danger of not being able to accept this philosophy inasmuch as we have focussed our attention primarily on credulity as such. Now this does not imply that incredulity, as a later stage of reflection, does not raise some serious problems; we can even say in this connection that the mind will have to confront an antinomy which it cannot really resolve in a definitive way; on the one hand, incredulity appears to be only another name for the critical intelligence and implies the refusal to admit anything without proof; in considering the truth or falsity of any objective statement I refuse to justify any deviation from a certain attitude of inquiry, however important the values involved may be; on the other hand, from the specifically religious point of view, doesn't incredulity always appear to be related to a certain pride in one's reason which should be considered sinful? Our concern here is not with the question how this antinomy can be resolved within the context of a revealed religion; nor, in particular, with the validity, whether recognized or not, of some sacred text. It is possible for faith to accept what to profane thought seems a vicious circle. I have no desire to adopt any position on this question here. The metaphysical question is quite different; it consists in discerning at what point incredulity coincides with a certain fundamental infidelity and to examine its nature.

"Being as ground of fidelity. How does it happen that this formulation which came to my mind at a certain moment in time exhibits the same inexhaustible fecundity that is shared by certain musical ideas?" [7] This undated remark in *Etre et Avoir* is of paramount significance at this stage in our reflections. For it implies an interrelationship between the philosophy of being and the philosophy of freedom which to my mind the metaphysician can never overstress. However, if we want to see behind those formulations which seem so vague and indefinite to start with, we will find it appropriate to progress slowly, arriving at our goal by means of successive approximations: in any case I can do no more here than outline a dialectic which each person must pursue within himself.

To begin with, I can consider the affirmation: *I believe,* and then ask myself what it is I believe in; in answering this question, I cannot be satisfied with the enumeration of a certain number of propositions which I hold to be true; it seems clear that these propositions themselves express something far more intimate and profound; it may be said that what we are concerned with here is the fact of being in an open circuit with the reality recognized as a Thou, as assimilable to a Thou.

I can still treat the affirmation *I believe* as a datum which becomes the object of my reflection; however, I at once begin to wonder whether this belief is something that I possess; I venture to say that on scrutiny, it will be disclosed that the expression "having faith" is particularly open to criticism; a careful analysis of *having* is indispensable here; the fact is that belief, construed in terms of what is characteristic and significant about it, is not something I can hold, and it cannot be identified with a having; what is more, as soon as I treat it as a possession, it is in danger of becoming an object of suspicion to me, if only because of all those others who do not *have* it. Hence we are prompted to think that belief not only refers to being—it is quite possible that what follows suggests no precise meaning—but that it stems from being, that it is my being, that it is in fact the ground of what I am. And it is certain that this is a much more acceptable and significant interpretation of *I believe*. Here again, however, self-examination intervenes to compel a subtle adjustment of this view. My belief is perhaps the very ground of my being; but is there complete parity between the two? am I my belief as overtly manifested? is my life indentifiable with this belief become entirely explicit? It is clear that this is not the case; how can I ignore the fact that, instead of letting this light which can illumine my belief appear and shine through me, I obscure it most of the time? insofar as I am not transparent, I do not believe. Here incredulity merges with opacity; and what I have tried to express in terms of belief, can and should also be expressed in terms of love or of charity.

Hence I cannot affirm that I believe without careful reflection on my insufficiency which leads me to recognize at the same time that I do not believe; but the *I do not believe* can only be elucidated in terms of the initial *I believe* which is therefore limited rather than nullified by the former.

Any other approach to the question will eventuate in an analogous conclusion, and this is particularly the case if, as I have done elsewhere, we consider the idea the non-believer forms of the belief of others.

I think that the foregoing observations however, will offer us a glimpse of the response that can be made to the question what the place of *I believe* is in the spiritual economy. The response is evident as soon as we agree to substitute the term *permeability* for the somewhat ambiguous term *participation.*

Again, we have to guard against ascribing a materialist meaning to this term. Moreover, here as elsewhere, an initial consent is required, and this consent can be refused at any time.

Despair and betrayal are there at every moment waiting for the opportunity; and death, too, at the termination of our visible career, like a permanent invitation to a complete self-abandonment, as an incitement to affirm that there is nothing, that nothing is of any value. Remember the terrible passage in Claudel's *la Ville:*

Nothing exists.
I have seen and touched
The horror of what is useless, adding the proof of my hands to
    what is not.
The Void does not fail to declare itself by words which say: I am.
This is my prey and the revelation I have made.[8]

The thought of our death, i.e. of the only future event we can acknowledge as certain, can exercise a fascination over us in a way that somehow invades our whole field of experience, extinguishing all our joys, paralyzing all our efforts; it is, I think, appropriate, to emphasize as strongly as possible that this metaproblematic of death and of non-being is possible, that suicide is possible—and that in a way it is the temptation-type, the betrayal type, and that all other temptations and betrayals can perhaps be reduced to it. Therefore, it is not sufficient to affirm (and this is a truism) that as an existent being, I am subject to death, but it must also be affirmed that I am subject not merely to the feeling of being swallowed up by it, but to a view of the world as a palace of illusions where death ultimately has the last word. If I were really satisfied with the naturalistic affirmation that *I am my body,* that *I am my life,* if I could abide by these affirmations, it would no doubt be necessary to recognize that the judgment was true; but such a view is in fact untenable; we have to recognize a vascillation at the root of our being; and in our supreme moments there is a scintillation of belief which corresponds to this existential scintillation. It is not entirely true that I am my life, since I can sometimes judge it, and can fail to recognize myself in it; and this judgment is only possible on the basis of what I am, i.e. of what I believe. It seems therefore that an act is born which will free me from an objective pessimism and from death. I repeat "is born": it is not possible—at least not without an act of grace the possibility of which the philosopher can barely apprehend—not possible, I repeat, for this liberation to be achieved and for it to become for us a *fait accompli.* Nevertheless it seems that what warrants the most scrupulous reflection on our condition, on what is on this side of the datum that is revealed to us, is that constantly making ourselves more actively permeable to the Light by which we are in the world, we can hope that death tear us from ourselves in order to better establish us in being; allow me to conclude with the words of one of my heroes, Arnaud Chartrain in *La Soif,*—a pledge, or prophecy, or more fundamentally, an act of faith: "It is death that will open the door to all we have lived on earth." [9]

NOTES

1 E. M. Forster, *Howard's End* (London: Edward Arnold & Co., 1910), p. 78.

2 *Revue Hebdomadaire* (Jan. 27, 1923).

3 [In English in the text. Transl. Note]

4 [This quote is omitted in the Aubier edition of *Etre et Avoir*. Transl. Note].

5 *Etre et Avoir*, pp. 76-79.

6 *Journal Metaphysique*, p. 131.

7 *Etre et Avoir*, pp. 55-56.

8 *Théâtre*, 2 Vols. (Paris: Editions de la pleíade, 1951), Vol. I, première version, p. 326.

9 (Paris: Desclée de Brouwer, 1938).

IX

Meditations on the idea of a proof for the existence of God

What in the final analysis does it mean to *prove* something? It means to make another person, who may be myself moreover, acknowledge that whenever he accepts a certain proposition, he is also required to accept some other proposition which only seemed to be independent of the former and the truth of which he doubted when it was considered by itself. But we need not restrict ourselves to purely logical considerations: a number of other points deserve to be clarified.

In the first place, to prove is *to prove to;* to oneself no doubt, in many cases; but to oneself construed as the other. In any case, I must seem to occupy a more advanced or a more dominating position with respect to the other: but always relative to the other, and so far as he too occupies a certain position in this connection, and not in an absolute sense. Let us use the expression *field of apperception* to designate the set of propositions which, whether explicitly entertained or not, seem to be certain to a particular individual, propositions which he holds and which he can therefore be responsible for, propositions of which he can say: I distinctly see that . . . etc. When I venture to prove to the other that . . . , his field of apperception is in a way also mine, i.e., I claim to apprehend it through the idea I have of it; but I admit at the same time that the converse is not true; that my field of apperception transcends, extends beyond, his. The proposition I am concerned to prove is for him part of a zone of darkness, contrasted with the zone which is illumined for him as for me. What then is the nature of this operation which I am trying to perform? I believe one can say that I am concerned with prevailing on him, i.e. on his attention, really, to focus an intense enough light on his field of apperception to enable him to reach that adjoining region in near proximity which was already illumined for me but is still in the shadows for him. This of course is a phenomenological description rather than a logical schema. It is quite evident that the moment we raise the question of validity— and we cannot describe the nature of a proof without raising it— we have to move to another level as it were, more precisely, we have to construe the above in terms of certain universal forms which *must be acknowledged,* a proof consisting in eliciting the organic unity of an idea where it seemed at first that we were confronted with disconnected elements, i.e. statements capable of being completely isolated from one another, some of which for example were true, others indeterminate or even false.

Let us try to apply these preliminary observations to the notion of a proof for the existence of God; and let us examine the phenomenological implications of the act of proving or wishing to prove that God exists. First of all, there is an "I am certain that . . . ," that something is the case which I do not doubt and do not specify insofar as I am concerned with proving to the other person that it is well-grounded (this certainty, for example, can be based on some striking personal experience or on a complete subjugation to some unquestioned authority). On the other hand, I am, from a conceptual point of view, sufficiently identified with the position of the other to be able to say to him: you admit that . . . , and if need be, i.e., if I find that this is denied, I can retreat to a line further back where I can be certain that I will meet him on the same ground (for example, our agreement that something exists). Once I have forced him into this corner, I will try to make him admit that if he really commits himself to the minimal assertion, i.e., to what he apprehends as necessarily true, rather than to the mere utterance of it, or better, to a blind countersigning of it, he will see it expanding, so to speak, to the point where it coincides with the other affirmation to which he refuses to subscribe: God exists; it is true that God exists.

Hence if the act of proving implies a claim, an "I commit myself to . . ." it must be added that this claim seems to be based not on a proud awareness of a power I know I possess, but ontologically on a unity which is invariably disclosed to the mind which achieves a certain degree of inner concentration. It is clear that whoever acts or claims to do so as a conjurer, who passes himself off as unequaled in the art of . . . , will appear to the other person not as a philosopher or a theologian, but as a charlatan of theology or philosophy, i.e., as a non-philosopher or a non-theologian *par excellence*.

On reflection, however, it seems that we are confronted with a scandal from which the classical philosophers have too often been tempted to avert their glance, and which is the following: generally it happens that this argument which claims universality, since it passes itself off as grounded in being, encounters the same kind of obstacles, ends in the same failure, as the performance of a hypnotist, conjurer, or medium who has lost his hand.

Can this scandalous situation be avoided if we urge that:

the argument fails either because it rests on a sophism which can be unmasked once and for all, and which the other, as it happens, has managed to identify;

or it fails because it happens to encounter what is essentially ill will, a stubborn obduracy?

The first solution, it seems to me, is not really tenable; we periodically witness the renewal of efforts to rehabilitate, to revamp, the traditional proofs of rational theology; I refer not only to neo-thomism, but to examples such as the more or less second-rate paper on the proof *a contingentia mundi* delivered by Professor Orestano at the International Congress of Philosophy. There is reason to think that at a certain level of philosophical reflection, it is just as impossible to declare the classical proofs adequate or completely adequate, as it is to reject them out of hand, the way we discard already postmarked stamps. The fact remains that certain distinguished minds found them adequate, and we cannot simply affirm that we are situated at a more advanced position than they on a road which is the highroad of reason. Don't we have reason instead to assume that something essential is implied in their argument which cannot be completely expressed, something we try to explicate without being altogether confident that we can do so?

We must regard the second solution as completely vulnerable. When I accuse the other person of ill-will, I have to ask myself on reflection whether his attitude suggests this to me because it is opposed to my own will, my will to persuade him, to subjugate him. When I claim to prove to the other that his doubts are mistaken, and *a fortiori* capable of denial, I have to acknowledge that in a sense I am trying to exercise my will to power over him, to get the better of him—and that I thereby tend to put him on the defensive and to provoke his will to resist. This is not all there is to it, however, nor does it even reveal the fundamental aspect of the situation: assuming that this ill-will in fact exists, we still must try to understand it and not confine ourselves to stigmatizing or lamenting it. It is much more useful to try by an effort of sympathy to situate oneself on the inside of what may be justifiably called ill-will, although to itself it must appear to be something quite different. There are grounds for the view that if the other person gave a full explanation of his rejection, he could in fact qualify it by saying: I refuse to take this road, I do not agree to take it because it leads where I do not want to go. In a sense this is instructive, but there is also a sense in which it is completely ambiguous. Why doesn't the other person want to conclude with the affirmation of God's existence which is discovered at the end of a road that had been masked from his view? Perhaps the reason is that the affirmation seems to him to be inconsistent with the elementary data of experience, with, for example, the existence of suffering and of evil in all their forms; it may also be the case that the affirmation blunts his *élan* which prompts him as a free creature to consider himself as containing an inexhaustible potential; in this case, "where I do not want to go" means "I do not wish God to exist, for if he exists I become limited in my being, i.e., I am negated." This is of paramount importance and, in effect, expresses the peculiar fact that what the "demonstrator" advances as a perfection is construed by the person who contradicts him as an obstacle to the expansion of his own being, a being which is more or less tacitly divinized, hence which is a negation of the Sovereign Good. This implies that there isn't even a minimal agreement between the two—for there is disagreement not only on the means, on the course to choose, but also on the ends, on what is essentially better. However, both reflection and history seem to point to the same fact, that the notion of a proof is inseparable from a prior affirmation, the truth of which one is later led to doubt, or rather, led to put in parentheses; we have to remove the parentheses. Proof is a phase of an inner eristic, and is always subordinate to an unvarying condition, or more precisely, to a system of values which cannot be questioned. Hence the less one acknowledges these values, or in other words, the weaker the spiritual tradition embodied in this system becomes—the more difficult it will be to produce a proof, just when the need for it becomes correspondingly pronounced. Thus we confront the paradox that generally, proof is efficacious only when we can if necessary do without it; while on the other hand, it will always seem circular to the person to whom it is directed and who must be persuaded. It must be repeated that we cannot substitute proof for belief; but what is more, there is a profound sense in which proof presupposes belief, in which it can only help to evoke an inner reaffirmation of the person who feels within himself a cleavage between his faith and what he takes to be a special requirement of his reason.

In a more significant sense, I think it is necessary to observe once and for all that the fact of *proving to* implies the existence of

a communication between oneself and the other which is only possible on the basis of a concrete situation which philosophy—or
theology—must take into account if it wants to avoid being
isolated in a zone of a false or at least indifferent abstraction. Such
a concrete situation implies the active presence or rather absence
of a κοινόν τι, [a common ground] or better, the presence of a
vinculum, which is itself concrete, although in a distinctively ideal
sense of this term.

One of the most serious mistakes made by a certain philosophical
view which is not essentially thomistic but which nevertheless represents the current interpretation of thomism, seems to involve
the postulation of *natural man* as a transhistorical constant. This
notion of *homo naturalis* is itself dangerously ambiguous, because
we are not justified in identifying the natural man whose nature
develops on the hither side of a revelation of which he is unaware
but which he is perhaps ready to receive—with the natural man
who pits himself *against* a supernatural power which he conceives,
combats and rejects. What is more: natural man is an historical
reality and is defined with respect to an image of a universe
changing in time; he is in history even when he tries to envision
himself in a world conceived as alien to history, for this world still
expresses his nature in its various forces and exigencies as these
are realized in any given era. Given the truth of this view, it is
clear that natural man not only evolves, since *homo naturalis* is
chiefly *homo historicus,* but that he can also disintegrate; I believe
that this disintegration in large measure explains not the impossibility—it would be inappropriate to use this word—but the
relative ineffectiveness on the apologetic level at least, of so-called
rational theology: and there are many people of "advanced"
opinions in social or artistic circles who cannot decide to give this
up. In the final analysis, it is because the unity of man has been
shattered, because his world is broken—that we confront this
scandal of proofs which are logically irrefutable but which in fact
exhibit a lack of any persuasive power.

This scandal, however, cannot be an obstacle in any absolute sense for the philosophical thought which comes into collision with it. I fully agree with Mr. Le Senne that the obstacle as such has a positive, stimulating value; and the problem here is to determine precisely how that change can take place whereby the obstacle becomes a spring-board. This change is only possible insofar as I succeed not merely in elucidating but also in accepting the fully vital and dramatic value of the situation in which I am involved whenever I unsuccessfully attempt to convey my certitude to the other person.

I am a believer confronting a non-believer. And as I have indicated: I am sorely tempted to interpret this non-belief as implying bad faith or ill-will; we have also observed that I have to resist this temptation and open out to an understanding of the other such that I will be able to imagine this inner attitude as it is for him (and not in terms of my own). For else I will be induced to think that something has been *given to me* which has not been given *to him;* further, I must reflect on the nature of this gift and of its counterpart. An examination of the conditions under which faith can be construed as a reality is appropriate here; I believe that this inquiry will help us to see that the word "reality" cannot be construed in this context either in terms of validity or practical efficacy. The question is rather one of discerning whether the believer—or rather whether I who claim to possess faith, have truly understood how to respond to the appeal addressed to me; such a response involves a testimony to which my life may or may not bear witness, a life construed not only in terms of specific, enumerable acts, or not mainly so, but in terms of what I give to, or radiate for, the other. In other words, the essence of real faith completely precludes assimilation to a possession of which I can avail myself; as soon as I claim this to be the case, faith is denatured; hence I am now led to judge the discrepancy between myself and this faith which I thought was my due, i.e. to take into account my non-belief which exists at the center of what I call my faith. A communication is immediately established, therefore, between me and the person who avows simply that he is a non-believer—a communication established in the light of truth which is also a light of charity; this communication can also eventuate in a transposition, which is not objective, to be sure—for this is meaningless—affecting the relation I established between myself and the other; for I can arrive at the point of acknowledging that the other who avows he is a non-believer, bears witness more truly and more effectively than I who claim to be a believer, to the reality embodied in my act of faith.

It is clear, however, that this dialectic must itself be reflected. I must examine why it is that I oppose the fullness of faith to those rudiments of belief which I discern in myself. Is it sufficient to reply that I judge a factual datum in terms of an ideal which overflows it on all sides, but one of which I can only have a conception? This would be tantamount to degrading faith to the point where we can see in it nothing but an impulse; it would at the same time resurrect the problem of the object of faith, a problem which, as both history and reflection concur in showing, offers no solution whatever; in short, it means a regression to the shabbiest and most sterile agnosticism such as we find at the end of the 19th century. In this connection it is reflection and reflection alone which as always, enables us to ask whether the distinction between the ideal and the real is still viable in this context, whether it is not wrongly transposed to a zone other than that of objects to which it is alone applicable. Nevertheless, it is here that traditional philosophy and the dialectic of affirmation as I conceive it, meet. However, it must be stressed that this reflection, however close to the ontological argument it may be, is directed on an *I believe* which can be explicated only when construed in the form of *I believe in You, who are my sole recourse.*

We can distinguish between problem and mystery in terms of the above complex train of reflections; for this reality to which I am open when I invoke it can in no way be identified with an objective datum the nature of which must be comtemplated and cognitively determined. It may be said at once that this reality gives *me* to myself insofar as I give myself to it; it is through the mediation of the act in which I center myself on it, that I truly become a subject. I repeat, *that I become a subject:* the fatal error of a certain species of idealism really consists in a failure to see that being a subject is not a fact nor a point of departure, but a conquest and a goal.

X

Orthodoxy versus conformism

It is not without serious apprehension that I have here consented to express all too briefly my thoughts on a theme which is of really paramount importance to me, but which I cannot deal with without feeling that I am walking the narrow edge of an abyss. In the first place, there are a number of things a person may affirm which are particularly intimidating to him because they lead him to see how unworthy he is of uttering them. On the other hand, it is next to impossible to avoid causing serious misunderstandings within the scope of a few pages, and in particular, to avoid shocking some reader without being able to offer him later the assurances he rightfully demands.

When we say "we catholics" in the context of some problem or other that has been raised, we are ripe for trespassing the bounds of catholicism and we almost cease to think as catholics. The following remarks revolve around this somewhat paradoxical assertion which occurs in one of my own books. Perhaps I shall be better understood if I say that I am concerned with separating as much as possible two ideas which we are all in danger of confusing with one another, i.e., orthodoxy, on the one hand, and conformism on the other.

It seems to me that the essential characteristic of orthodoxy will elude us if we persist in thinking that it is merely a question of maintaining certain correct tenets of dogma. On the level of affirmation, orthodoxy is an absolute fidelity to the *Word* which has been made flesh; it is the fidelity of an adhesion or a response; it is incarnated in the *Credo* which is intoned at every hour of the day and in every place by the voice of the *Universal Church,* and in every man of faith so far as he participates in this living Body. "Nothing more strangely indicates an enormous and silent evil of modern society," Chesterton wrote, "than the extraordinary use which is made nowadays of the word 'orthodox.' In former days the heretic was proud of not being a heretic. It was the kingdoms of the world and the police and the judges who were heretics. He was orthodox. He had no pride in having rebelled against them; they had rebelled against him. . . . The man was proud of being orthodox, was proud of being right. . . . He was the centre of the universe; it was around him that the stars swung. . . . But a few modern phrases have made him boast of it. He says, with a conscious laugh, 'I suppose I am very heretical,' and looks round for applause. The word 'heresy' not only means no longer being wrong; it practically means being clear-headed and courageous. The word 'orthodoxy' not only no longer means being right; it practically means being wrong." [1] Chesterton's observation is more true today than it was thirty years ago. It would be easy to show that a certain religious and even christian philosophy of the present-day has arrived at the point of treating heterodoxy as a positive value. This has been possible only because of a fundamental contempt which, it must be openly acknowledged, allows the essential characteristics of christianity to elude it; which in effect lets evaporate the revealed content without which christianity ceases to be a religion and degenerates into what one should not even call a philosophy, but an anemic and contradictory ethics.

Orthodoxy is fidelity to the word of God, but this is tantamount to saying that the word loses its meaning and application as soon as it moves out of the supernatural order which is that of the incarnation. To be sure, we hear of Marxist orthodoxy, for example, but I venture to say, only so far as Marx is made super-human, and where his thought is treated not as a doctrine, but rather as the Absolute tidings, or as a Revelation; and this is clearly absurd and even self-contradictory since the very idea of such Tidings or Revelation is inconsistent with the purely materialistic content of Marxism. The more we move out of the zone of prophecy, whether it be true or usurped, to bury ourselves in the realm of an impersonal science, the more impossible it becomes to talk of orthodoxy, or indeed, of heresy.

Conformism, whether intellectual, aesthetic, or political, implies submission to a certain order emanating not from a person but from a group which claims that it incarnates what *must* be thought, what *must* be valued, in a particular country at a specific moment in time, but a group which is careful, to be sure, not to acknowledge the stigma of relativity which affects every mode of knowledge or taste.

Contrary to what was claimed by a fundamentally sophistic philosophy, grafted in the 19th century onto the positive sciences on which it was but a parasite, it is absurd to see in the exercise of virtue a moral conformism; for any virtue worthy of the name, whether practiced by believer or non-believer, is not a mechanical obedience to an order, but the characteristic act of freedom.

Moral conformism may be encountered among those who practice a certain virtue only because it—or more frequently its image —is of advantage in the milieu to which they belong, and more particularly, to those who set the fashion. Today when we speak of "right-mindedness" and the expression is interpreted in the ironical and pejorative way with which we are familiar, it is certainly moral conformism we have in mind. Two observations, however, must be made.

In the first place, nothing in the final analysis helps us to decide on the reasons why a certain person practices a certain virtue;

considering that such reasons are indiscernible to him most of the time, we cannot determine whether behind what seems to us to be a simple submission to certain usages, there is not concealed a moral spontaneity expressive of his very soul.

On the other hand—and this seems to me to be *fundamental*—the moment I denounce the "right-minded individual" whom I see in the other person, i.e., as soon as I set myself up as his judge, thus violating one of the major precepts of the Gospel, it is I who act like a pharisee; for I implicitly claim a "greater right-mindedness" for myself, free of the banal constraints which to my mind fetter the behavior of the other. We need not linger any longer in the barren regions of abstraction: it seems to me quite clear that with respect to many catholics of the left who do not spare their sarcasm for the catholics of the right who are treated as "right-minded" and as whited sepulchres, we witness the development of a reversed conformism which is in danger of degenerating rapidly into a conformism *tout court*. With the advent of the frightful Spanish civil war which has convulsed the world and the individual conscience for more than two years, we are confronted with two inverse and clearly opposed theses, both of which are expressed in an equally categorical manner: "we catholics must pray for General Franco and for those who wish to free Spain from marxist domination."—"we catholics must take sides with those who refuse to surrender their country to a dictator supported by moroccan mercenaries and the forces of fascism." From the catholic or christian point of view, it is inadmissible that a temporal cause can possess an absolute value when abstracted from the means used to serve it. Even if it is conceded that this distinction of means and ends is acceptable on the political level—and in this realm too, there are many things which can deeply wound the conscience—it is, on the contrary, the essence of christianity to reject it completely. I venture to say that when catholics of the left and right confront one another on the Spanish civil war, they actually represent two clashing conformisms each of which is carrying out a command issuing from such-and-such an organ which daily supports and reinforces the preconceived opinions of its readers. But a drama such as the one which is unfolding on the Iberian peninsula is so complex that it transcends the schematic ideas which are formed of it by badly informed readers, who are in any case, fed on tendentious news; the consequence is that the adoption of a seriously thought out position, i.e. one which is not based on emotion, may be held to be practically impossible. How can we avoid the conclusion that, however paradoxical it may seem, if catholicism is primarily a *need for universality,* our responsibility as catholics is to recognize first of all that there is surely no sense in wishing to think here *as* catholics; but the question rather is that when confronted with something which brings out both the best and the worst in us, we must adopt a critical attitude (wrongly discredited today and often on behalf of a fallacious and simple-minded notion of intuition); and secondly, not to swerve towards one side or another from that justice and charity without which there is only partisan warfare.

I know from experience that this attitude is a thankless one, and that it is even opposed to our natural bent. What is more, it seems to me that there is an almost insuperable temptation for a catholic more than for anyone else, to organize his convictions into a seemingly coherent whole each part of which supports the other; there are two reasons for this: on the one hand, it represents a way of strengthening the parts of the whole which are the weakest; and on the other hand, systematization satisfies the need to confront the adversary with a compact unity which one believes can intimidate him. Hence it is entirely natural that conformism in every sphere is construed as the pure and simple extension of orthodoxy. Nonetheless, this is an optical illusion whose real consequences are always in danger of leading to disaster. It is hard for orthodoxy to avoid infection, so that orthodoxy itself is treated as religious conformism and thus seems to be exposed to all the criticisms to which submission to some watchword is exposed. It is easy to show how this is so in every sphere; for example, in the realm of science. To say: a catholic as such has to adopt a position which is opposed to the law of evolution or Einstein's theory, is to forget at one's own peril the complete incommensurability between the realm of transcendence to which he is related as believer—and the zone which, to be sure, has limits but which is nevertheless autonomous, of positive knowledge. Nothing can be more mistaken than the idea of a continuity of principle and of fact between the invariants of Faith and some conception which is essentially relative and hence capable of modification, and which expresses the state of science at some given time; and I might add that nothing would be more imprudent than the effort to exploit on an apologetic level a physical or biological discovery which one isolates from its context, and whose consequences are unjustifiably extrapolated.

If this is true, are we not then induced to create a gulf between the order of Faith on the one hand, and thought and even life, on the other? I think it is particularly important to clear up any ambiguities that may arise in this connection.

How often have we heard non-believers scornfully declare to us: "You Christians begin with a premise which is already accepted as true, and do not advance under your own power; which is the same as to say that in the game of knowledge and of life you use loaded dice." Now this accusation would only be justified if we had reason to concede that orthodoxy must inevitably give way to conformism. And this is precisely what I reject without the slightest hesitation. We must indicate the existence of a certain discontinuity here so that we can disclose the nature of that freedom whereby we become men. We must, however, be clear about this discontinuity.

The profound distinction made by Bergson in *Les Deux Sources de la Morale et de la Religion,* between a closed and an open morality, is well known. The first or closed morality is that of a being who is an integrated part of the society to which he belongs; he and it together are absorbed in the single task of individual and social preservation. The society therefore is supposed to be immutable. The other morality implies an impetus, a need for movement. The morality of the Gospel is essentially that of the open soul. "The act by which the soul opens out broadens and raises to pure spirituality a morality enclosed and materialized in ready-made rules." ² The open morality is expressed in a set of appeals made to the conscience of each of us by those who represent what is best in humanity. I believe the bergsonian philosophy should be extended here beyond the boundaries of the ethical: not only is it true that authentic christian thought is an open thought *par excellence* (and we can say that it denies itself as such whenever it closes in upon itself) but it can be held that a real orthodoxy creates those conditions rooted in the supernatural which unfold the most spacious and unbounded horizons for human knowledge and action.

If this is so, what I said a moment ago about the discontinuity between the order of Faith and that of experience must be complemented, or more precisely, counterbalanced. To be sure, we are in no way concerned with extricating some revelatory content from certain corollaries possessing the same certainty as, and drawn for example from, the domains of science or politics as the latter manifest themselves at some particular moment in time. On the other hand, however, the person who lives in the light of Christ and of his Promise finds that he is thereby oriented in a way which permits him to better grasp, not in the abstract or in theory, but *hic et nunc,* the conditions of truth and of right action. But this only remains true insofar as his fidelity does not degenerate into that self-complacency or self-sufficiency, that satisfaction with oneself which characterizes the pharisee—the pharisee whose presence we can all recognize with a little attention, within ourselves.

What distorts everything for the non-believer or heretic—at least for the person who is proud of his heresy—is the view that open thought has the responsibility of remaining suspended in connection with the ultimate character of human destiny. Hence indecision with respect to what is essential seems to be the mark and the privilege of an illumined mind; sometimes, in fact, one goes even further than this and agrees more or less overtly that only negation can satisfy the deep desires of a free being, and that affirmation is a prison. These assumptions which, when distinguished by reflection, seem disconcerting to say the least, are really implied in what we may appropriately call free-thought; and a lengthy analysis would be necessary to show how they have been able not so much to impose themselves on the lucid mind, as to insidiously permeate the very mental tissues of many contemporary minds; it is clear, however, that orthodoxy, when it is thought of and willed as it really is, creates the spiritual climate in which affirmation can expand the most freely. "If we want reform," Chesterton declares, "we must adhere to orthodoxy"; for, as he continues, "Men who begin to fight the Church for the sake of freedom and humanity end by flinging away freedom and humanity if only they may fight the Church." [3] Events of the past few years throw a brilliant light on the relation linking orthodoxy in the real sense with the safeguards of what may appropriately be called *the positive element* in man—a positivism which all the new masters of our ravaged Europe implacably pursue with the same violence. And it is both right and necessary to add that if a small group of protestants in Germany put up a heroic resistance which deserves all our admiration, against an official church infected by neo-paganism, it does so only so far as it remained faithful to the Word of Christ, i.e., to the extent that its roots were still anchored in the orthodoxy which it seemed to repudiate.

Perhaps in the last analysis—and in concluding I wish to stress this point—perhaps it is with respect to interconfessional relations that we should be most on our guard against the kind of latent pharisaism into which we are constantly in danger of falling whenever we construe orthodoxy as a superior sort of conformism instead of as fidelity.

Few controversies to my mind are more futile and ultimately more exasperating than those which periodically oppose catholics to protestants, both of whom are nevertheless endowed with the same good will, with the same desire for mutual understanding, but who try to sharpen the nature of their agreement and disagreement. As soon as the catholic declares to the protestant that he, as a catholic, or more precisely, the Church, is a guardian of a universal truth of which the protestant grasps only a few fragments which are tainted with error; in short, when he wholly denies that he is on the same level as his adversary, he destroys the conditions which are requisite for debate, and even though the encounter takes place under seemingly favorable auspices, it is practically impossible for it not to end in bitterness, despair, and incurable misunderstanding. No doubt the latter is not altogether avoidable in fact if not in principle; yet the fact that christians do find it impossible to understand one another is such a scandal from the viewpoint of the Gospel that it must be rejected with the same unequivocal and abiding refusal that evil in its various forms should wrest from us. If we fully exploit the distinction I have tried to make between orthodoxy and conformism, we can, I believe, glimpse the path we have to follow here.

In Father Congar's *Ecumenicalism,* an admirable book in many ways, we find this courageous statement which is marked, as it were, by an heroic evangelism: "Whenever we act against someone, even if only to combat error, we do not act like catholics." [4] Whatever other effect this statement may have, it could be offensive, and I can see quite well the sort of objections it might raise. It seems evident to me, however, that here the catholic is not merely permitted—the fact is, he is required—to categorically oppose all claims. It is to the extent that a heresy claims to be the truth that it can be condemned. Nevertheless—and the whole problem is here—it is still necessary to oppose to this claim something else besides an inverse claim or assertion which the other person can identify with an opposed claim. And it seems to me that in this respect it is Charity and Charity alone which transcends such opposition and which can refute; and this is precisely the fundamental lesson of the New Testament on every level of interpretation. If this is so, Orthodoxy can be recognized as such by the Other, that Stranger towards whom we tend in our anguish, only in the light of that plenary Charity which it is the nature of Orthodoxy to radiate, inasmuch as it falls short of being that Absolute Fidelity which is its very essence. Can it not be said, therefore, that any lack of Charity, not so much on the part of the Church as on the part of those whose tremendous mission it is to act in its name, constitutes an attack on Orthodoxy itself; that a failure of this kind obviously tends to make orthodoxy appear to be a claim in the other person's eyes, when the fact is that it is a perpetual witness? that to this extent it betrays orthodoxy and Christ whose witness it is? Hence the sighing, disdainful condescension many of us feel towards our separated brethren, verbally expressed by the phrase "we catholics" as opposed to "you poor, blind devils," may be condemned, I think, in the very name of catholicism. The same dialectic I tried to exhibit above in connection with right-thinking is again discerned here. Election, in the christian sense of the term, is measured primarily by the increase in responsibility resting on the person who is elected. It seems to me that this is entirely true of the catholic as such. If it is true that it is granted to him to think of the heretic quite differently than the heretic can think of the catholic, this can only be so on condition that he divest himself of anything that might resemble a feeling of superiority, privilege, or a possession, that he rather sharpen his inner awareness of his personal shortcomings and his obligations with respect to the heretic; it is only on condition that he assume the burden of the other's errors, not impute them as a crime to the other or congratulate himself as the pharisee does on being so wonderfully exempt from them himself. In fact, how can we forget that our status as christians makes us witnesses? We can only bear witness for orthodoxy, i.e., for Christ, if we have a humility which is not an attitude, but rather implies the recognition of a real and inescapable situation; but we should not forget either that although we cannot fail to bear witness for all, we can on the other hand bear witness against our Master and thereby augment the number of those who daily re-enact his Crucifixion. The mistake of every conformism is to believe that a middle term can be inserted between these two kinds of witnesses, between this Yes and this No into which every spiritual destiny has to crystallize, without which there is room only for the fleeting mists of opinion. But these mists are dispersed in the night when there is no sun to absorb them.

NOTES

1 G. K. Chesterton, *Heretics* (New York: Dodd, Mead and Co., 1927), pp. 11-12.
2 Henri Bergson, *The Two Sources of Morality and Religion,* Transl. by R. A. Audra and C. Brereton (New York: Henry Holt and Co., 1935), p. 51.
3 *Orthodoxy* (London: Bodley Head, 1908), p. 247; 256.
4 [Editions du Cerf, p. 320. See the following chapter. Transl. note.]

XI

On the fringe of the ecumenical

I am not qualified to give an appraisal on either historical or strictly theological grounds of the distinguished work Father Congar has recently published on the problem of Ecumenicalism entitled *Chrétiens Désunis-Principes d'un Oecuménisme Catholique;*[1] in what follows I shall be careful not to venture onto strange ground, leaving to others more competent than myself the task of providing commentaries or expressing the reservations they think necessary in connection with the above dual perspective. After indicating what I believe to be the essential features of the author's position, I intend only to offer some observations of a philosophical nature which will render that position somewhat more comprehensible.

Father Congar begins by drawing up a concise list of the chief dissenting viewpoints which have arisen in Christianity from its beginnings. He forcefully points out that the continuance of our divisions has become like "a heavy stone rolled before the tomb where unity has been imprisoned by early misunderstandings."[2] Personally, I am deeply grateful to the author for having stressed in passing two essential points.

In the first place, in contrast to a number of tendentious or crudely superficial interpretations, he has reminded us that "the Reform in the given circumstances, was opposed to a part of these circumstances, and was, with the complicity of the remainder, an essentially religious movement, an attempt to renew the sources of the religious life"; that its concern at the outset was "to rediscover the inviolable mystery transcending all conceptual thought; to rediscover behind a literature of edification a Gospel which lived and which flowed freely from its source; behind pious practices which were sometimes debased by the highest bid and by various irregularities (Indulgences), a religion which was simple, pure, virile, chaste; behind a priesthood of every cloth, and titled prelates, a dialogue with God in the privacy of one's conscience." [3] It may be said that, by and large, at the origins of the great schisms—those having a positive spiritual value—there was usually an authentic spiritual feeling, and an authentically catholic one insofar as it was positive and pure. This must be fully acknowledged if we want to make an unbiased judgment on the Reformed Churches.

In the second place, Father Congar has very *courageously noted* that while heresy provides the opportunity for orthodox theology to progress in the sense that it leads the latter to emphasize and even significantly deepen a truth which is in danger of being gravely ignored, the same heresy on the other hand threatens to initiate a train of thought among its critics which is too unilateral. "Every time an error is made with respect to some question, the organism of the Church stiffens, its forces become polarized in order to resist the evil; confronted with the false affirmation which is . . . the exaggeration of a truth, the true affirmation is presented, is more precisely stated: in most cases, one does not fall back on the whole body of dogma but is satisfied to throw into greater relief, provide greater precision to, the truth which is ignored or denied by the error; hence error, always being biased, the opposed truth of dogma is also in danger of being biased." [4] Thus to cite one example among others, "doesn't the massive crystallization of sacramental realities around the *seven* sacraments which are amenable to a precise theological-canonical formulation,[5] contribute to a forgetfulness of the sacramental nature of the whole Church, of the whole of the christian life, at the expense of symbolical and liturgical meaning?" [6] The two are not logically related, but the one is a psychological effect of the other, linked, it seems to me, to the conditions on which attention is based, an attention oriented too exclusively towards areas that are threatened as one masses an army in a particularly vulnerable sector.

I am prepared to elaborate this crucial observation by adding that it is misleading to assume that heresy leaves intact the organisms it has abandoned; here bio-medical metaphors are no doubt the most reliable. Such a separation evokes from the organism a defensive reaction which is very similar to a fever, but which, while both necessary and beneficial to the organism, is itself opposed to the state of health strictly speaking. I venture to go even further than this, although I am not sure Father Congar would choose to follow me. I am not satisfied with affirming that heresy provides the theologian with an opportunity to recognize the necessity of stressing one aspect of the truth which had hitherto been insufficiently emphasized. It seems to me that heresy ought to initiate the kind of reflection with which repentance provides an inner analogy; for in the final analysis, if our behavior as christians was always up to the doctrine we professed, the aberration called heresy would have no cause to arise. Hence when we oppose it, we must not only accuse the heretic and transfer the whole weight of error to his sinful pride, but we must also accept the fact that we are at least partly responsible for the error into which he has fallen. From the philosophical point of view at any rate—I have sufficiently warned the reader that I do not speak here as a theologian—it seems evident to me that heresy, even as it is viewed by the Church, cannot be considered a kind of external calamity which the church has only to take note of; in a way, heresy is within it, although from another point of view, the Church as Church, as Body of Christ, is supreme, is in all eternity clearly untouched by it, and the idea of a sin of the Church as Berdyaev conceives it, for example, should be firmly rejected by the catholic. Here we touch on a paradox which is in reality a mystery, and which is at the very heart of our subject.

Father Congar sums up in a few fairly simple propositions what we understand by the unity of the Church. I apologize for having to cite them here, but they will help to clarify what follows.

"The Church is the family of God, established through the communication to mankind of the trinitarian life of grace, faith, and charity; it is one as God is one."

"The communication of the trinitary life is accomplished in Christ and in Christ alone. The Church is the Body of Christ, linked with the life of He who alone may return to the bosom of the Father from whom he comes."

"We are related to the life of Christ through the sacraments in which our faith is expressed and vivified. Baptism and the Eucharist are the ultimate grounds for our forming a single body which is the Body of Christ." [7]

Furthermore, it should be added that in accordance with all that we know about our condition as "incarnate beings, members of the same species, destined by nature to live our human life in a society, communicating with one another and nourishing our minds only on sensible things," it is entirely understandable that "the society of the Holy Trinity which is being formed in this world develops in a way connatural with this same humanity, i.e. into a Church which has the form of a society, embodied in sensible realities, teaching, governing, active, and militant." [8] In particular, it is the essence of the sacraments to be sensible signs, symbolic and collective gestures, adapted to the fact that we are progressing towards the substance of heavenly realities. We might consider in this context the very characteristic passage of Hugo of St. Victor: "*Usque hodie Christus amicos suos in Scriptura sacra et sacramentis Ecclesiae atque aliis visibilibus virtutum exercitiis quasi quadam corporali praesentia consolatur.*" [9] The Church on this earth, insofar as it accomplishes the destiny of Israel, according to the very logic of the Incarnation, will be wholly sensible and wholly divine, theandric as is Christ. "Since faith is manifested in the Church in human terms and through the ministry of men, it will be dogmatic and authoritarian; since the life of Christ is manifested there by means of sensible sacraments and the ministry of men, it will be sacramental and sacerdotal." [10]

Hence from the catholic viewpoint we are led to distinguish between both the Mystical Body of the Church which is and will be eternal, where Christ is its sole authority, and where only a hierarchy of saintliness and virtue is conceivable such that a Pope in this respect can be further from Christ than a humble and ignorant woman,

and the Church as a Society or Institution, where there is a sovereign and subjects, which is a body in the sociological and juridical sense of the term, something therefore which is of a certain magnitude deployed in the world and which possesses distinct parts; but

we are also led to conceive of a unity of the two, an "organic unity similar to that which links body and soul, or better, which exists between the divine and human nature in Christ; this unity is created on the level of and by means of the Sacraments; the Church itself, with respect to its terrestrial being, is like a sacrament in which everything has a sensible meaning, which attains an inner unity of grace." "It is just as true to say: *Ubi Christus, ibi Ecclesia*, since as soon as the Spirit of Christ is communicated the Church exists, as it is to say: *Ubi Petrus, ibi Ecclesia* since the inner community of life is realized through human means, by an apostolic ministry which had in Peter himself its visible criterion of unity." [11]

It is particularly important to notice not only that the fundamental differences which have arisen in the course of history have been concerned with the nature of the Church, but also—and contrary to what some protestants have said—that these differences by no means represented an extrinsic aspect of christianity, but rather something essential to it, involving, in sum, the Church as the prolongation of the Incarnation. What is more, I am personally tempted to ask whether the heterodoxy which cropped up at the ecclesiological level, was not already present in the manner in which one thought of the Incarnation itself, of Christ himself, although this perhaps went unnoticed because of terminological ambiguities. In any event, this was the feeling the audience could not help having when Pastor Boegner and Mr. Florowski met with members of the catholic clergy including Father Congar himself, at the *Union pour la Vérité* to discuss the results of the ecumenical meeting which took place at Oxford in the summer of 1957. At that meeting it was obvious that the misunderstandings which accumulated were primarily caused by the concept of catholicity.

In his book Father Congar points out that by catholicity we must understand the universality of truth, of *redemption* of spiritual goods and gifts, as well as universality in time; the dynamic universality of which catholicity as a body consists, directly stems, moreover, from the unity and unicity of the Church; and these express the indissoluble bond uniting the Church as Mystical Body with the Church as Institution. This universality is not only compatible with an extreme diversity of religious experiences and ways of approach to God: *it also requires it.* However, it at the same time proposes to purify these elements that it gathers up, i.e., strip them of their particularistic or exclusive claims. In the present context I shall confine myself to summarizing in a few words certain propositions the different applications of which the catholic reader should have no difficulty in perceiving. On the other hand, I should like to show what form the problem threatens to take for the non-catholic christian and indirectly, for the non-believer.

It is hardly possible for the non-catholic christian to refrain from rebelling here against what for him seems dangerously akin to a presumptuous claim; and I have personally felt this very acutely at the meeting mentioned above. "This universality, this catholicity taken in the full sense, the protestant will ask especially, how can you make such a categorical claim for your Church, when it is after all only one Church among others in the observable pattern of world history? Why are you not aware of the offensive and even scandalous nature of your affirmation that you alone are the guardians of the Truth in its wholeness, while we only possess some broken fragment or other, some tainted residue?"

As far as I am concerned, I note that if we consider the question on the level of *having,* if we take the word "guardian" literally, the non-catholic's feeling of indignation is not only explicable, but is in large measure justified. The fact is that we can only be guardians of what can be identified with a thing, not of a truth in the spiritual sense of this term, but of a formula or a recipe. It is almost inevitable for a protestant to attribute this claim to a catholic who makes imprudent statements to the effect that his Church *possesses* all the true formulae, all the supreme recipes; and far from envying him for this, he is rather in danger of turning away from these, with the feeling that they are linked to a presumption contrary to the very spirit of the Gospel.

We must not have any illusions about the "soothing" value of a distinction invariably made for the benefit of the non-catholic between the spiritual quality of the heretic considered as an individual soul or as a person—and his doctrine which is repudiated without qualification (even when it is conceded that it is true in what it affirms and false in what it denies—since affirmation and denial here are not really separable). For it seems to me that in this context we are not concerned with any doctrine; or more precisely, what is thought and condemned as an heretical doctrine by the catholic, is grasped and lived from within as tradition, as Church; *a tradition, a Church which includes martyrs in its bosom,* and this is a serious matter which perhaps is not ordinarily weighed. For me the existence of these martyrs is sufficient, even if this view should raise protests; is, I repeat, sufficient to confer reality on a determinate community which in a way completely transcends the judgments one is justified in making relative to the doctrine professed by its members. And we return here, but on a much deeper level, to the observation I made at the outset following in the steps of Father Congar, with respect to the impossibility for the catholic of relieving himself of his responsibility for not merely the causes of heresy but for its development as well.

It seems to me that this is why any controversy in this area should be considered not only as obviously sterile, but also as external to what is really in question, to something which can barely be captured in words. In fact it would be far too simple-minded to admit that there is on the one hand someone who, be-

cause he is a member of the Roman Catholic Church, possesses
the truth in its organic wholeness (even if, as is inevitably the case,
he grasps it only to the extent that his inadequate capacities allow),
and on the other hand, a heretic who pridefully clutches a few
fragments of this same truth which he has been taught to isolate
from the whole of which they are parts, and who claims to establish
these fragments as an absolute. Thus construed, this opposition, although we cannot go so far as to assert that it is completely meaningless, is only a faulty schema of what should actually be interpreted as a drama taking place within the christian conscience
itself. By an inexorable dialectic, we are stricken with the same
blindness we claim to discern in the other person. I am well aware
that I shall be held guilty of obscurantism here: someone will point
out that if I must practice humility for myself as a christian, this is
not the case with respect to a transcendent Truth of which I am no
more than an insignificant witness. Nothing can be more true; but it
is just this word "witness" which seems essential to me here and
which we must consider. The whole question is one of determining
the conditions under which I can effectively be a witness for this
Truth.

The other day, when the discussion I have often alluded to took
place, I could not help observing that despite the relevance of the
arguments advanced by the catholics, the effects these had on their
questioners was obviously the opposite of that which they had
hoped to produce; I mean that they strengthened the feeling of indignation on the part of their separated brethren with respect to the
intransigence of the Church and its exaggerated claims. On the
other hand, how could they be blamed for having tried to eliminate
all ambiguity? As learned men they were obliged to speak plainly.

Does this not confront us then with a real antinomy? What positive conclusion can we infer from this contradiction? For me at any
rate, the latter is embodied in the fact that any discussion, as I
have noted, is probably harmful; for whoever professes a doctrine
does not have it in his power to avoid the appearance of claiming to
hold it as a privilege. I mean that the fact of exhibiting a truth does
not imply merely an ideal presentation of the truth by itself; it is a

concrete act performed by a particular person; in a way it is an act of aggression which threatens to compromise this same truth by converting it into a weapon. And this is especially serious when what is at issue is not a truth but the Truth, i.e., Christ.

Personally, I think I may venture to infer fom this that any testimony established at the level of discourse or of polemics, is always impure in some measure and is, as it were, essentially inadequate to the cause which it claims to make triumphant.

These remarks which may appear very meager, seem to me necessary for anyone who wishes to be fully cognizant of the problem raised at the present time by the ecumenical movement.

Father Congar has vigorously indicated the steps of this movement from the meeting at Stockholm in 1925, and the progress made since, to the meeting in Oxford last summer. While the Stockholm meeting was still permeated with the optimistic and evolutionary pathos characteristic of post-war liberalism, in the aftermath of the crisis which has spread everywhere since then, it has been acknowledged "that the Church, must not only better man's condition, but must be what God wished it to be in faith; . . . it is more clearly understood now than in 1925 that unity can be neither decreed nor created by human will, but that it will be the work of God in his own time." [12] Real ecumenicalism begins when it is granted that others—and not only individuals, but ecclesiastical bodies themselves—are also right, even though they assert something different than we do; that they too possess truth, saintliness, God's gifts, although their Christianity is not our own. "Ecumenicalism exists," an active member of the movement has remarked, "when one believes the other person is a Christian, not despite his particular religious confession, but as a member of it and through it." [13] In examining the possible justifications for this attitude, Father Congar shows that we cannot justify it in terms of a refusal to view any Church as the true Church, i.e., by placing the existence of the true Church at some uncertain time in the future; unquestionably we should rather summon it beyond any ecclesiastical or confessional truth (which is in any case indisputable), to participate in a sphere of action available and open to the renewed efforts of the Holy

Spirit which are not reducible to the ordinary frame of reference and logic of theology.[14] Some orthodox writers like Mr. Berdyaev, who, because of the audacity of his personal convictions cannot be considered a reliable representative of the confession in which he claims membership, believe that they can distinguish between their own Church as such a confession, which, while being more true than others in their opinion, nevertheless, and on their own admission, bears the signs of human limitation; and on the other hand, the ecumenical Church where plenitude is to be found and which is called to realize itself both within and beyond that Church, beyond its present limitations. Since the orthodox, even while maintaining the superiority and, we can even say, transcendence of their Church, have agreed to take part in ecumenical conferences, we perhaps may ask why the catholic Church has not considered it possible to adopt the same attitude, Father Congar justifies this refusal as follows: besides the fact that we cannot commit a body as large and as complex as the catholic Church to a movement which is still in its early stages and which seems destined to pass through many vicissitudes, he says, the catholic Church is justifiably afraid that if it does participate, the sense of unity which is essential to its being will tend to be weakened, to become enfeebled by contact with the variety of separate confessions; on the other hand, it perceives that in these meetings and conferences it cannot define the plenitude that it bears without attenuating it, and that it is forced to appear as a party when it is really a living whole which transcends any linguistic formulation. Finally, if it fully recognizes the existence of a government of the Holy Spirit transcending ecclesiastical government strictly speaking, one with which it furthermore believes it is in harmony but on which alone the final reunion of all christians into a single whole depends; if it is therefore ready to admit the existence of the sphere indicated above, hence of a metalogical zone, it largely distrusts the risks inherent in counting on an act of God's will which lies ahead of us and which will manifest itself in the future;[15] all this, I suppose, because of the perilously conjectural nature of those claims which assume that a government of this kind can be realized—and because it is of the essence of the catholic Church as such to keep its eyes fixed on the promises and the creative words on which it is founded, in a sense which implies a history to be sure but which at the same time rises above history.

Setting aside for the moment Father Congar's discussion of anglicanism and orthodoxy, I should like to lay stress here on the two final chapters of his work where the author tries to clarify the situation of dissenters and dissent in regard to the Church, and to outline a concrete program of catholic ecumenicalism.

If the dissenter, whom we assume to be in good faith, by nature never finds in his sect or Church the totality of principles on which the life with Christ is based, principles which are equally applicable to the realization and unity of the Church, he is nevertheless a member of the Church insofar as these principles are immanent in his confession however imperfectly embodied they may be. Hence the Church has members who really belong to it however invisible and incomplete this relation may be. In revealing a parallel between the "good dissenter" and the "bad catholic," Father Congar observes that "if the latter is worse than the former, his Church is still right and in itself offers him every means to saintliness; and that if the former is better, his Church is in error and only offers him an inadequate or illusory assistance." [16] According to my own point of view, i.e., one involving the sharpest possible understanding of *the other as other,* I can say that these affirmations which are perfectly natural for a catholic to make cannot fail to shock his "separated brethren" to whom they are nevertheless addressed. How could the latter avoid objecting *a priori* to a verdict which in their opinion must be biased by definition. The rejoinder to this is: we do not form a party since we are the whole, and it is only you who form a party. Now it is all too clear that this way of thinking is completely alien to the conditions requisite for any eristic; moreover, all discussion is in fact barred, since one claims to place oneself above all possible controversy.

I am not concerned with condemning this claim, but simply with showing that it is by nature unacceptable to anyone to whom it is addressed. When Father Congar further on defends the Church against the charge of imperialism, asserting that "what we desire is not the triumph of either an institutional apparatus, or even of a system of truths as such, but the triumph of life," [17] he says something which can only appear to his questioner as tainted with a remarkable presumption. And I think it necessary here to subject the ideas of *whole* and *part* to a more rigorous metaphysical analysis; or, what comes to the same thing, to carefully examine the meaning of the idea of plenitude. It is impossible, Father Congar vigorously maintains, for the reunion to take place, if instead of seeming to be a plenitude, our Church seems to those christians who still view it from the outside as a particular confession, one system among others, an "ism" which is as particular and as exclusive as the other "isms." [18] Nothing can be more true; but on the other hand, as long as the doctors of the Church proclaim that the dissident Church is in error and "only offers to its members inadequate or illusory assistance," it is impossible for the Catholic Church not to appear to outsiders precisely as the most exclusive, the most particularistic Church of all. The moment the other is induced to acknowledge that he is only a part which takes itself for the whole confronting the only real whole, he is converted; this is a mere truism which I nevertheless do not hesitate to emphasize because it is particularly important to point out that we are not gravitating around a problem here; I mean by this, around a difficulty which can be resolved, a difference which can be settled by some dialectical process or other, however conspicuous the good will which inspires it. Occasionally, one is tempted to ask whether any effort at clarification, even something ventured in a fervent spirit of charity, does not frustrate its purpose and is not, as I pointed out above, in danger of exacerbating a conflict the elimination of which one wishes with all one's heart.

We are compelled to accept the conclusion—as a matter of course, nor will anyone argue the point, that reunion—the word "reconciliation" seems to be unacceptable from the catholic point of view—can only be accomplished by means of grace and not by reason; for we are dealing here not with a problem but with a mystery. Nothing, however, would be more fallacious than to adopt as a consequence an attitude of passive resignation, or, if you like, of pure expectation. . . . Father Congar himself has said as much in a memorable formulation in which the essence of my own remarks is condensed [19] but what he asserts here is tantamount to saying that error can be attacked far more directly by some non-polemical yet positive action whereby catholics attempt not to purify their doctrine but rather to incarnate it and radiate it more effectively. They are not so much concerned with proclaiming: "Our Church is *the* Church, is Plenitude," as with making this truth evident not to their adversaries—for on this level the word no longer has nor can have meaning, but to our separated brethren, long suffering and partly blinded, to whom they convey a Life and a Light which is lent to them so that they may spread it in turn to others.

I may add myself—and I think that Father Congar will agree—that at the point we have reached in history, any collaboration between catholic and non-catholic christians for the purpose of establishing justice, helps in a manner to clear the way for that reunion which in itself is so difficult to conceive—insofar as such a collaboration eliminates the fatal distinction between "we others" and "you others" which is itself the basis of mutual friction and conflict.

Finally, Father Congar observes very courageously that there is after all a sense in which the Church, completely catholic from the point of view of the dynamic possibilities of its living substance, "explicitly realizes this catholicity only in an imperfect way, and that the division between Christians plays an important role in this imperfection"; that "what our separated brethren have taken away from the Church and realized outside of us is that in which our explicit and visible catholicity is deficient." [20] We need not confine ourselves to the statement that "because Russia is Orthodox and the Scandanavian countries Lutheran, the Church is deficient in a slavic representation or in a nordic expression of the single yet multiform grace of Christ; we may equally assume that in the measure that the existence of the schismatic forms of Christianity as represented in the various religious bodies is due to the affirmation of certain values of which they were acutely aware, these religious bodies also represent spiritual families which have their own message to convey and have in a sense their own mission." [21] "In the measure that Luther had an extraordinarily keen awareness of certain authentic values that he had as his mission to reveal for the benefit of the whole Church in becoming one of its elect, but by drawing them away from communion with all the other values, warping them, mingling error with them, he created the soul of dissent," [22]—yes, perhaps what is true of Lutheran religious experience is lacking, not to be sure to the substance of the catholic Church, but to the incarnation, to the full expression of its living principles. I am extremely grateful to Father Congar for having stressed so vigorously and so tactfully this nuance of meaning, which if it were expressed less forcefully, would threaten to give rise to a relativistic and therefore essentially heterodoxical interpretation. I recall having shocked a very saintly priest once by impulsively stating: "We have no idea whatever of what God thinks of the Reform." "But I know," this clergyman replied—wherein I think he was mistaken. Error, even transgression, has a mysterious role to play in the economy of providence; no creature, not even the most knowledgeable doctors, can be permitted to treat it simply as "what ought not to have taken place." More precisely, there is another far more real and meaningful perspective beyond the present one which we can only glimpse and of which we can only have an intimation, which only unfolds with the consummation of time. We might ask in the light of a parable such as that of the Prodigal Son, whether differences which are so shocking when considered by themselves, have not contributed to the end of history, to a deepening of the content of faith, which in their absence, would not have been realized with the same measure of inwardness.

The positive conclusions at the end of Father Congar's book are not of the kind that can be accepted without reservations, if only because of the patently irenic imprint they bear. Let us have an evangelical soul which is fraternal and friendly. Instead of being the adherent of a system, let us be beings of communion. And "for reunion to first seem possible to the others, and then desirable, let the Church reveal itself to the others as the catholicity of the whole heritage of Christ, in which they may keep all their poor treasures, but enriched and transfigured by a fullness of possession and communion; let us present them with the spectacle of an authentic, full, and radiant freedom, which yet does not deny authority,—the spectacle of a deep sense of the merciful action of God, yet one which does not deny the free collaboration of man—with a faith which is inscribed in the orthodoxy of the Church, an abiding submission, which however does not cease to be a mystical reality, fully inward and spontaneous. . . ." [23]

NOTES

1 (Paris: Editions du Cerf, 1937.)
2 *Ibid.,* p. 29.
3 *Ibid.,* p. 23.
4 *Ibid.,* p. 34.
5 [The third chapter of the liturgy, which is the form of public worship, deals with the seven sacraments and sacramentals—Baptism, Confirmation, Communion, Penance, Extreme Unction, Holy Orders and Matrimony. Transl. note.]
6 *Op. cit.,* p. 35.
7 *Ibid.,* p. 77.
8 *Ibid.,* pp. 82-83.
9 [Now Christ consoles his friends through the Holy Scriptures and the Sacraments of the Church and through other outward signs of His power which affect us as though He were still in the flesh. Transl. note.]
10 *Op. cit.,* p. 93.
11 *Ibid.,* p. 109.
12 *Ibid.,* pp. 172-173.
13 *Ibid.,* p. 173.
14 *Ibid.,* p. 176.
15 *Ibid.,* pp. 179-181.
16 *Ibid.,* p. 293.
17 *Ibid.,* p. 296.
18 *Ibid.,* p. 338.
19 [See Supra, p. 226. Transl. note.]
20 *Op. cit.,* p. 316.
21 *Ibid.,* p. 318.
22 *Ibid.,* p. 319.
23 *Ibid.,* p. 339.

XII

The phenomenology and the dialectic of tolerance

I believe that I was first led to raise the question around which the following remarks revolve as a result of my reflections on the relation between belief and faith. My use of the term "phenomenology" rather than "psychology" is not unintentional; in the final analysis, I am not at all sure that tolerance is a psychological reality in any sense whatever, and I hope to show you why shortly. We have to recognize that tolerance is located in a frontier zone and on the mutual boundary, as it were, of feeling, and attitude or behavior. *A person shows that he is tolerant*; this expression is significant; I do not know whether one *is* tolerant; I believe that one *is* on the hither or far side of tolerance. But I shall clarify this in what follows.

Let us first ask what tolerance refers to. It is clear, in fact, that a person shows himself tolerant *with respect to something*. It is not at all clear that in absolutizing the idea of tolerance, so to speak, it is not annihilated, or that it does not at least undergo significant modification. Tolerance generally refers to the manifestations or expressions of belief or opinion; it must be admitted that it refers to the belief or opinion itself: in itself, the belief or opinion is unattainable and by and large is not considered except in certain limiting-cases. The fact is that there is only tolerance of what can be prevented; and prevention is only possible with respect to what is overtly manifested, what happens (as distinct from what occurs in consciousness). However, it must be emphasized that if the exercise of tolerance has to do with simple manifestations (and we shall see in what sense), it nevertheless refers beyond these to the opinion or belief which they express. Hence it somehow involves a relation to an other, or to the other *qua* other.

Is it sufficient to say that tolerance is non-prevention, non-prohibition? I do not think that this is the case. It is clear that the verb "to tolerate" can mean simply to support; but here we are concerned with something more. Furthermore, the word "support" is ambiguous since it can signify in the extreme case, undergo; but we are not concerned here with any kind of undergoing. If, as is clear, there is a spectrum of experiences to which the term "support" vaguely refers, it is to the other end of the spectrum that we have to go. When I assert: I supported the presence of L. in the room adjoining mine (at the hotel), I mean that I have accepted— or that I have resigned myself to co-existing with—when I was able to expel him or have him expelled. In this sense, to support is practically the same as to undergo. In tolerance, however, there is much more to it; I venture to say that there is not only the recognition of a fact but of a right, and this recognition can become an act of guarantee. This should lead us to perceive (and this is paramount) that tolerance is ultimately the negation of a negation, a counter-intolerance; it seems difficult for tolerance to be manifested before intolerance; tolerance is not primitive; it is to action what reflection is to thought. In any case, it is inconceivable without a certain power which sustains it and to which it is, as it were, attached; the more it is tied to a state of weakness, the less it is itself, the less it is tolerance.

However, this power does not appear to be isolable from a certain realm of its own, that is, one in which it exercises its authority, or more precisely, in which it arrogates to itself the right to exercise that authority. It can even be asserted that this power implies the awareness of having a certain mandate. This will become clear if we but keep in mind the distinction between tolerance and the fact of tolerating—or again between tolerance and the fact of not tolerating. I think it would be helpful here to pause a few moments on what may be termed the negative slope of the problem. The distinction made above is not incisive enough; here as elsewhere, we have to do with a spectrum of meanings. If I say that I will not tolerate that certain remarks be made in my presence, tolerate here has almost the sense of support. There is, however, the vestige, as it were, of a mandate. Suppose that I declare: I cannot tolerate a defense of pederasty in my presence; this by no means implies only: this is extremely disagreeable to me in so far as I am the particular individual that I am, but: as a representative of all gentlemen, I cannot permit it; the english expression *to stand for* is here preferable to the word "represent." It seems that here we have the confused image of a class of decent men whose absence is exploited by a defense of pederasty; but it must not be said that I who am present, I who act, as it were, on their authority, will tolerate that these shocking remarks be made with impunity. The matter can be further clarified if we introduce the implied reference *at home*—no longer referring to something which is simply before me. The subject here really seems to be placed in charge of a type of sanctuary inside of which certain words or sacrilegious acts are not permitted. And here the signification of the expression *in my capacity as* is crucial. The head of the family who does not tolerate subversive remarks to be made by a stranger at his table and in the presence of his children, may quite well say afterwards to the stranger: "You understand that when we are talking privately, you can say whatever you like, but in the presence of my wife and children its different. As head of the family I cannot tolerate. . . ." We should not refer here to intolerance but to non-tolerance; for on reflection, I wonder whether intolerance in the strict sense is not frequently a counter-tolerance. The refusal to tolerate is in this case justified by the obligation to safeguard something. "It is not a question of myself or my feelings, but of a certain responsibility entrusted to me which I neither can nor have the right to endanger. Again, my own person is not involved; but in the name of the sacred trust for which I am responsible, I must forbid you to. . . . It can be said that I am a sentinel at the advance-posts. I cannot permit you to encroach on the zone under my protection. To do so would be to disobey my orders. It is for their sake that I exhibit intolerance."

This indeed opens up a broad field of investigation. I am not considering merely the inner sincerity of someone who talks like this, an inner sincerity which we can always impugn. A more adequate formulation would be that we have to examine the nature or validity of the mandate itself. Who has given me the authority to represent these higher interests which I claim are not mine in the restricted sense of the term? We shall no doubt have the occasion to return to this point in the sequel.

If we turn now to tolerance itself, we shall see our problem grow in complexity. It shares with intolerance the fact that it is also manifested in the name of . . . in the higher interest of. . . . And it is very interesting to note that in both cases, the allegation can introduce hypocrisy and *cant*.

It seems to me, however, that we must immediately distinguish two different cases: a case according to which I personally adopt a position contrary to the one expressed by the behavior which must be tolerated,—and a different case in which I maintain a state of neutrality, i.e. of indifference with respect to both this position and its contrary.

Let us take the first case: I have some fairly dogmatic beliefs, but I exhibit tolerance towards those who maintain contrary beliefs; and this does not simply mean that I am careful not to deal harshly with them: In so far as it depends on my action, I guarantee them complete freedom, I prevent anyone from trying to interrupt their meeting, desecrate their rituals, etc.; and this involves the counter-intolerance I mentioned above. But what makes this attitude possible? does it or doesn't it imply a contradiction? We have to examine here the relation I have to my opinion, the way in which I inwardly adopt a position with respect to the other's opinion. The question raised here is that of determining whether it isn't because of a certain loosening of the tie which relates me to my opinion that I can exhibit tolerance towards an adversary (who thus ceases to be an adversary and becomes a neighbor). In sum, don't I tend to show the greatest tolerance to the other in the measure that I attach less importance to my own opinion—where (therefore) I have less confidence in it? Hence my tolerance is the fruit of a certain skepticism of which I can yet be insufficiently aware. Thus the prefatory remark I made at the beginning of my exposition is relevant here: is it not to the extent that belief has become opinion or more precisely, has tended to become qualified as opinion, that tolerance has been able to emerge into the world? To be sure, I do not believe that this hypothesis should be categorically rejected; but the truth in this case seems to me far more complex. It is conceivable—and I now have to insist on this point —that a dialectic which is precisely the inverse of the present one, may be engendered by the above. To the extent that I hold to my opinion, am aware of sticking to it, it may be—provided that I clearly envisage the *other* together with the tie relating him to his opinion—that I put myself in the other's place such that I can conceive his opinion to be worthy just because of the intense conviction with which he holds it; it may be that my awareness of my own conviction is somehow my guarantee of the worth of his,—instead of it being the case, that I cannot as a skeptic take seriously any conviction whatever (and if there is tolerance from this point of view, it will be of a degenerate form, to the extent that it is indifference and nothing more). I said that this *can* occur; but it is not at all inevitable, and we must determine the reasons why this is so.

Where is the emphasis placed in the example I have just brought to your attention? solely on the *subject*, on what essentially characterizes it, or better, on the movement whereby it proceeds towards a certain self-affirmation. This may be more clearly expressed in the following: I recognize within myself that the validity of a belief consists in the fact that it expresses my actual being; my subjective reality; hence a belief which is alien to my own will also seem to me to be the expression—although different —of another personal reality which must also be safeguarded. Any personalist attempt, in the broad sense of the term, to ground or to justify tolerance, must, it seems to me, rest on this postulate.

On the other hand, a difficulty arises here which we cannot evade: in treating belief as a mode of realization of the person, do I not tend to abstract from the *object* to which it refers, or, in other words, abstract from the intentionality of the belief? In considering my own belief as an expression of myself, isn't it the case that I not only place myself outside of it, but also in a way betray it by switching its center of gravity from the object to the subject? and isn't tolerance rooted in this very betrayal? Let us reconsider the question, this time orienting belief and the question of the validity of belief towards the object. What do we find? I believe in a certain reality; i.e., this reality possesses a certain magnetic force for me, and the modalities of my belief are governed by this reality, the possibility of my exercising a choice being completed excluded here. In the measure that I believe in this reality, however, it must seem to me to impose itself on everybody; it is as though it endowed my belief with an indefinite power of expansion; but in the course of its dessemination, my belief encounters obstacles, those contrary beliefs with which it collides. We may note, by the way, that insofar as I am a believer dedicated to the task of making proselytes, I confirm what was said earlier with respect to the role of representation, of mandate or of investiture in connection with the act of tolerance or intolerance. (It seems as though I were responsible for spreading my faith, and it even seems that I should be guilty of a lukewarm attitude if I gave up converting those who did not believe as I did.) The more my thought is centered on the object of my faith, the more inevitable my tendency to attribute error to the adversary who encounters my proselytizing. For if before, when I considered the subject exclusively, I could readily concede an equivalence or equipollence of beliefs construed as modes of expression of the personality, now this is no longer true. How would I be able to grant the right to ascribe to the object of a false belief anything comparable to the absolute privilege possessed by the object of my own belief? I could not do so, without falling into a self-contradictory agnosticism, or without my belief ultimately becoming nullified.

It should be noted that this proselytizing is not in itself intolerance. However, if we revert to my description of an effective tolerance—as a recognition and a guarantee bestowed on the other —the difficulty will readily come to light. Insofar as I consider the object of my faith sacred, doesn't this prevent me from taking any action which would confirm the disbeliever in his disbelief? What is more, am I not in the final analysis enjoined or at least advised to oppose the invidious use he makes of his own freedom? (in the same sense that I have to prevent a child or a simple-minded person from performing acts which would endanger his own safety or that of his fellows).

However plausible this argument may seem, we feel that it is not and cannot be conclusive; it has a flaw; more precisely, we feel that any cause which enlists this kind of dialectic is thereby discredited; we hold it to be evident—although this conviction is not sufficient and must be justified—that the means employed ultimately compromise and debase the very end to which they were supposed to be subordinated.

"The frightful thing about crimes committed against the spirit," Henriette Waltz has written, "is that as soon as we want to unmask or punish them, we find ourselves swept along in the same path of violence, the same abuses, the same excesses which aroused our indignation in the beginning."

However, the fundamental question is to determine the principle on which we can base a tolerance which is really a counter-intolerance, but which is not, at the same time, the expression or mark of a complete skepticism, but rather the living incarnation of a faith.

The fact is that we must first of all subject to detailed analysis the set of presuppositions concealed by an intolerance which is fully cognizant of itself and which seeks to justify itself; presuppositions whose nature, whether cognitive or affective, cannot be wholly determined, but which nevertheless involve a state of distrust or apprehension. "If I do not see to it that is is halted, i.e., if I do not find a way of checking its development and preventing the overt manifestations of the subversive belief, a good many evil consequences will inevitably follow." In other words, I acknowledge a responsibility analogous to that which would fall on me if, as a doctor, I had to check an epidemic; in this event, I would not only have to prescribe certain preventative measures, but also seek the cause of the disease and attempt to act directly on it. In any case, I must reject the argument that people have the right to poison themselves if they want and eventually infect one another; such a right does not exist, is null and void, and must be categorically denied. Possibly the objection may be raised that this case is quite different, for the doctor acts on the basis of an objective certitude sharing nothing in common with a religious or moral belief which necessarily offers a minimal certitude; hence we are not justified in urging the latter kind of belief against a different belief which may be true. But I do not believe that we can pose the problem satisfactorily in these terms. To put the problem in a nutshell, we must instead put ourselves in the place of someone who has absolute faith and for whom the possibility of being mistaken does not arise. The real question is that of determining whether the supposedly complete certainty such a person has of possessing the truth precludes the possibility of manifesting a genuine tolerance for those who think differently.

The truth is, we have to examine just what it is we are affirming. I have just expressed myself in a manner which would lead one to believe that we were concerned with an individual soul; reflection discloses that this is impossible; if it is really a question of religious belief in the deepest sense, the subject in question would concentrate in himself a temporal power and authority on the level of dogma which rightly belongs to the Church. It is clear that the possession of such a conjunction of powers is something which we find it difficult to conceive of today, and that such a subject is only a limiting-case. However, we are entitled to ignore this difficulty to a certain extent and to proceed as though the question can be raised in connection with a believer actually possessed of such a power.

If we return to the example of the doctor fighting an epidemic, we will note that the concern here is to reestablish a normal state of affairs; actually this state can only be restored if different volitions are exercised with respect to their objects in conformity to a normative judgment which is apparently irrevocable. It is inconceivable that the doctor, acting in his capacity of doctor, can be restrained by the idea that the epidemic is perhaps due to the anger of the Gods, that it is therefore respectable, and that one would be transgressing a higher law in trying to check it. If he thought of it in this way and acted in accordance with such an idea, the doctor would be treated as a madman and would be banished from the human community. Now the case of a heterodox belief considered from the orthodox point of view is clearly quite different: but we have to determine the nature of this difference. The end which the orthodox believer has in view or is supposed to have in view, is service to God, to the divine will. But we must ask whether the believer, in construing this will or using it, in a certain way, does not convert it into a simple idol; whether, without knowing it, he is not guilty under these circumstances of the subtlest kind of betrayal. The fundamental datum here is *transcendence,* the fact of transcendence one can almost say, although this expression may shock certain people, since what in one sense is the absolute fact, in quite another sense is not a fact at all, cannot be a *given.* We shall observe how the meaning of the word "transcendence" can be clarified in terms of the type of relationship which may be established between the divine will and my own will; more concretely, by the kind of appeal we hold the divine will to make to my own will, in an area where I have to exercise my freedom relative to other freedoms. Here we are dealing with a triadic relation. How ignore the fact that to serve this divine will means in this context to act as a mediator between it and the other consciousness whom I assume is blinded in the present case? and this means: to act in a way such that this blinded consciousness turns towards the will that I serve, that it unfolds to the light which is supposed to illumine me. With this in mind, I must be absolutely sure that the other consciousness does not feel that I am acting out of personal motives, that it is not inevitably made to think that what I call divine will—the will which it does not yet acknowledge—is only a mask behind which I deck out those opinions to which I am wedded as one is wedded to oneself; that it does not reveal a desire to exercise my power; to maneuver the other into a region of which I am the center. It is evident that it is only by showing love to this person that I can evoke the feeling that this is not so, that I am really a mediator between him and an unknown will which refrains from revealing itself as a material power; and this love must go out to the soul as it is, with the belief which nourishes it and which must also be included in my embrace; my love must be strong enough to allow this soul to be transformed and to renew itself, to expand and to be reborn; and this must occur in such a way that at the same time its belief, somehow bursting of itself out of the narrow framework in which it had been confined, is transfigured and throws off the elements of heterodoxy, the fate which threatened to strangle it.

It is also evident that I am an instrument in the entire situation, that I am absolutely not a cause, that nothing issues from me, that I preserve a state of absolute humility relative to God's will which safeguards the latter's transcendence. Nothing of this kind can happen, however, if I claim to place at the service of God's will instruments of force which by their nature cannot fail to engender in the other the conviction that I am acting out of self-interest and in order to satisfy my desire to proselytize; or, what is still more serious, that I am a servant of a God of prey whose goal it is to annex and enslave. And it is precisely here that we find the frightful betrayal I alluded to earlier: I impose on the person I claim to convert, a loathsome image of the God whose interpreter I say I am.

On the other hand, however, we must recognize that from the moment the divine will is served in a way which fully protects its transcendence, we have gone far beyond the tolerance mentioned earlier; here nothing is conceivable without charity, without grace;

and I tend to think that conversely, whenever I act towards my fellow creature in this way, whatever the actual contents of my mind may be, God's transcendence is really embodied in my action.

To be sure, the case I have just described which is in sum that of an absolute religion, is really a limiting case; it is evident that we have to examine some intermediate cases where the solution I have tried to discover does not fully apply or does not apply at all. I am thinking here, of course, of political situations strictly speaking. Consider for example the attitude a head of state or of a government labeled democratic can and should adopt against a revolutionary party whose goal is the destruction of the existing order. Any transcendent considerations are here excluded by definition; but at the other extreme, and by the same token, it is scarcely possible to identify categorically the spread of the revolutionary sentiment which one proposes to combat, with an epidemic which must be relentlessly combatted by every means possible. In principle, it is difficult to admit the justice of treating conscious or ostensibly conscious beings as rats in a plague or as mosquitoes that must be exterminated, even if the ends they pursue seem completely evil to us. At most we can make this identification only in the case where, in adopting whatever measures are required, we find it necessary to eliminate the capacity to harm of those individuals who obstinately pursue a path of pure destruction, even if this path according to their conviction is designed to prepare the way for some Salentum or other.[1] Generally, we must think up some compromise measure, a measure which besides, would be fundamentally unreliable, which would imply fairly stringent sanctions capable of intimidating, although not capable of arousing in its victims an awareness of themselves as martyrs since we should then run the risk of making them invincible. To be sure, the notion of such a compromise is misleading from the point of view of reflective thought. But the social realm is one of deception to my mind, and in the present case we are precisely at the core of the social. Whatever the nature of the situation, it does not seem possible to me that the head of state or of the government concerned can exhibit here anything like tolerance; nor does he have the right to do so if he does not wish to be guilty of a weakness which can very easily involve the destruction of the society whose temporal destiny it is his task to safeguard.

We find therefore, that while earlier we were above tolerance, we are now below it. Or to express this more adequately, tolerance in the strictly political sphere can be practiced with impunity only within certain limits which it is perhaps impossible to trace out *a priori*; and only to the extent that the divergent opinions which are permitted free expression, can be considered as relatively innocuous. We here return to the example I had put aside earlier in which the agent maintains a neutrality with respect to antagonistic positions. But we have to examine—and this is the subject of another inquiry—the limits to which such a neutrality can actually go. The significant thing to note here is that it is dubious whether such neutrality is a psychological reality. As a matter of fact it can only be expressed negatively or on the level of precepts, and we can always demand what becomes of these negative formulae, what they mask to the concrete beings who have the task of applying them in practice.

In conclusion, and as I intimated at the outset, it seems to me that what we understand by the word "tolerance" is really a rough and ready compromise between certain psychological dispositions which are moreover distributed between benevolence, indifference and aversion, a machiavellianism in the larval state—and a spiritual dynamism of a completely different kind whose ground and main driving force is to be found in transcendence.

NOTES

1 [Ancient city of Magna Graecia. Cf. Paul Hazard's reference to the utopianism of Fénélon in the former's *The European Mind* transl. J. Lewis May (New Haven: Yale University Press, 1953), p. 425: ". . . he sets to work to build with his own hands the ideal city, Salentum. There vice and misfortune shall be no more. . . . At Salentum, peace shall reign, and justice, and social order, and abundance. Riches shall be borne in upon a flowing tide, and, as the tide recedes, it will leave other riches behind it. Every problem finds a ready solution." Transl. note.]

XIII

The fundamental and the ultimate situation in Karl Jaspers

I shall not be concerned in the following pages with giving a comprehensive account of Jasper's metaphysics as it is presented in his *System of Philosophy*.[1] My concern is rather to provide as detailed an analysis as possible of certain ideas which govern its development. It would, of course, be interesting to determine the extent to which these ideas are original. In large part they are derived from Kierkegaard. As to contemporary figures, Heidegger, who maintains a personal relationship with Jaspers, has had an obvious influence on his thought. It seems to me, however, that it is of paramount importance to assimilate in *itself* a philosophy which has been remarkably worked out and in which we may discern a particularly vigorous effort to exhibit the essential strata of what it is tempting to call the orography of the inner life.

I

If we focus reflection on some basic philosophical question such as: what is Being? why does anything exist? or, what am I? what do I really want? we will observe that these questions are all based on a certain fundamental situation which must first be analyzed by the philosopher *in the measure that this is possible.* We have to make this qualification since it will not take us long to see that an exhaustive analysis of this situation is precisely what is impossible.

I note first of all that I am involved in a certain process. There are certain things I apprehended or thought I had apprehended, and that I subsequently had to drop—and this is in fact an experience I am moved to generalize. Confronted with an incessant flux, I reach a point where I must ask: since everything passes, what does *is* mean, strictly speaking? The question is especially urgent because *I was not there* at the beginning and *will not be there* at the end—of that spectacle at which I was privileged to take part. I who am situated between the beginning and the end, I question this beginning and this end. The response I seek to elicit must assure me of a foothold or at least the possibility of a resting-place in the midst of this flux. Because of this ceaseless transformation wherein I pass from the shadows where *I was not yet* into the shadows where *I will no longer be,* I am filled with an indeterminate anguish. The thought occurs to me that perhaps something will be lost forever if I do not grasp it right now. But what is the meaning of this "perhaps," this "something"?

When I awake to myself, I note that I am situated or thrown into a world within which I have to find my orientation. Won't I succeed in discovering what `this is by exploring this world, by determining why it is that I should find myself in this peculiar situation and what it implies relative to both the whole and to myself? Assuming that these inquiries help me to find the response I seek, what are the essential features of this response? Being will be transformed into an *object* of whose nature I shall be informed (or taught), as I would be with respect to the structure of the Cosmos. But such a doctrine of being can only be one more object presenting itself in the company of other objects in the midst of which I previously had to find my orientation, without this involving any change in my situation as it is in itself, without the discovery of any remedy for this sliding away of reality which is the cause of my anguish. If I claim to stick to the question why this being of which I am informed is given to me, I can only succeed if I first forget myself: I thereby convert myself into one object among others, and I avert my glance from that particular object. It may seem at first as though I had thus avoided the situation in which I thought I was imprisoned. But this escape is illusory; it is only a dream from which I will have to awake sooner or later; it is sufficient that the objectivity of the principles in terms of which I tried to forget or repudiate myself are suddenly found to be unreliable, for me to find myself once again in my original situation. In other words, I shall not find an abiding refuge, a means of freeing myself from the in-between nature of my condition, in the world of objects, whatever the latter's metaphysical status. If, as the result of my decision and of my own free choice, as it were, I do not dare to be what I am, I am destined to remain a prey to the anguish of non-being. I must not assume that I can elevate myself to a comprehensive view of reality so as to cast my glance from the lofty eminence of this high observatory into the depths of my own being and destiny. To be sure this does not deny the possibility of a knowledge of the universe which is objective and capable of improvement. The things in the world in which I orient myself are knowable, lend themselves to our knowledge, and even up to a point, to the techniques we use to control them. And Jaspers uses the almost untranslatable term *Weltorientierung* to designate the ensemble of unlimited investigations which help us to clarify our situation *from the point of view of the object*. Our mistake consists only in wishing to transform this knowledge—which takes its start from a certain fundamental situation—into an objective science of being, the sort of claim a rash idealism would risk making. This knowledge issues from our past, rests on historical foundations, is never fully realized, yet conceals within itself the possibility of the future. It is the unique mode in which reality reveals itself to me. However, we must observe that when I try to conceive it, I can only draw from it outlines or schemas; as something real, it is always more than anything I can say about it. We have observed above that it is never pure immediacy or actuality, nor does it ever imply pure universality, although it is possible to discern a certain general structure in the situation enabling us to proceed to an analysis of our empirical condition (*Dasein*).²

Hence it is clear that I can neither hope to know myself in an exhaustive way when I begin from some particular objective, historical presupposition, nor inversely, can I understand the world starting from my situation. The latter is essentially mobile and that in a dual sense: both in the measure that it participates in the world of events, and insofar as it implies a free decision. Hence its basically unrealized character, one which is moreover communicated to philosophy itself. We reach therefore, the following conclusion: finding myself as an indeterminate possibility, in the situation in which I am placed, I must seek Being in the strict sense, if I am to find myself. This, however, is only possible if I fail in the quest which I have managed to consider in philosophical terms. And the philosophy to which I give my assent has its source—i.e., its principle—in *possible existence,* and its method is that of transcendence.

The above are the points of departure for Jaspers philosophy; he has presented them with a remarkable clarity in the first few pages of his System; but it may be noted that he returns with great insistence to these fundamental themes throughout the three volumes. The fact is that we are immediately confronted with a radical choice—the significance of which is strikingly presented for example, in the first chapter of Volume II, p. 21. Do I pretend to find repose in a knowledge which relates to something self-subsistent and which constitutes a principle of objective security? Or will I instead discern in this inquiry and in this desire a self-betrayal? and separating the notion of being completely from that of subsisting, shall I side with a philosophy which puts in my hands the highest stakes and which establishes (in a sense which must be carefully examined) the primacy of the *existential?* Such is the problem around which the thought of Jaspers revolves. It must be further recognized that according to him, any indecision is impossible for the person who has become aware of the true nature of philosophy, for the individual who realizes that it is not a simple, abstract stratagem, game, or poem, but rather the road leading us to ourselves.[3] For Jaspers, a self-subsistent metaphysic of being can only be an *impasse*; doubtless, it can only succeed in becoming a doctrine at the price of paralogisms which reflection discloses to us—and in any case, it completely ignores what it is that makes a man a man in the strict sense—something we can tentatively designate equally well by the term "existence" as by the term "freedom." An analysis of what is meant by *I* will help us to better understand the thought of Jaspers in this context.

When I examine what it is I have in mind when I say *I*, I find first of all a particular empirical being; on the other hand, however, I, as such, am essentially identical with any other I to the extent that I am *consciousness in general*. In the third place, I do not merely wish to know what is there, what I in fact am, but also to apprehend myself as a possible source of actions which are avowedly mine. There are times when it is clear that it is really myself who wills and does something. On those occasions I am, as it were, flooded with a certain conviction of myself which is not connected with any kind of knowledge. In this third sense to which we must devote our attention exclusively, I am neither an empirical being (an objectified subject) nor consciousness in general (a subject which construes objects as universally real and valid), but rather *a possible existence:* a being confronting his own possibility who is not a datum of any consciousness whatever. Possible existence may be construed as a break in the circle formed by the self and the object when these are considered in terms of their constitutive functions. It can open a way for us which is barred to consciousness in general in its world of objects.[4] "Existence, Jaspers affirms, "is what can never be an object, and which is the source of my thought and actions";[5] it is, he continues, what underlies the relations one has with oneself and one's transcendence; [6] and he explicitly affirms that he has borrowed the term from Kierkegaard although the meaning he ascribes to it is obviously remote from the meaning Kierkegaard ordinarily assigned to it. In order to clarify his meaning which is extremely difficult to grasp, Jaspers multiplies his assertions instead of giving definitions since existence strictly speaking is indefinable. It is dubious whether they are all able to throw light on the main issue; here and there, however, there are rifts in the clouds through which daylight appears. "We speak of existence, of the being of this reality, but existence is not a concept but a signum (*Zeiger*) which refers to a realm transcending all objectivity. [7] Again, Jaspers also asserts in a simpler and more forceful manner: existence is only something I can be, not something I can see and know; yet it is only found in the universal medium of a thought which can clarify it. [8] Such a statement is logically contradictory, for the existing being does not belong to an objective category. It is here worthy of note that all these propositions which are largely negative and which seem on the surface to be self-refuting, revolve around a basic non-cognitive apprehension of something which we can identify with our awareness of our radical freedom; with an absolute certainty which is unverifiable (since it is supra-objective) that there is something in the final analysis which depends on me and and on me alone. "Whenever I cease to consider myself from a psychological point of view, without however acting in a naively unconscious manner, i.e., when I act positively and in accordance with my own personal impulse, in the light of a certain evidence no knowledge is able to convey, but an evidence which is the basis of my own reality—then I decide on what I am." We can say that Jaspers is here engaged in a very audacious elucidation—on a level which neither is nor can be that of causality—of the traditional idea of the *causa sui*. One observation however, must be made immediately. This free realization of the self appears as a response; doubtless it is only possible at the center of what Jaspers terms *communication*, a word which requires as much explanation as "existence."

"In contrast with the contingent nature of my empirical being left to its own volition, I experience myself in communication: I am never more certain that I am myself than when I am completely disposable with respect to the Other, so that I become myself because the Other, in the course of a struggle for self-revelation, also becomes *himself*." [9] Furthermore, Jaspers refers to the para-

dox that while I am only through the Other, I am still myself. [10]
It is clear that—so far as there is a correspondence as we shall see,
between the categories of the objective world and the conceptual
schemas which can be extracted from existence by a process of
abstraction which is in a measure always specious—we are inevitably tempted to place communication alongside of mutual action.
However, the same observation must be made with respect to the
causa sui mentioned above. Under no circumstances should we
forget that here every objective language is inapplicable, and one
of the chances Jaspers takes in his work involves just such a
desperate effort to remain with it because of the simple fact that, on
his own confession, existences are not assimilable to the parts or
members of an intelligible whole. [11] It is evident that his premises—
assuming that this term is appropriate—necessarily entail this
negative conclusion; but we have to examine whether the use of
the plural in these circumstances (existences) is not justified;
doubtless we are not justified in assuming one existence into which
the other existences may be absorbed; but if so, aren't we in a
realm in which the categories of the *one* and the *many* are at once
transcended, so that discourse itself becomes impossible?

The essential point to recognize at the present stage of our inquiry, is that the questions Jaspers forces us to raise, proliferate
because of the heroic effort he makes to grasp at the point of their
maximal intensity the basic paradoxes of our human situation,
paradoxes whose uncomfortable edges are concealed by the conceptual veil we throw over them. It is unfortunate, however, that
the overly flexible syntax of his language often leaves a residue of
ambiguity behind in his statements, to which—at once its merit and
the counterpart of its deficiencies—our own philosophical language which we French use, cannot adapt itself. When Jaspers
writes for example: *Aus moglicher Existenz ergreife Ich das
Geschichtliche meines Daseins,* it is impossible to find a French
equivalent for the preposition *aus* whose meaning here has such a
rich indeterminateness. Literally, the sentence would seem to
mean: beginning with possible existence I grasp the historicity of
what I am (I am ignoring at present the difficulties raised by the

word *Dasein*); however, it seems very dubious to me that *aus* should be rendered here as *beginning with*. "Beginning with possible existence" has no meaning, in fact, and I may add that if we use the article in French, as we must, this suffices to falsify the meaning. It seems to me that *Aus moglicher Existenz* should rather be translated as: from the point of view of possible existence—if this expression itself was not in a sense contradictory, since existence does not itself depend on knowledge; we shall note that to designate the act whereby thought becomes immersed in existence, Jaspers uses the word *erhellen*, a word which is not currently used very much in philosophy, it seems, and which does not mean "elucidate" or enlighten, but rather "illuminate," strictly speaking (as someone would let light into a room where the shutters were drawn). So far as I move on the level of possible existence, I recognize the deeply historical nature of my situation. "Historical" here must be construed as *Geschichtlich*. It is evident that we must be careful not to interpret the word "historical" in terms of its commonly accepted meaning in this context (and we shall understand why we must not do so more clearly as we go on), a meaning to which the adjective *historisch* is related. The awareness the self has of its historicity, Jaspers says, is originally a personal one. I become aware here of myself communicating with another personal reality; as for myself, I am linked in time to a succession of situations and data each of which is unique in time. While the historical being of objects to which my knowledge refers is historical for me and not for itself, I am aware of myself as historical for myself. [12] It is hard to resist the thought that Jaspers has discovered on his own initiative the distinction Peguy illumined with such extraordinary force, notably in *Clio*. Didn't Peguy adhere to such formulations as: "What has bounds and is determinate when viewed from without, is inwardly the manifestation of authentic being. The person who loves only humanity does not love; he only loves who loves a specific human being. The person who is logically consistent and keeps his commitments is still not a faithful being, but only the person who shoulders his act and his past love as his own burden and admits that they are binding on him.

He who desires a just organization of the world which will endure forever desires nothing, but only he who in his own historical situation grasps the possible as something which derives from himself." [13]

Hence existence is not separable from communication, i.e., from a certain *coesse* which is spiritually apprehended, any more than it is able to be grasped outside of its rootedness in time. Time then ceases to be a pure flow and becomes a manifestation of Existence which the latter wins by its own decisions. Time can thus be transcended, not to attain to a timeless abstraction, "but in a manner such that while I am in time, I am nevertheless above it without being outside of it." [14] So far as I unqualifiedly act and love in time, I will find eternity itself there. Furthermore, this is what my reason does not comprehend, for it is only a momentary illumination and occurs at a later date through a recollection which does not preclude doubt. In any case, it is never a possession which I obtain from the outside. Eternity is neither the intemporal nor a ceaseless duration, but rather the profundity of time construed as an historical manifestation of existence.

We are now prepared to see that existence is in a way eccentric relative to the world. There is a being whose nature it is to be there (*dasein*) and which compels me to acknowledge it, to create something out of it later on, and we can say that the very stuff of what is called the world is made up of this being-there. Existence, on the other hand, *is not there;* it is neither given nor able to be drawn from the given by some extractive process or other. Between the world and existence, between what can be known and what can only be illumined, between the being of the object and the freedom characteristic of existence, the gulf cannot be filled, but only bridged by a jump (*Sprung*). Nevertheless, the contact between these two modes of being is actually such that distinguishing one from the other is an infinitely long undertaking, the accomplishment of which implies both a knowledge of the world and the illumination of existence. The formulations which are designed to render this distinction have only abstract validity. [15] Objective being (mechanism, life, even consciousness) is given; so far as I am existence, I am a source, not to be sure of being in general, but of myself *im dasein*. Being, construed as something which subsists, and being construed as freedom are not two coordinate species; they are linked with one another but it is completely impossible to compare them. "What is—or is valid, always, is objectivity; what vanishes in an instant and yet is eternal is existence. One is only for the subject which thinks it, the other, to be sure, is never without an object, but is only real for an existence in communication." [16] This proposition seems to me to be of particular significance; only so far as I *participate* in existence (and this term would doubtless shock Jaspers), can I think it—and not know it, of course, since it completely eludes objectification in a judgment. If I adopt the point of view of the world (identical with the objective point of view), it is impossible to understand the meaning of existence. If, on the other hand, I establish my being in existence, every non-existential factor will seem to me a pure loss or a fall. The fact is, however, that my situation places me on the boundary of the world and existence; hence the radical ambiguity which characterizes my faculty of apprehending; and I expressly use here a term which is as vague as possible and which can, if need be, cover the whole terrain of thought and not merely that of knowledge. In any case, we must perceive that being can by no means enclose itself within a whole which is, as it were, capable of being surveyed by the mind. If I conceive a being, it is always some determinate being and not being itself. While I have an assurance of possible existence, this does not mean that existence is an object for me, and the assurance I have is not in existence in general but of myself and the existence which communicates with me. We cannot take one another's place as though we were interchangeable units or copies. Existence in the final analysis is a signum, a token, which designates the direction taken by this assurance the self has of itself; it does not refer to anything cognitive or universally valid, anything which can be known or significantly affirmed either of one's self or of others.

Under these circumstances we must recognize that the actual meaning of the problem of being, the question: what is being?

depends for its answer on the person who raises it. At bottom, it has no meaning for consciousness in general. Consciousness in general is dispersable among the variety of determinate beings, beings which are such-and-such. Furthermore, Jaspers affirms that this consciousness does in fact acknowledge the rupture between the various modes of being; but it remains indifferent to these because, oriented towards objective being, cognition presupposes without question the unity implied by objective being even if that unity is not known. [17] It is only on the level of possible existence that a passion is engendered which causes the question of being in itself to issue into an act which transcends all objectivity. Being, so far as it is relative or the object of an inquiry, is only a phenomenon, i.e. the manifestation of something which is theoretically its substratum. Hence at the core of the being which appears, we must recognize an irremediable cleavage for the consciousness involved in time; between an inaccessible *in itself,* a transcendence which cannot be cognized as an objective substratum, and that being to itself which is present in existence and which cannot be identified with empirical consciousness. [18] Existence and transcendence are linked to one another even though they are heterogeneous. This relation is revealed in the empirical consciousness.[19] Hence scientific inquiry will remain dominated by the idea of a substratum, whereas the philosopher apprehends being through the phenomenon by means of a process of deciphering as well as through that thought which summons or appeals to existence.

On the above view, the principle of immanence is false if consciousness is construed as an object of inquiry; but the principle is valid to the extent that for us "consciousness" is only what appears, i.e., what enters into consciousness. When consciousness is divided from itself as an object of inquiry, either the unconscious in the various interpretations it possesses as an object of inquiry, or the meaning transcendence has for existence, alternately open out to, or conceal themselves from consciousness. This complement to consciousness, however, is necessarily *in consciousness*—playing the role of theory of the unconscious for inquiry and cipher of being for existence—assuming a form which is self-contradictory and therefore evanescent. Again, we must carefully distinguish between the existential meaning of the word *manifestation* and its objective meaning. From the existential point of view, *manifestation* means a becoming aware of and implies objectification, where what is completely present as being simultaneously grasps itself.[20] "The manifestation of consciousness as an object of inquiry is related by us to the substratum which remain radically alien to us. The manifestation of existence, on the other hand, is related by us to what we originally are, where we must answer for what we are." [21] The one is a universal object of knowledge, the other reveals itself in existential communication. This surely is sufficiently clear; but do we have the very same situation with respect to the relation between existence and transcendence? Here too, there is an essential feature of Jasper's thought which must be exhibited with the greatest possible clarity. The essential point, it seems to me, is the following: "Being as a whole is not and cannot be exhausted in a being who is still in the process of deciding *if* it is and *what* it is; the latter is linked to a being which is not identifiable with existence but rather with its transcendence." [22] The fact is that the act whereby I search for being carries with it limitations which preclude the very possibility of this discovery; on the other hand, however, if my inquiry is interrupted it is as though I myself ceased to be. What I must therefore obtain is the unity of presence and of inquiry. In the last analysis, it is "only by an anticipation, an anticipated prehension of what must be found, that the inquiry itself is possible; transcendence must already be present where I am seeking it." [23]—The modes of this inquiry into being, beginning with possible existence, are roads to transcendence. Their illumination is the task of metaphysical philosophy, and it is clear that Jaspers lays the heaviest accent on the inadequacy of any being which is not transcendence. We cannot regard freedom as ultimate. For freedom is still in time, still on the route taken by possible existence. Freedom is not being in itself. In transcendence freedom is in abeyance because it no longer constitutes the realm of decision; in transcendence there is neither freedom nor lack of freedom. Being viewed as freedom, as the most meaningful appeal addressed to us, so far as what we are still depends on us, is not the being of transcendence. "Even freedom when isolated in itself, is destined to decay. It is in transcendence which is only accessible as such to freedom, that freedom seeks its realization. . . At any rate, the elimination of power as a phenomenon which suffices to itself, is for freedom the ultimate satisfaction that the temporal life can offer it." [24]

When the time is ripe to consider carefully the meaning of transcendence, however, we must not retrogress to the hither side of the essential, to an objective philosophy which is incapable of ascending to an apprehension of existence and freedom.

Finally we must note that it is in the ultimate-situations, in the confrontation with death, suffering, sin, for example, that the mysterious transition from existence to transcendence is seen to take place; because they are essential to an understanding of what is most significant in Jasper's thought as well as of the close relation between him and Heidegger, I shall transcribe a few lines describing the meaning of ultimate-situations. [25] "Situations such as those which consist in the fact that I am always involved in a situation, that I cannot live without conflict and suffering, that I must inevitably assume my Guilt, that I have to die—these are what I term ultimate-situations. They themselves are never altered, and only the manner in which they manifest themselves, changes; they are definitive with respect to our condition. We cannot see beyond them; in our condition we can see nothing more behind them. They are like a wall against which we collide, which we run our head against. We do not have the power to alter them, but only to illuminate them without being able to explain them or deduce them in part from anything else. They are bound to our very condition."

This insistence on the role of ultimate-situations seems to me one of the strongest and most outstanding points in the philosophy of Heidegger and Jaspers, in contrast with an idealism which tries to eliminate them by coating them, so to speak, in a syrup of pure abstraction. The price of such sugar-coating is the complete loss of all contact with life, with the tragic reality of man, and a glaring inability not so much to provide a response to the specific problems which compel us to posit an existence whose principal feature is strictly dramatic, but rather to understand these problems and to offer to those who live them the consolation, however humble it may be, of an unqualified sympathy.

II

The image we have of a situation is essentially spatial; it is the position certain things occupy relative to one another in a topographical order. But if we want to define a situation strictly, we can say that it is a reality in which a subject is involved *als Dasein,* and which defines both his field of action and its limits. A reality which, because concrete, is neither solely physical nor solely psychical, but both at once, and which involves both advantages and disadvantages for me, which is to my benefit or is detrimental to me, which represents an opportunity or a prison, or both at once. As *Dasein,* that is, as empirical being, I find myself in situations in which I act and am acted upon, without understanding them except in a schematic or partial way. These situations subsist only by changing, by renewing themselves, and it is my responsibility to contribute to their transformation, to create new situations technically, juridically, psychically speaking. These situations are linked to one another and scientific inquiry discloses these connections which unify them and which enable us to understand them. Because empirical being is being "in a situation," it can never abandon one situation without becoming involved in another. Ultimate situations are those situations which cannot be altered with respect to their essentials but only with respect to their mode of manifestation. So far as they are related to our empirical being, they exhibit a final, ultimate character. As we have already indicated, they cannot be controlled by a mind which contemplates them, and they are more like a wall against which we butt our heads. We can only illuminate them without being able to explain them in terms of something else from which they might be logically inferred.

It is at once worthy of note—and this observation is of paramount importance—that the ultimate situation is not a situation for consciousness in general; for the latter, so far as it knows or acts relative to certain determinate ends, can only treat it objectively, or else consciousness evades, ignores, or forgets about it. Empirical being *qua* consciousness, is either unaffected by ultimate situations, or else is obscurely and confusedly agitated by the feeling of impotence it has in its regard. Actually, as empirical being, I can only try to escape the ultimate situation, stop up my eyes and ears in order to avoid the shock of contact with it; and I do so because I cannot hope to find any ground on which to stand in order to elaborate those thoughts about it which would enable me to overcome it; I can only react to it by a completely different kind of action which transcends the plane of *Dasein,* the plane of a being which is empirically given, viz., by becoming myself a *possible existence.* We become ourselves by entering an ultimate situation with our eyes wide open. The ultimate situation is only accessible to cognition from the outside, superficially; as reality, it can only be existentially experienced. We can therefore give the following formulation which should be kept in mind: *experiencing ultimate situations and existing are one and the same thing.* [26] We here accomplish a leap in which consciousness imparts to itself a reality, actuality, and historical fullness.

It is appropriate to remark that Jaspers does not ignore the possibility of a contrary attitude, the attitude, for example, of Valery. I can, Valery declares, oppose everything, confront everything including my own being with an astonishing, empty attitude of independence. Hence I affirm my solitude, my absolute insularity with respect to the world. Strictly speaking, I am no longer concerned with anything, and instead contemplate everything as an object of cognition, the latter becoming my only support. I am in this case no more than a will to knowledge construed in its universality. Nothing but an eye, a look. This solitude, however, cannot be ultimate, and it hides other possibilities. It is after all the look of a being who attempts to transcend himself and who seeks the proper path to follow. Even after this first leap, I still am a being who appears as a possible existence in situations, a being involved in, and in the deepest sense interested in, reality. The second leap consists in becoming clearly aware of ultimate situations as possibilities which touch the very essence of what I am; I acknowledge that it is impossible for me either to actually escape these situations or to render them wholly transparent to myself; furthermore, these two possibilities are related to if not identified with one another. For I cannot escape a situation by controlling it through my understanding of it, unless this situation is transparent to me. [27] Hence I find myself confronted with a cleavage between the world from which I can cognitively detach myself,—and existence from which on the contrary I cannot detach myself in order to observe it, but which *I can only be or not be.* The theory of existence is therefore paradoxical in the sense that it represents an effort to illuminate what is non-transparent and to exhibit this very non-transparence. Furthermore, the theory is not to be identified with the realization of existence; it reveals ultimate situations from the point of view of possible existence—it constitutes a preparation for the leap, but is not the leap itself. This leap—the third leap—represents the transition to the philosophical or philosophizing life in which philosophy finds its ultimate expression, its final achievement.

As empirical being, I therefore find myself in situations; as possible existence, I find myself in ultimate situations. Once the leap is made, I confront an irreducible dualism: I am not merely in the world, but I exist only so far as I manifest myself in it. I can try to free myself from this dualism in either of two different ways but these efforts are futile. I can still find a refuge outside the world in mysticism. But this, Jaspers affirms, is an illusion; for the mystic in fact continues to live in this world. If this is true, then: either his life outside the world and his life within it do not communicate with one another, and his mysticism may then be reduced to an experience, to an ecstasy; or, on the contrary, this connection is continuously preserved, and then the dualism implied in the ultimate situation reappears. On the other hand, there is another possible evasion besides dualism, viz., positivism construed as a denial of the being of anything which is not in this world, but this solution is no more viable than the first.

In this connection, Jaspers forcefully reveals the limitations and deficiencies of positivism which shows itself incapable of taking account of all those things which give to human life its tragic dignity, which does not recognize either the reality of death or the reality of destiny or guilt; which reveals its inability to understand the nature of doubt and despair or to present a response to them.

Hence we must relinquish the hope of freeing ourselves from this tension between the world and what transcends it—which provides, as it were, the impetus for our existential condition."Everything in the world is wholly indifferent, and again everything in the world can take on a decisive significance; existentially, I am above time, while relative to phenomena I remain completely temporal; the inessentiality of time in connection with the manifestation of existence, is the absolute weight which decision bestows on it; the passion in an action is linked to the awareness that all this means nothing, but passion is related to it in such a way that the significance of the act is deepened and not mutilated . . ." [28]

III

We are now ready to construct what Jaspers terms the *systematic* of ultimate situations.[29] One of these situations dominates all others in the hierarchy however, and consists in the fact that as empirical being, I always find myself in a determinate situation which is this particular one and not another; I live at a certain period, have a certain sex, am of a certain age, occupy a particular social position, etc., and this basic limitation can be contrasted with the idea of man in general and with the attributes or perfections which characterize him. The situation however, also leaves room for the future as an indeterminate possibility.

Now we must note first of all that it is specious to hold that my determinate situation belongs to me in the sense that it is an instance of a universal; for the fact is that it is only on the basis of my situation that I can rise to a comprehensive notion or pseudo-notion of the universe. It is an illusion to think that I can place myself above my situation, as it were, and to treat my situation as one among a number of possibilities, viz., the one which happened to be realized. This is the path taken by cognition to find its orientation, but it is one which does not lead to being; in the last analysis, it is a way of trying to eliminate the ultimate situation or, at any rate, of trying to conceal it. I collide with the given everywhere; everywhere data on the basis of which I think and act confront me. My situation implies the existence of material, psychical, spiritual, or ideal obstacles with which I have to reckon. Doubtless, we can distinguish two limiting cases: one, related to matter, which implies a freedom possessing complete control over the object; another, related to mind, which implies a freedom consisting in completely mutual understanding. But these are only ideal limits; mind is only real to the degree that it is in a measure subject to nature. "My necessary dependence on the materially given and on another's will is a fundamental aspect of my ultimate situation considered from the point of view of its restrictive character." [30]

My historical determination will thus seem to me to be somehow constitutive of *existence* when the latter is apprehended in its fullness. This depth of meaning, however, is not simply given with the historical consciousness. It is a significance which is only achieved through the existential illumination of the ultimate situation. And this illumination can only be realized by each individual for himself;—it is not an abstract operation which can be performed by anyone and which is able to be transposed. I exist in the measure that I am active in the unique situation which is my own, in the measure that I therefore take into account what is unique about it. On the other hand, when I act only as another person would act in my place, i.e., when my act is an instance of a universal, I experience a feeling of emptiness, of dissatisfaction towards something which is, in short, only a pastime.

Finally, we may observe that I can by no means think of myself as an absolute source; in a way, I can look beyond my own beginnings, beyond my birth, can therefore view my origins objectively. However, I have to adopt a certain spiritual attitude towards these origins; the paths both of fidelity and disownment open before me. And disownment is to Jaspers a truly spiritual suicide. I have not chosen my parents. They are mine in an absolute sense. Even if I wish to do so, I cannot disregard them; even if their being should appear alien to me, it is linked to mine by the closest community of interest. The objectively empty concept of parents only becomes determinate and receives a content in *my* parents who belong to me in an irreplaceable way. Further, my existential awareness condemns me to recognize either that I am incomprehensibly responsible for what they are or were,—or, if I do break my ties with them, that I cut myself off irrevocably from my own roots. Needless to say, however, my parents cannot be a simple, objectively subsisting datum for me; they are beings, they participate in possible existence, hence a real or virtual process of communication which includes the possibility of crisis, is established between us. But even where the situation prohibits or excludes communication, piety remains, with what I am personally tempted to call its ontological character; and there also remains, in the measure that it expresses an unbreakable community of being, a basic *Mitseyn* which can only be separated from my own being by an unjustifiable act of violence.[31]

Inasmuch as I consider the circumstances of my own destiny, I oscillate between the notion of chance, of a set of chance events, themselves fortuitous, and the idea of an absolute necessity, of astrological predestination, for example. When I am obsessed by one of these images, the other seems to set me free, and conversely. Here however, there is a kind of infernal circle which I can only break out of when I become aware of the ultimate situation. As an acting being, I cease to be for myself simply *other* than the situations in which I am involved, I am only myself in them, and they are like the manifest body of what I can be. In the ultimate situation I experience myself as one with the chance I have apprehended as my own, beyond all formulations. The ultimate situation only becomes clear when I somehow appropriate the chance event to make it my own. I and my circumstances are united, and I actually refuse to separate one from the other. My destiny ceases to be something alien to me. I love it as I love myself. This is the *amor fati* a being existentially experiences for something which seems to be a limitation when considered from the objective point of view. In the final analysis, our concern is to eliminate both the superstition for the general and for the totality, and the capricious desire for pure variety, in order to attain the indissoluble unity of particularity and existence which is manifested or illumined in the historical consciousness of *amor fati*.

The foregoing account is that of the original ultimate situation which in a manner dominates all the others. We must now examine those situations which are, as it were, the secondary keystones of the existential order. The first of these is death.

DEATH. It is clear that death, construed as an objective datum, is not an ultimate situation. As long as death plays no further role than that of providing man with an incentive to evade it, man behaves as a mere living being, not as an existing being; and as we know, it is existence which implies the awareness of ultimate situations while conversely, this awareness is characteristic of existence. The fact that one vanishes is constitutive of existence. In the absence of this fact I would be, *qua* being, a duration without end and would not *exist*. It is neither the desire for nor the fear of death but the disappearance of the phenomenon which testifies to the truth of existence as a presence. Existence is lost to me if I view life as an absolute and act like a pure living being continually alternating between forgetfulness and anguish. As possible existence, I am only real if I manifest myself empirically, yet only if, as a phenomenal embodiment, I am something more than this phenomenon. This statement, however, must not be construed as a universal proposition. For such a proposition could refer only to an objective fact. Death in the ultimate situation is a specific, determinate death, the death of someone near to me or my own death.

The death of the beloved with whom I effectively, existentially communicated, is first evidenced as a cutting off, as a break. I remain irrevocably alone. Solitude in the presence of death seems inevitable, of the dying person as of the survivor. Yet communication can be established on a foundation that is so deep that even the decision of death can seem to be a further manifestation of it, while communication itself preserves its being as an eternal reality. In this way existence is transformed. The simple living being, the *blosse Dasein,* can, of course, forget, console himself, but in the other case a *saltus* is accomplished which is like a rebirth; death is gathered up, as it were, into life. Life reveals the truth of the communication which survives death. Death ceases to be simply a gulf. It is as though through it, I again bound myself to an existence with which I was in the most intimate communication. The loss of what was, although it does not provide any tangible consolation to the living being that I am, is transformed into a positive reality through the fidelity which it depends on me to attest to.

The death of my fellow-creature is not absolute and does not become an ultimate situation unless he is unique for me.[32] Even so, it is my death, my own death, which is the decisive ultimate situation, and not something objective, not something which is comprehended in a purely general way. As a process, death is by definition the death of the other person. My death cannot be experienced by me; but there is no experience which is not a function of death.[33] In dying, I suffer an utter lack of knowledge which is tied to the fact that I am committed to a path from which there is no turning back; I am, as it were, at the point of petrifaction of my empirical being: "The rest is silence." But this silence in the absence of knowledge, construed as a will to ignore what I am forbidden to understand, still implies a question which is without a response capable of enlightening me as to what I am; rather, is it a claim to lead my life and to experience it by confronting my death. Hence there is an inner breach at the core of my actions: what remains essential when it is confronted with death is existentially realized and it is the pure empirical or vital datum, the pure *Dasein,* which reveals itself as in process of decay. However, it should be added that I tend to founder existentially when, because of death, I can no longer discover any significance in anything and abandon myself to a nihilistic despair. Death ceases to be an ultimate situation when it is interpreted as the final disaster which is characteristic of objective destruction. And I do not succeed in better evading the existential when I adhere entirely to the particular as though it were absolute, when I allow myself to become wrapt up in my cupidity, jealousy, desire for self-affirmation or pride in the prison of my vital being. Death can then appear as the mirror of existence, for every such manifestation on the phenomenal level must be ephemeral if existence is indeed the meaning of life. Death is gathered up into existence, as it were, is like a confirmation of the self, insofar as it stamps with relativity everything which is only *Dasein*. For the individual who exists in the midst of the ultimate situation, death is neither near nor remote, neither friend nor enemy. It is both of these in the actual movement of its contradictory manifestations.

It is evident that the inevitability of death can only be a source of despair and of a despair which is without appeal, to the will to live which interprets duration as the criterion of being; to seek to forget it is to evade the problem and not to resolve it; and it is futile to try to persuade oneself like Epicurus that the fear of death rests on a confusion, and to say to oneself: "As long as I am, death is not, and as long as death is, I am not, hence my death does not concern me." Each of these ideas is clear in itself, but not one of them is of the kind to extinguish our fear in the presence of non-being. Jaspers, furthermore, judges just as sternly the effort to represent to oneself a sensible and temporal immortality, another life after death. Any hypothesis of this kind seems highly improbable to him, and even inconsistent with the data of experience. It is curious to note here to what degree this critique of positivism nevertheless allows itself to be intimidated by positivistic negations of the most crudely scientist sort. Moreover, it seems to him that courage in confronting death is only courage when every image of what is beyond the grave has been banished; and to his mind, the believer who bases his supra-terrestrial hopes on dogmatic guarantees, destroys the ultimate situation and the existential privileges which are in a manner associated with it. Furthermore, he is of the conviction that two types of fear or anguish can be distinguished: one of these is related to non-being and is inherent in the will to live, in *Dasein* itself; the other is *existential anguish* which I feel in the measure that I am conscious of not having lived, i.e. of not having ordered existence to my own advantage. The more conscious I am of having realized myself, the more readily will I accept my demise to rejoin those who have departed. But if the threat of death only evokes a desire to have as much pleasure as possible before it is too late, I fall back into the circle of *Dasein* and repetition, fully realized only when manifested as fidelity.[34] Here, however, it is the realization alone which is significant. Death reaches down to the depths of being only in the measure that it is not repose but realization. In life, everything that is attained or consummated thereby becomes like death. Nothing completed can live. To move towards realization, therefore, is to move towards death. For us, accomplishment is but a stage, a step. Life is overflowing by definition. It is contradictory to try to bring it to completion. It exhibits this characteristic of a fulfilled or accomplished reality only when it is for another, when it is a spectacle; but it is a spectacle only because it is not lived, i.e. not real. Thus so far as the most active life tends towards its own fulfillment, it tends towards death. And death is doubtlessly violence, a brutal interruption, not a completion but an end. Existence, however, confronts death as the necessary limit of its own possible realization. Jaspers, who is obviously thinking of Tristan and Iseult in this context, shows the value of the revelation which may be associated with the death of love, the *Liebestod;* but only in order to quickly remind us that real achievement excludes any incapacity to support the weight of life, as it excludes that mixture of anguish and voluptuousness which is self-hatred. Death can have no depth of meaning if it implies evasion. Its significance lies precisely in the fact that its alien character fades, that I advance to meet it as that principle in which I incomprehensibly find my consummation, as a mysterious hospitality.

SUFFERING. Suffering is manifested in various ways, but it is always a partial destruction and behind it waits death. As long as I behave in the presence of suffering as though it were not final, but capable in principle of being averted,—I remain on the hither side of the ultimate situation. I combat it, and in so doing, I imply that it can be eliminated in principle. The victories over suffering are never more than partial and limited; but it is generally maintained today that when biology and medicine are sufficiently advanced, when the art of politics permits the establishment of absolute justice, suffering and illness will come to an end, and death will become but an extinction without any pain, evoking neither desire nor fear. But the fact is that these encouraging thoughts cannot save us. Whoever refuses to confront unblinkingly the necessity of suffering, is nursing illusions (insincerity concerning illness, his own spiritual deficiencies, etc.). We accuse the other person of stupidity, of malice. Or else we flee the suffering of others, avoiding those whose disease seems incurable. Thus a gulf widens between those who are happy and those who are not, and we end up by feeling hatred and contempt for those who suffer.

In the ultimate situation, we have just the opposite, for I acknowledge my suffering as an integral part of myself; I do not mistakenly try to conceal it from myself; I live in a kind of tension between the will to say *yes* to my suffering, and my inability to utter this *yes* with complete sincerity. I discover that if happiness was the last word in life, possible existence would remain dormant, as it were. Just as suffering annihilates our empirical being, so happiness seems to threaten our true being. From deep within me an objection against my own happiness arises,—an objection stemming from a knowledge which does not allow it to subsist in a pure and simple state. Happiness is something which implies risk and it must be won. Between the resignation of an active being who renounces all knowledge and who struggles without respite, and the passive resignation of the person who takes refuge in immediate pleasures, there is a polarity which I overcome at the core of the ultimate situation. My suffering ceases to be a contingent fate and the sign as it were of my dereliction, and instead reveals existence to me. A transcendent expression for suffering may be sought in the view that when I see the suffering of others, it is as if they suffered in my place, as if existence were asked to support the suffering of the world as though it were its own.[35]

CONFLICT. Death and suffering are ultimate situations which are created without my active collaboration. Conflict and Guilt, on the other hand, are ultimate situations only because of my own participation; the fact is that I would not be if they did not have being. Any attempt to evade them results either in their reestablishment under another guise, or to self-annihilation. Conflict is revealed to us in forms hierarchically arranged between the struggle for life at the bottom which is completely unconscious—and love or the strug-with oneself to become what one really is, at the top. We must therefore distinguish two kinds of conflict which are quite different: one is vital, a conflict employing all the means of coercion, the other is existential and is a conflict in and by love. Not only is the struggle for life inevitable, but it must also be conceded that exploitation of a kind is a necessary condition of any effective spiritual life. No doubt there is solidarity too, but only within very strict limits; solidarity is successful in the creation of certain limited wholes which fall into conflict with one another. Here too, just as in the case of suffering and death, I can undoubtedly try to put my-self on the hither side of the ultimate situation and vaguely envisage a life where justice, peace, and the generally accepted conditions of life shall reign. As long as my own conditions of life are relatively stable, I am able to forget the fact that conflict remains a necessary condition and limit of life. I take refuge in a certain neutrality and delude myself about the objectivity of my evaluations. But as soon as there is an external danger, I feel something weighing on me, I become aware of the injustice of which I am the beneficiary and which has permitted me to adopt the attitude of the impartial judge. If my will to see things in a true light triumphs over my un-conscious resistances, I would recognize the real conditions which permit me to be what I am.

Now we can indicate two apparent solutions to the problem re-sulting from the ultimate situation: I may either attempt to realize an existence without conflict, a utopia in which I would negate my-self; or I will affirm the value of conflict for its own sake whatever the stakes, surrendering to the will to power which animates me. In both cases, the ultimate situation is a moment which has been grasped but just as quickly lost. The first solution entails the illusory view that life is possible on the level of absolute non-resistance; the second assigns an intrinsic value to conflict which it does not really possess.[36] Further, it must be noted that all this may be turned inwards: austerity too, implies an exaltation of conflict—the struggle against oneself and one's instincts. And we are familiar with the inverse attitude which consists in encouraging us to follow our inclinations and which enjoins an inner non-resistance. "Both of these contrasted attitudes may be clearly and rationally considered, for they are both outside the ultimate situation." We must bear in mind this observation since it is of the utmost significance. Actually, however, non-resistance and pure violence both lead to destruction and despair, even if the despair in question is due to the fact that we have no adversary. The understanding seems to be presented with an inescapable choice. Doubtless, we will attempt to dispute the view that life implies conflict and the use of force,—or it will be maintained at any rate that it is our duty to establish an order in which force is not the deciding factor. But consider the vast number of objections based on empirical evidence that there are to this optimism! A sharp increase in the world's population, the relative inadequacy of the resources designed to provide for its needs, forms destructive for the individual but indispensable to the life of the species, etc. . . . Actually, every fair and rational organization of society is but an enclave; the notion of a universal organization is a chimera. The view that force is but an instrument to be used in the cause of justice is illusory, inasmuch as justice itself is at best the expression of determinate historical forces; forces which subsist as ideas of Existences in a realm of reality whose order is rooted in decisions evoked by conflict, and which only endures as an order because of the constant threat of a resort to force. The idea of a concrete, universal law is a pure abstraction and impossible of realization. A definitive peace of the human community can be neither established as an empirical possibility, nor intuitively represented as an ideal. For the ultimate situation subsists; if I wish to live, I must accept the fact that any benefit I receive is the result of an act of violence committed somewhere; I must therefore support it myself; I must assist it and accept the assistance of others; I therefore tend towards unity and compromise. Thus there is no objective solution which is permanently valid, but only certain historical solutions which are indispensable *hic et nunc.* The whole question is that of determining *when and where* we must adopt force and exploit it to our advantage, when we must yield and submit, when struggle and take risks. And the decision in such cases cannot be justified by appeal to general principles, (although it cannot be made without their aid either), but is rather based on our historical existence which is involved in its particular situation. In contrast with abstract and unilinear limiting representations, we are beings who discover our reality and existence in temporal situations involving conflict. Our reality is not something which is complete in itself nor is it intemporal.

There still remains the question of conflict which is no longer for life and for power but for an existence which surrenders itself to love. Since existence is only realized in communication, and communication in turn, in situations which alter in time, the pure harmony which is realized in such a mutual comprehension can only be momentary and ephemeral. The fact that the certitude of being can only issue from a conflict whch leads up to the manifestation or revelation of the self, is for existence that ultimate situation which makes it the most profoundly aware of itself as it also makes it utterly despair of itself.[37] Existentially, nothing possessed by the phenomenon has definitive value; existence as a revelation of real being, is in the very conflict which manifests it. Conflict points towards the primordial source of our being which is freedom and not a basic tendency of our nature. And this apart from any nice calculation, any kind of objectivity. Conflict continues without any violence; it is impossible for either one of the parties to the conflict to either win or lose, for victory and defeat are shared by both. And in whatever shape violence appears (through suggestion or through intellectual prestige), it puts an end to the conflict. Conflict is only possible on condition that it turn against both oneself and the other; individual existences who love one another literally cease to ask anything of one another, since they wish everything to be held in common. To be sure, there is something within me which desires that I dispense with the conflict, which wants me to welcome both myself and the other unconditionally. But existential love, in the measure that it is extended in time, cannot be the peaceful *éclat* of two souls, the one shining in the light of the other. At best this would be but an uncomprehending debauchery of feeling concealing the reality which lies behind. Existential love implies an ardent and mutual questioning. We are readily aware of the degraded manifestations of which this conflict is capable: dictatorial behavior which intellectual superiority occasionally indulges in; the passivity of the person who unconditionally submits to the will of the other; the substitution of pity and of an entirely external solicitude for love itself. And it can also be that a lie of sorts alters love in a fundamental way: when one of the lovers actually tries to affirm only himself, or when through self-hatred he tries to drag the other down with him to destruction. Reciprocity is lacking, conflict, i.e. love itself, dies away, existence is annihilated.

GUILT. Each of our actions entails consequences in the world which the agent could not predict. He becomes afraid when he considers these unpredictable consequences. Actually, I accept the fact that my own conditions of life imply the toil and suffering of others; I can live only by exploitation, even if I pay for my evil by my labor, by my suffering, and ultimately, by my own disappearance. What then, is the nature of this soul whose purity I seek to preserve? I don't know at all, I am thrown back on a concrete awareness which guides me and somehow persists in finding me guilty. Purity of soul is the characteristic of an existence constantly aware of its guilt which actually risks and realizes the impurity in the world so as to apprehend the attainment of purity as an infinite undertaking amidst the tensions of temporal life. Here too, as in the case of suffering and conflict, the understanding envisages a simple solution which consists in attributing to each individual his just deserts; but this abstract distribution of deserts would entail the elimination of all existential reality. I cannot act without wronging another; should I therefore find refuge in not acting? but not to act is still to act; if practiced systematically, not acting would also have certain consequences, and would be a form of suicide. If I have the power to do something, and do not do it, I am responsible for the consequences of abstaining; I cannot escape my guilt in this way. Responsibility means being ready to assume the burden of one's guilt. Hence I can at all times keep myself on the hither side of the ultimate situation and can say for example: "That's the way things are, I can't do anything about it, I'm not responsible for the order of things; if it makes guilt inevitable, I am not to blame for that." We know, however, that we cannot retrogress to the hither side of existence. Existence requires that I do not close my eyes to my, as it were, intrinsic or essential guilt, I must build a spiritual reality on an awareness of my primordial responsibility.

In conclusion, we may observe how the whole of empirical reality exhibits a problematic character. No achievement in the world is possible since even the communication existing in love reveals conflict. Every reality which presents itself as authentic Being is swallowed up when confronted by the spirit in search of the absolute. Search, questioning, *Frage, Fragwurdigkeit,* these are the words which continually obtrude themselves; the fact is that we are everywhere confronted with fissures, cracks, which somehow penetrate the presumed integrity of being. Being as *Dasein* actually exhibits a structure which is fundamentally antinomic.

Generally, to think, to think objectively, is to struggle for domination against the contradictions and oppositions which one encounters, in order to be able to make use of them afterwards.

What is characteristic of the antinomies, however, is that instead of my being able to resolve them or bring them together, they become deeper as soon as I try to think them clearly.[38] To affirm the antinomic structure of *Dasein* is to affirm that only the particular oppositions and contradictions found within *Dasein* can be resolved whereas the speciousness of all solutions is exhibited as soon as we claim to continue on to the limit and apply these solutions to everything. And in this notion of the antinomic structure of *Dasein* we perceive the same element shared by the ultimate situations which we have examined in detail. It is here that we find the evil without remedy which exists in the world. We may observe in this context that values are actually tied to conditions which deny them. Opposites are so intimately linked with one another that I cannot rid myself of my adversary without affecting the polarity of contraries itself, or without ultimately losing the very thing I wanted to preserve as real. Freedom is bound to dependence, communication to solitude, historical awareness to universal truth, myself as possible existence to the manifestation of my empirical being.

(a) It is possible for this antinomic structure to be hidden from me behind a veil, as it were, if I consider it as a spectator. Thus I can set my mind at rest by urging that these contradictions enrich our experience and that without them both the world and mankind would lose their fulness of meaning. In so doing, however, I regard the ultimate situation from the outside as something in which I am not involved instead of existing in the ultimate situation. I confine myself to an antinomic representation of the world.

(b) I can also close my eyes to one of the two opposing terms; this is an attractive choice because of the seemingly rational clarity of the simplified judgment on which the choice is based; since I know in the abstract what is good, I need only subsume whatever appears under the abstract principle I have chosen.

The fact is, however, that as an existing being, I only have access to myself within the ultimate situation involving the antinomies. The situation, however, demands that we think these antinomies, not that we become hobbled by them, caught in a trap, as it were; as for example, when I claim to know some being in itself as absolute, or envisage a totally rational order of the world which satisfies all the requirements of reason. When I adopt this course, the world as such becomes everything for me; I deny transcendence. A world without antinomy, entailing the presence of an absolute and objective truth, would be a world in which existence would cease to be together with the very being who is able to grasp transcendence within the area of his experience.

We have here reached the central issue in Jasper's theory and perhaps in his philosophy taken as a whole. In his book on transcendence, he shows how the failure of all theodicy is transformed into an appeal made to our freedom of action, an appeal which may still be met with defiance as well as with its contrary possibility, self-abandonment.[39] Such abandonment, however, entails that all knowledge must be repudiated; it is authentic only in the absence of knowledge; when it attempts to justify itself by appealing to any kind of understanding, it loses its authenticity. Furthermore, in the last chapter of Volume III, Jaspers focusses his attention on establishing the inevitability of failure, together with all that this implies with respect to ruptures or disappointments, on the level of *Dasein* or of the will to live which is a condition of freedom. Freedom, he further declares, only has being because there is a natural being, and only in opposition to the latter. Hence it will either perish as freedom—and this is what occurs if it identifies itself with nature —or it founders as *Dasein*—and in doing so, compensates for it as freedom. Two kinds of *ethos* are manifested in the world: one with a claim to universality, is expressed in terms of an ethic of measure, wisdom, and is a relativism, but does not take account of failure; the other implies an absence of knowledge which persists in its questioning attitude, and is expressed by an ethic of unconditional freedom governing what Jaspers terms in an untranslatable phrase, *Die Chiffre des Scheiterns,* i.e. the transcendent meaning of failure. The basic illusion implied here, which is itself tied to individuation, is not simply something that must be dispelled; it is rather the indispensable mean term which permits us to bring into play those forces which, when frustrated, dispell our illusions, and thus reveal a sensible Being to us. Without such illusions, being would remain lost to us in the darkness of the possibility of non-being.

I shall not discuss further this theory of transcendence which I have not yet examined thoroughly. It is clear, however, that the theory is closely related to what I have said above. The indissoluble relation which we have asserted and even acknowledged between *Dasein* and *Sein* is, in a sense, still completely unintelligible; being is, only if *Dasein* is, but the former is not reducible to the latter; *Dasein* as such is not being. And when I affirm that there must be *Dasein* if there is to be being, I myself do not understand the meaning of the term *must* in this context. We end up with the paradox that the absolute is ephemeral for us, as it were, because of the fact that freedom is a reality, or because what is relative can only subsist in time and in what has objective validity. This inversion of the relation which we might have forseen, is due to the historicity of *Dasein*. In a world which does not offer the image of something at once unified and true, and which instead appears to be all the more split up as it is more truly observed, possible existence can only be realized by a freedom which must struggle with obstacles. The word "shattered" characterizes this aspect of it. Furthermore, Jaspers affirms that "existence, although possessing its own certitude, is a temporal being in a shattered state, as it were, as though there had been antecedently a perfect reality which had been lost, and which we had to seek again without ever being able to find it." [40] The fact that *Dasein* appears to metaphysical intuition as an historical fact, however, means that intuition grasps it as a manifestation of freedom in which each individual participates as a co-responsible agent.

The foregoing is an account of the theory of ultimate situations, construed as so many articulations of existence, so to speak. If I were to describe my own personal reaction to this body of ideas, I should say that it is, in a sense, contradictory. I find in the notion of antinomies a systematic and profound expression of a basic intuition which has always been my own.

On the other hand, however, Jasper's conclusions, whatever else they may be, seem to represent an attempt, or at any rate one he imagined he was making, to overcome both positivism and idealism, an attempt which is marked in places by the doctrines against which the author is struggling and which he claims to transcend. In the course of my discussion I have indicated the contempt he displays for all conceptions of immortality; does he not affirm that it is mortality, on the contrary, that can be demonstrated? And we must not be misled in this respect, for what we have here after all is a psycho-physiological dogmatism. To be sure, it must be acknowledged that within the framework of this dogmatism of the here-below, he makes an heroic effort to elevate himself as high as possible to the transcendent. But how evade the fact that he moves within a certain *enclosed space?* It is useless to be told that this space has no assignable boundaries, for this only makes it still more bounded, more confined. And without realizing it, he forces us in the final analysis to ask whether he is not simply effecting an unjustified secularization of certain essentially religious ideas whose vital springs, however, have already been broken. I am thinking here, in particular, of his notion of guilt. Jaspers uses the word *Schuld* in this context, and not *Sunde;* but how ignore the fact that this ineradicable guilt which is coessential with us, represents the trace or abstract vestige of original sin? I make these observations with a certain timidity because I have not subjected Jasper's thought to a thorough examination; but it seems to me that the manner in which he presents his religious philosophy directly confirms my remarks. Doesn't he actually finish by telling us that everyone should remain in the religious faith in which he has been brought up—because it is a part of his fundamental situation—but that he cannot escape the fact that he will most certainly cut the figure of a heretic within the religious faith of his upbringing; and doesn't he refer to the spontaneous tendency of philosophy towards heresy? This point seems to me extremely significant. Jasper's position with respect to existence necessarily tends to make him reject any idea of religious canonicity or orthodoxy, and this is only an expression on the religious level of a radical rejection of the ontological as such. We have here reached the central point of his doctrine, the point at which I shall conclude my remarks. I believe that if we sanction this rejection, it would not be easy to find a body of thought today which is more profound, more supple and more hospitable to the mind, than Jasper's. I also believe that if we proclaim his doctrine to be a fundamental perversion of reason, we shall be led to revise all of Jasper's positions and to add another dimension to his thought whereby it becomes completely transfigured.

NOTES

1. *Philosophie*, 3 Vols. (Berlin: Springer, 1932).
2 We must note once and for all that the word *Dasein* has no French equivalent. To render its meaning we have been forced to use terms which detract from the clarity and rigor of our account.
3 *Ibid.*, Vol. I, p. 336.
4 *Ibid.*, p. 15.
5 *Ibid.* [Marcel's transcription of the German in this and subsequent passages has been largely omitted. Transl. Note.]
6 *Ibid.*, p. 26.
7 *Ibid.*, Vol. II, p. 16.

8 *Ibid.*, p. 22.
9 *Ibid.*, Vol. I, p. 16.
10 *Ibid.*, p. 236.
11 *Ibid.*, p. 265.
12 *Ibid.*, Vol. II, p. 119.
13 *Ibid.*
14 *Ibid.*, Vol. I, p. 16.
15 *Ibid.*, p. 17.
16 *Ibid.*, p. 18.
17 *Ibid.*, Vol. III, p. 2.
18 *Ibid.*, Vol. I, p. 20.
19 It should be noted that empirical consciousness here includes the sphere of consciousness in general which for Jaspers, is clearly a part of *Dasein.*
20 *Ibid.*, Vol. I, p. 21.
21 *Ibid.*
22 *Ibid.*, Vol. III, p. 2.
23 *Ibid.*, p. 3.
24 *Ibid.*, Vol. III, p. 5.
25 *Ibid.*, Vol. II, p. 203.
26 *Ibid.*, p. 204.
27 *Ibid.*, p. 205.
28 *Ibid.*, p. 209.
29 [See Kurt Hoffman's essay "The Basic Concept of Jaspers' Philosophy," in *The Philosophy of Karl Jaspers* ed. P. Schillp (N. Y.; Tudor, 1957), p. 95, for the distinction between a "system" and a "systematic:" "Jaspers terms his philosophical work not a system; but rather a systematically connected, but open structure. . . ." Transl. Note.]
30 *Ibid.*, Vol. II, p. 213.
31 *Ibid.*, p. 216.
32 This is closely related to what I termed the pure Thou in my *Journal Metaphysique.*
33 *Ibid.*, p. 222.
34 *Ibid.*, p. 228.
35 *Ibid.*, pp. 232-233.
36 *Ibid.*, p. 238.
37 *Ibid.*, p. 242.
38 *Ibid.*, p. 250.
39 *Ibid.*, Vol. III, p. 78.
40 *Ibid.*, Vol. II, p. 348.

Index

trial (test), 72-73, 76, 93, 101
Tristan and Iseult, 244

Vahinger, 78
Valéry, Paul, 63, 236
values, evaluate, 43-45, 73, 108, 112,
   116, 125-127, 138, 145, 153, 172,
   179, 207-208, 246, 250

verifiability, verification, 6, 108, 127,
   145, 227
Voltaire, 129

Wagner, 122
Waltz, Henriette, 216

Zola, Emile, 131